NAAFI, KNICKE...

Second edition, 2010
First published in 2009 by

WOODFIELD PUBLISHING LTD
Bognor Regis ~ West Sussex ~ England ~ PO21 5EL
www.woodfieldpublishing.com

Some names have been changed
to protect the innocent (and the guilty!)

ISBN 1-84683-071-0

Naafi, Knickers and Nijmegen

The Postwar Adventures of a WRAF Airwoman

JOAN BLACKBURN

Joan Blackburn
(nee Ratcliff)

Best wishes

Woodfield

Woodfield Publishing Ltd

Woodfield House ~ Babsham Lane ~ Bognor Regis ~ West Sussex ~ PO21 5EL
telephone 01243 821234 ~ **e-mail** enquiries@woodfieldpublishing.com

Interesting and informative books on a variety of subjects

For full details of all our published titles, visit our website at
www.woodfieldpublishing.com

To those who were there...

Also by Joan Blackburn

Granddad's Rainbow
Adventures of a War Baby 1939 – 1951

It is 1944 and three-year-old Joannie listens to the tall stories told by her Granddad as he tries to bring normality to a very abnormal time. Born into an upstairs/downstairs world that is fast becoming history, her grandfather, the Head Gardener at Coxhill Manor, near Chobham in Surrey, had seen it all before in 'the first lot'. Now his son, serving in the RAF in France and Malta, is just a face in a photograph to little Joannie, who one day will follow in her father's footsteps and join the Royal Air Force.

Joan Blackburn has returned, in this, her second book, to her rural working-class roots. With access to her father's RAF Record of Service and an Aunt who lived to be over 100 years old, together with the aid of her own memories, she has been able to piece together the events contained in the book accurately and informatively to create a create a realistic and warm-hearted portrayal of the life of an ordinary English family caught up in the extraordinary events of World War II and its aftermath.

The Tailor's Daughter
Adventures of Charlotte Adshead 1858 – 1929

This is the true story of the author's great-grandmother. Born in the 1850s in Clapham, London, she emigrated on her own to New Zealand at a time when to do such a thing was fraught with danger. It is also the story of Frederick Gosley, the seafarer whose life changed when he met Charlotte. It changed even more when he went blind and it took all the will-power and tenacity the plucky Cockney girl had been born with to overcome the difficulties that were to follow.

The book follows the couple through the years of their lives, which included events ranging from the sinking of the Titanic, the devastating First World War and Votes for Women until their deaths in 1929, within a few months of each other. From Charlotte's father Thomas to her Granddaughter, Lily Dorothy, it traces over a century of history.

The conversations are of necessity imagined but the facts and most of the people (including the passengers on the SS *British King*, on which Charlotte sailed to New Zealand) are real. Only a few minor fictional characters were added for the purposes of continuity.

Both books published by Woodfield @ £9.95
www.woodfieldpublishing.co.uk
www.amazon.co.uk/shops/woodfield

~ *Contents* ~

Preface

Joan Blackburn (nee Ratcliff) joined the WRAF in 1959 just one week after her eighteenth birthday and signed on for four years. Following basic training, she first went to RAF Medmenham, a tiny little station in Buckinghamshire, fondly known as 'Gods Little Acre' where she and her friends, who were still in their teens, spent many a happy hour ghost hunting and generally trying to outwit their superiors. Then, in complete contrast, she was posted to Rheindahlen in Germany, the largest non operational station in the RAF. It was here that she was introduced to the famous 100-mile Nijmegen Marches in Holland and her account of this event so graphic and entertaining that readers have reported that it made them laugh and cry at the same time! Above all, it is a heart warming and nostalgic tale of youthful exuberance that makes one proud to be British.

Being in the WRAF at a time when Rock 'n' Roll was in its infancy and young women had to overcome the disadvantage of being locked into their accommodation at 11pm, it is a snapshot of a different world.

Her adventures, in this innocent time, were typed on an old fashioned typewriter within weeks of her return to civilian life in 1964 and taking up a job as a secretary for British Aircraft Corporation (BAC) at Weybridge, Surrey. Every detail of those four years was fresh and clear in her mind as she typed away during quiet periods at work or after everyone else had gone home. It was typed straight off, with no rubbings-out or alterations, in the days long before spell-checking and ease of correction.

The 150 pages of foolscap manuscript were read by her family and then put in her parent's loft and forgotten about...

In the meantime, still missing the WRAF, Joan joined the RAF Association and was asked to be involved in the formation and running of a Girls Venture Corps cadet unit in the grounds of BAC. Back in uniform again, albeit as a hobby, it wasn't long before – with the backing of the ATC and the RAF – Joan was able to arrange a coach trip to take the girls to Nijmegen for the marches. Initially it was just her own unit but, over the following years, teenagers from other parts of the country joined in and it became an annual event for the girls as well as the boys.

Eight years passed and, as the watershed of Joan's thirtieth birthday approached, she left the now well-established GVC Unit, and her job and family, to go back into the Royal Air Force in the role of WRAF Admin. It had been twelve years since the eighteen-year-old had first marched into the Recruiting Centre, following a bet with her father and the book she had written back in 1964 still lay undisturbed and forgotten.

In 1971 Joan marched into the same Recruiting Centre, but this time gaining permission to take leave to continue to take her cadets to Nijmegen. Within two years she met the man who was to become her husband and Corporal Joan Ratcliff became Mrs Norman Blackburn and a civilian once again. Two children were born and raised and Joan saw her son join the RAF before her old manuscript was finally turned out of her parents' loft after they had passed away. By now computers had been invented and in 2009, fifty years after she had first walked into that recruiting centre, the account of her original four years – four happy years of rock and roll innocence – was published in its entirety.

Anyone old enough to remember the fifties and sixties – and particularly anyone who served in the UK armed forces at the time – will be taken on an emotional journey down memory lane and reminded just how much times have changed in the intervening years. For younger readers it is a window into a gentler, more innocent world, far removed from the lives of today's teenagers but perhaps none the worse for that...

1. Being a 'Plus Type'

The sun glinted on scores of windows along the sides of dozens of brown wooden huts standing in rows, like long straight worms, all around the large RAF parade ground. It seemed to be a giant conductor for the midsummer heat and I was momentarily dazzled by the sight before me. For a minute I felt as though I was in the blistering desert instead of rural Wilmslow and about to join the Women's Royal Air Force. The summer of 1959 had been exceptionally hot and it seemed as though today was breaking all records.

Just a few days ago I had celebrated my eighteenth birthday – not that eighteen was much to write home about. It was just like any other birthday really. Twenty-one was when you officially became an 'adult' and 'teenagers' were still a novelty, along with rock and roll and *Six Five Special* on black and white television. However, I was old enough to become an airwoman – or so I thought.

I put my case down on the ground and shielded my eyes as I looked at the large, square, pale blue board at the side of the entrance gates. *Royal Air Force Wilmslow – Recruit Training* was the legend, in bold letters, over an RAF roundel.

Subconsciously I was aware of the other girls, much my own age, chattering around me as they got off the Air Force bus, but I was too preoccupied to take in very much. I had said a very tearful farewell to my parents a few hours earlier, although God knows why I was upset! After all, it was *my* choice! Nobody had twisted my arm. Suddenly I remembered the last words my father had said before we parted company that morning.

"Now remember, my girl, you behave yourself, and..." he had smiled his lovely warm smile as he put his arm around me, "watch out for the dark corners!"

I must have grinned to myself, because my thoughts were rudely interrupted by one of the girls, who had been standing nearest to me, rubbing the sweat from the palms of her hands after putting down her heavy case.

"Jee-zuss H. Ker-riste!" she exclaimed. "I don't see that this is anything to smile about. It looks like a bloody concentration camp! By the way, I'm Pat Seymour, what's your name?"

"Joan Ratcliff," I answered coyly, ignoring the choice of language. "Pleased to meet you. Perhaps we should go and find out what we have let ourselves in for."

"I think I know already," muttered another girl following close behind us.

We struggled with our cases again and walked through the gates, little knowing that we had taken one step into another world. The rest of the group followed behind us as an RAF Police Sergeant popped his head out from the Guard Room just inside the gate and asked us for the paperwork that we had been given at the Recruiting Centre. He looked very impressive in his well-pressed uniform, white peaked cap and webbing belt.

"He's called a 'Snowdrop'," said Pat, knowledgably.

I didn't know where she had got that from, but bowed to her superior knowledge.

"A few more lambs to the slaughter," the Snowdrop grunted. He disappeared back into the Guardroom, like a villain leaving the scene of a crime that hadn't quite been committed yet, and left us to think about his comment.

Almost immediately, and certainly before I had time to think about changing my mind and retracing my steps, a WRAF Sergeant came down the road towards us, looking very hot and bothered, despite the fact that she had left off her jacket and her shirt sleeves were neatly rolled up to just above the elbow. Her face was red with the exertion of it all and she wasn't a bit like the cool and composed Sergeant that I had previously met at the Recruiting Centre in London. She screeched to a halt in front of us and immediately started shuffling through a bundle of papers she was holding.

"Whew! What a day for you to arrive on," she panted. "You are the new D Flight, come on, follow me."

She mopped her brow with the end of her tie and we trailed behind her in a 'crocodile', like a group of schoolgirls out with their teacher. She was chattering to anyone who happened to be listening, but I was far too busy taking stock of my new surroundings, little knowing that within a few years the whole place would be pulled down and consigned only to our memories.

Most of Wilmslow was made up of wooden huts, some grander than others, like the Officers Mess. That looked very splendid indeed, with its dark brown wooden walls, white paintwork, well-kept lawns surrounded by white stones and a profusion of roses round about.

On the other side of the road, and to my left, stood a 'memory' of not very long ago – a well cared for and obviously highly-prized fighter plane. It was now set into the ground, with gardens all around it. It had probably saved our lives just over fifteen years ago, in the War, but now it was going nowhere. For all that, it looked very majestic and proud.

"Imagine flying in that," whispered Pat. "They had some guts, those pilots, you know."

I certainly couldn't argue with that observation.

The road now came to a T junction, with the left hand side going towards the NAAFI and our spirits were immediately lifted by the sound of music. There was obviously somebody with good taste in there, as we could hear Cliff Richard singing 'Living Doll' coming through the open windows. All, therefore, was not entirely lost! The place *was* civilised after all.

"Hurry up," panted the NCO. "You can enjoy listening to that young man later – that is, if you've got sixpence for the jukebox."

Despite our protests, we were taken the other way, towards the billets which, of course, were not as glamorous as the Officers Mess that we had just passed, as the sound of Cliff faded away behind us.

On closer inspection it could be seen that the rows of huts were all joined together by means of a long concrete corridor running from the front of No. 1 hut through the width of all the wooden huts until it reached No. 20. All the front entrances to the living quarters came out onto this corridor and, opposite the front doors, on the other side, were even more doors, leading to the washrooms and toilets. All the passages were made of bleached stone, which we were to get to know very well during the forthcoming weeks!

"If you want a bath you need camping equipment to get there," joked the sergeant brightly.

It didn't take us long to find out that she was only stretching the truth by a small amount, because the bathrooms were down endless stone passages, at the end of which we found half the taps did not work or, worse still, the plugs were missing.

She seemed to enjoy her little jokes at our expense.

"You know," she went on, "it is said that the only things keeping Wilmslow together are the Death Watch Beetles holding hands."

We all laughed politely.

"Anyway, here we are – your home for the next six weeks or so..." (I was almost expecting cackling laughter, like the witch out of the Wizard of Oz.) She opened the door of the second hut along the row and my first impression was of gleaming, unbelievably highly-polished floors, with a couple of dozen beds spaced evenly around the room. Alternately spaced between each bed were narrow wooden wardrobes and smaller bedside lockers.

In the porch, as we entered, there were two small rooms, the broom and store cupboard on one side and the Corporal's room on the other. In the centre of the billet was a large, black, coke stove with a box of coke on either side of it. This was the only source of heat in the winter and so I was very glad it was summer! Apart from anything else, I did *not* fancy cleaning that thing!

"Look at that," whispered Pat. "Even the coke has been dusted."

It had too!

We all wearily bagged our beds, with sighs of relief, though we did not sit down on them until we had carefully turned back the striped counterpanes, in case we creased them.

Already we were learning!

"Hell!" I thought. "What have I done? And to think that I am only here because of a poster and a stupid bet with my Dad."

My teens had begun with Bill Haley. Until *he* came to London we sixteen-year-olds were merely 'older' children and I started my job as a Junior Clerk, wearing clothes not dissimilar to those I had worn to school, in dark, sombre shades. But things were starting to happen and it was always interesting to walk around the City in my lunch hour. New office buildings were being built, although around St Paul's, where I worked, there were still signs of bombing and piles of blackened bricks with foxgloves growing up through them, where people sat to have their sandwiches in the summer.

Then Bill Haley arrived!

He chose to do so at exactly the same time as I, and thousands of others, were trying to 'do battle' in the rush hour at Waterloo Station. For some it was a nuisance, but for people of my age it was exciting, chaos and a 'watershed' all in one. His taxi came right into the station and along the platform to pick him up directly from his train, but despite the pushing and shoving and the inevitable newspaper photographers, I did manage to catch a glimpse of him as he leaned out of the vehicle and waved, his black kiss curl quite visible on his forehead. I lost a shoe in the process and my train was an hour late but I didn't care about that – although my Mother did when I arrived home in my bare feet.

"You never walked down the road like that?" she had cried in horror. "Whatever will the neighbours think?"

Despite the neighbours, it was the turning point that moved us teenagers from 'black and white' to 'colour'. Suddenly, almost overnight, offers appeared in the 'Woman' and 'Woman's Own' magazines of 'cut-out-and-sew' skirts and dresses in bright colours. The fact that they were in *her* reading material legitimised them in my Mother's eyes and soon, like everyone else, we were sending for them and buying frothy underskirts to make them stick out all round.

My Father thought the world had gone mad.

"What do you look like, all done up like a Christmas tree?" he laughed, when he saw me in my latest creation and watched in amusement as I stretched a four inch wide elastic belt round my fairly ample waist.

"It's the fashion Dad," I explained patiently.

I often felt that being a 'teenager' was a lost cause and had not quite reached where I lived, so I quite often spent my lunch hours walking around London and looking in the latest magazines in the shops. By February 1959 my route took me past the RAF Recruiting Centre in Kingsway, where there was a huge picture in the window of a young airwoman, with the slogan underneath saying 'Be a plus-type girl'. I looked at my reflection and wondered briefly what you had to do to be a 'plus-type'. It was all very well having the fancy skirts but the London smogs and train delays did nothing for them and then, to really upset us further, came the awful news that Buddy Holly had died in a plane crash before any of us had even seen a picture of him.

We had heard his music and loved it, but I for one did not know what he looked like. I did now, for his bespectacled face was on all the newspaper hoardings I passed. For a while we thought that the music really had died and it was a very depressing time.

"Oh well, that's the end of it – poor young man!" my Dad had said. "Fashions change, my dear, and you'll forget all about Buddy whatever-his-name-is."

"Well, we have always got Elvis Presley," I retorted, sensing an opportunity to tease him.

"Well that says it all," said Dad. "What sort of a name is that for goodness sake? Elvis!"

It was a lost cause. I loved him dearly but I had to face the fact that we were a generation apart. I was too old for the Girl Guides and my strict upbringing kept me away from grown up dance halls. Instead, my life revolved around the Church Fellowship, where I could gather with my friends, who were also struggling to 'educate' their parents. We half-heartedly attended church services, in exchange for the use of the Vicar's record player to listen to our music on.

Then, one life-changing Sunday, after I had battled all week on the London Underground and had another wistful look at the poster of the 'plus-type girl', one of the older ladies who helped the Vicar organise our social and spiritual life bought some photos of her daughter to show us. She had just joined the WRAF and had recently completed her training and really *was* a 'plus-type' now.

"Look!" she said proudly, showing the pictures to anyone with the slightest degree of interest. "This is my Ruth at her Passing Out Parade. Isn't she smart?"

The photos were actually not that special but she certainly did look smart in her new uniform and very proud of herself. I didn't know anyone else who had joined the women's services and couldn't wait to get home and tell the family my bit of gossip.

"Hey Mum!" I announced, when I arrived back at the house. "Guess what! Ruth Hudson has joined the WRAF!"

"Oh yes?" replied Mum absently, too busy stirring the gravy for Sunday dinner to take any real notice, and my two younger brothers, Michael, aged eleven and Richard, just seven, were already sitting at the table, waiting to be fed. They weren't interested in anything I had to say. Even the death of Buddy Holly had gone right over their heads, much to my annoyance.

"Dad..." I persisted, "Ruth Hudson has joined the WRAF and she is a plus-type girl now."

Then I knew how I would get their attention.

"I think *I'll* join!" I suddenly announced, hardly believing my own words!

That certainly worked!

"Ten bob says you don't," laughed Dad.

"Right, you're on!" I replied.

There was laughter all round, but I was never one to refuse a bet with my dad. He knew it and I had fallen for it. My mother started to slice the leg of lamb and the smell pervaded the room. As I passed the mint sauce to my brother I was already wondering if I hadn't been just a little bit too hasty...

I could almost smell that lamb now as I sat and waited, surrounded by twenty or so equally shattered and bemused girls. At this precise moment in time my dad's name was mud

– and I was even blaming Mrs Hudson and poor Buddy Holly for my hasty decision.

My thoughts were shattered into fragments by the arrival of our corporal into the billet. I had been lulled into a sense of false security by the friendly little sergeant. Her deputy was a different story entirely. Though tiny, she seemed to fill the billet with a presence all of her own. Although we had not yet been taught to leap to attention, it was almost, already, a reflex action the minute she arrived. She marched down the centre of the room, all creases and shiny shoes.

"Bet she wears her tapes on her pyjamas!" I whispered to Pat.

"Good afternoon everybody," boomed the little corporal, who, as it turned out, was not much older than I was!

"I will be in immediate charge of you during the next six weeks and I will be living in the bunk at the end of this billet." Her eyes penetrated each one of us in turn as she spoke.

"She has eyes like pee-holes in the snow," said Pat.

"Shh woman," I cringed. "She'll hear us!"

I did not want to get on the wrong side of this NCO, who although lower in rank, looked far more forbidding than the sergeant.

"My name is Corporal Payne," she announced. "When I say jump you will jump and I *will* turn you into airwomen if it is the last thing I ever do."

With those words ringing in our ears, she swivelled on her highly-polished shoe and left the room, bellowing as she left that she would be back in half an hour and would expect us to be unpacked by then.

We all came to earth with an almighty bang.

I looked across at Pat, who was gazing open-mouthed at the empty doorway, as if in a bad dream.

"Bloody hell!" she gasped. "Hitler was a little corporal."

"Thank goodness we only have to put up with her for six weeks," I ventured, trying to look on the bright side.

"That will seem like a lifetime," wailed Pat.

She wandered off around the room, making herself known to everybody, whether they wanted to or not. I suppose I should have done the same but I was more concerned about not upsetting the little corporal, who I had taken an instant dislike to.

I began to try and fit my clothes into the tiny locker provided and was now able to take a look at the other girls, who, with the exception of my new friend, were trying to get unpacked and ready within the half-hour specified. There was a tall, freckle-faced Scots girl in the corner bed, busily swearing to herself in her native tongue every time she bumped into the girl trying to unpack in the next bed to her. It wasn't easy when petticoats were like something out of 'Gone with the Wind' and frothed up everywhere, with a life of their own. I had never heard so many swear words in all my life thus far.

Pat had the next bed space to me and on my other side was a little fair girl from Edinburgh, who we immediately christened 'Little Haggis', while the other Scots girl was, intelligently, called 'Big Haggis'.

"These cupboards are so wee!" moaned Big Haggis. "Ma claes wilna fit in there."

Opposite me and grumbling quietly to herself because she had apparently left her spare suspender belt at home, was Barbara, a tubby dark-haired girl from Lancashire, and somewhere further along the billet a Welsh girl, whom we 'boringly' called Taff, was grovelling about under the bed, trying to retrieve the dozens of hair rollers which she had dropped. There was no doubt that I would get to know them all eventually.

It took some time for Pat to decide that everybody knew who she was and what an asset she was going to be to the Air Force. It turned out that her brother was also in the RAF, though not through choice. He was a National Serviceman and thought his sister was totally bonkers to *volunteer* for it.

"Ker-riste!" Pat suddenly exclaimed, as she glanced up at the billet clock. "Look at the bloody time! That cow will be back in a minute."

Everyone rushed around to help her finish putting her stuff away.

"I'm sure your petticoat is bigger than mine," I grunted, as I tried to shut the door on it without any of the net sticking out.

Suddenly, without any warning, Corporal Payne marched into the room. Even then, some of the girls were still sauntering back from the washhouses as if they had all the time in the world. "Stand by your beds!" she yelled.

Not really knowing quite what she was on about, we did our best. Some of us stood at the foot of the bed, some on the right hand side, some on the left and all of us with varying postures.

She looked on in barely concealed amusement.

"When you get the order to stand by your beds," she roared, "it means that you stand to attention on the right hand side of your bed, at the foot, like this." She demonstrated for those of us that did not understand.

I was to find out that the order 'stand by your beds' was about the most common order of all at the Recruit Training Centre and if I had a pound for every time this command was given I could have bought myself a Rolls-Royce. Then we had to 'stand at ease', feet eighteen inches apart, arms behind our backs, heads up, staring straight ahead.

"Well I suppose that will do for now, D Flight," she snarled.

I didn't think we were doing at all bad after only having been in the Royal Air Force for half an hour, but who was I? Just a mere mortal.

She began pacing up and down the room as she spoke to us. Corporal Payne wore no makeup and her dark black hair was short and mostly hidden by her carefully placed beret, with its rim just one inch above the eyebrow.

"Now D Flight," she said. "The first thing that you must learn is how to address an NCO. You must always say your number, rank and name before stating your business."

"She does wear her stripes on her pyjamas!" I thought.

"You will soon be given numbers and you will find that these numbers you will never forget for the rest of your lives – your service number will be printed on your heart before you leave here. Until you get that number, however, you must just use your surname."

"Right..." she turned her eyes in Big Haggis's direction, "Macintyre, what do you call me?"

"Don't tempt me!" murmured Pat at the side of me.

"Corporal," whispered Haggis, who was visibly shaking.

"*What* Corporal?" screamed Corporal Payne.

"She's tempting me again!" whispered Pat. Suddenly I was having a job not to laugh!

"Macintyre Corporal," trembled the unfortunate Haggis, as she blushed bright red.

"That's better. Now... when you get your number, you would say 456 Macintyre Corporal, or Sergeant, or whatever the rank happens to be. Unless you prefix your sentence with that, then you will never be answered – not even if there is a fire in the NAAFI – do you understand?"

"Yes Corporal," we all muttered.

"I didn't hear you!" she shouted.

"*Yes Corporal!*" we yelled.

"Well, it is just about tea-time now and so I will march you to the Mess. In the broom cupboard you will find a large box containing eating irons – that is knives, forks and spoons to you – and another containing mugs. Get what you need and then form up in threes on the road outside, carrying your eating irons in your left hands – that's *this* one," she said sarcastically. She began to make for the door, but not before her parting shot over our heads.

"Oh, and I want you back here in an hour and a half because you will be taught how to spit and polish shoes and how to make a bed stack this evening."

"Payne by name and pain by nature!" moaned Barbara, as the corporal strode out of the billet ahead of us.

We gathered our 'eating irons', ran out to where she was waiting for us and formed up in threes, accompanied by much pushing and shoving.

"D flight, by the left – quick march!"

Poor Corporal Payne, you had to feel sorry for her! She must have been horrified when she saw the marching of her new flight. There we were, in our summer dresses with the big petticoats, some of us in sandals, some hobbling along in high heels, and all of us earnestly trying to look smart, on this, our very first effort at marching.

We were tripping over each other's feet and our arms just would not go in the direction that we wanted them to. In other words, we were 'camel marching.' Barbara, in the confusion, dropped her mug and I am sure that all the time Corporal Payne was trying her level best not to laugh at us. Another Corporal passed us coming in the other direction on a bike and shouted across to her.

"Good luck!" she laughed.

"I think I'm going to need it with this lot!" she shouted back.

"Damn cheek!" hissed Barbara under her breath.

The smell soon made it clear that the large wooden building we were approaching was the Mess. It was the smell of cabbage and fried eggs, and suddenly I did not feel hungry any more!

"D Flight – Ha-a-ate!"

We took this to mean 'D Flight halt' and promptly stopped in our tracks, causing those in the rear to fall over each other in their endeavours not to walk over those in the front.

"This is the Mess, D Flight!" she barked. "Enjoy your tea… and don't forget, I want you back in the billet in an hour and a half."

The place was heaving with about two hundred girls, all with plenty to say, and Corporal Payne, wisely, faded into the background.

It seemed that the term 'mess' was a good word, for far from enjoying our tea and being back in an hour and a half, it took no time at all to eat the 'mess' that RAF Wilmslow called tea in 1959! We filed in and queued up at the counter, holding our plates firmly as soggy potatoes and large pieces of pie were dumped onto them by four airwomen who, quite clearly, did not want to be doing the job. They were being watched closely by the only men in sight – two RAF cooks wearing blue and white checked trousers, white jackets and chefs caps. I was hungry, but promptly threw most of my meal in the waste bucket and made myself some toast instead.

"Well if that's tea…" moaned Little Haggis, "roll on breakfast!"

"Isn't it awful," I replied, and began to wish I was back home with Mother's cooking and, not for the first time that day, I wondered what madness had driven me to this.

I could well remember the rationing just after the war and the struggle to put food on the table, but this was something else. I lived on nothing but tea and toast for the rest of my time at Wilmslow. Well, after all, who can muck up toast?

Back in the billet after our 'tea' we listened in awe as we received our second lesson of the day – on how to spit and polish shoes and how to make bed packs. The former seemed simple enough, after all, anyone can spit, but my eyelids were too heavy with sleep to really take in the instructions of how to fold blankets into something resembling a liquorice allsort, to be placed at the head of the bed, with the pillows squarely on top, never mind 'aligning' the stripes on each of our bedspreads so that they matched from bed to bed around the room.

"Remember, D Flight," said Corporal Payne. "I can spot a spider's web before the spider has even thought about weaving it, and if I find one in this billet you will all live to regret it, so you make sure it is all up to inspection standard."

Just at that moment I was tempted to let Dad keep his ten bob ... and double his money!

It was only 9pm but, as she left us, with the cheerful news that we were expected to rise at 5am, all we wanted to do was drop onto our beds and die.

"Cow!" exclaimed Pat, with feeling.

Within half an hour we were all in bed, but any thoughts of going straight to sleep were shattered by Big Haggis. She decided that she wanted to find out all about everybody and began quizzing us all in turn. Bit by bit we found out who had left boyfriends behind and who had not. Most had not. Getting a boyfriend when you were in your early teens was not easy.

"Fat chance of finding a bloke in our age group when the minute they are eighteen they have to do National Service," said Barbara from the bed opposite me.

"Well, we are bound to find one on an all-female station aren't we?" replied Pat sarcastically.

"All those boys that have disappeared to do National Service must be around somewhere," said Taff, "and I am going to find them when I finish here."

"There is talk that National Service is going to finish soon," I ventured optimistically.

"Well, it will be a *bit* late for us," retorted Pat. "I could have done with it finishing two years ago when I was sixteen and then I might have kept my bloody boyfriend and not had to come into the bloody WRAF to find one!"

"Go to sleep!" demanded a voice from the other end of the room out of the darkness.

"I know," said Haggis, totally ignoring the request, "let's go round the room and find out who are virgins and who are not!"

"Oh for gawd's sake!" said the voice, "have a heart, I am shattered!"

"Come on Taff lassie," continued Haggis. "I am," she said proudly.

It was something to boast about in 1959. Not to be bashful to own up to if you were anything over the age of sixteen as it became a few decades later.

"So am I!" I answered, totally mortified, not at my answer, but at the whole questioning.

"I bet Pat isn't!" persisted Haggis, "not if she had a boyfriend when she was sixteen."

"I most certainly am!" retorted Pat indignantly. "I was too scared of getting pregnant. My parents would have kicked me out."

"What about you Maureen, are you a virgin?" Big Haggis was determined to do her Billet Survey no matter what. It felt like a week since I had left home that morning and I could feel my eyelids closing, despite my efforts to join in the conversation. However, they opened again wide in the darkness at Maureen's reply.

"I'm afraid I am not..." she sounded very embarrassed. At twenty-five she was the oldest in the billet by far, but her sudden confession stopped us in our tracks.

It was Pat who spoke first. "You were lucky not to get pregnant!" she whispered.

"I did," came back the casual reply.

There were gasps from around the room.

"I had to put my baby up for adoption, that's why I am here, to start a new life, I hope."

It was a sign of the times we were in that nobody was surprised at her parting with her baby. We were more surprised at her getting pregnant! Many 'unmarried mothers' had to go in a 'mother and baby home' and then the baby was taken away for adoption.

"Oh Maureen," answered Haggis, slightly chastened. "I am sorry. Did you know what it was?"

"A little boy," said Maureen. "I called him Robert, but of course he may have his name changed now. I doubt if I shall ever see him again."

We all felt extremely deflated but any further investigations into who was, or was not, a virgin came to an abrupt halt as the billet door was thrown open and the diminutive figure of Corporal Payne stood silhouetted against the light in the corridor behind her.

"Go to sleep D Flight!" she roared, so loudly that she probably woke up the Flight in the next billet to us. She had probably heard every word of our late night conversation too! We had forgotten all about her being in the end room next to ours. We wouldn't again.

"One more sound out of anybody and you will all be on a charge in the morning!" With that she slammed the door and we were all back in the dark.

"Night Pat!" I whispered.

"Night Ratty!" she replied, already giving me a nickname.

"What's a charge?" hissed Barbara from across the room.

I had an idea because my Dad had told me it was what he said would happen if I did not behave myself in the WRAF.

"You get hauled up in front of the 'beak' and sent to the 'glasshouse'," I replied, as I remembered his words.

There was the sound of thumping on the other side of the wall, between the corporal and ourselves, and we all went quiet. I heard the clock in a distant church strike ten. Is that all it was? I wondered if my Mum and Dad were thinking about me. I was certainly thinking about them. I pondered on what the next four years would bring.

Would I ever be a 'plus type girl' and – more importantly to me just then – would it all be worth ten bob?

2. *"Get your Number Dry!"*

"Come on everybody, rise and shine, the sun is burning your eyes out. Be out on the road to march to breakfast in half an hour."

The blanket of sleep fell away from me sharply as these words penetrated my dreams. I couldn't understand where I was – surely that wasn't my Mother's voice? And anyway, what did she want me to march to breakfast for? Surely I should be getting the rush-hour train to the office?

My eyes focused on the white painted wooden beams reaching up to the apex of the ceiling and the sound of the word "Ker-riste!" from the bed next to me brought me back into the real world. I crawled out of bed and almost sleep-walked in the direction of the washroom, finally coming to life after the feel of the concrete of the passage on my bare feet and the cold water on my face.

"Fancy having to get up at this time," said Pat. "People that expect others to get up at this time should be put-away in a loony-bin."

Trying to ignore her, I put on my best summer 'shirt-waister' dress with the frilly petticoats underneath and wide plastic belt.

"It's the middle of the bloody night," declared Pat again. "No wonder my brother thought I was mad for volunteering."

It was difficult not to agree with her when we went out onto the road, ready to march to the Mess at such an ungodly hour, and it promised to be a hot day again as well.

Haggis's idea of trying to find out all about us certainly had the effect of 'breaking the ice' and we felt as though we had already known each other for years as we sat together and had our breakfast. I was especially sorry for Maureen, having to give her baby away. She seemed like a nice, respectable girl too. She was tall and slim with dark curly hair and glasses and, because she was so much older than us, one or two of the girls called her 'Grannie'. It was all in fun though and she took it in good part. Most people would end up with nicknames before the next six weeks was over.

I was just beginning to feel a little more human when, to my horror, we were told that we were to have our first session of 'square-bashing'!

"Square-bashing!" cried Little Haggis. "At this time of the morning?"

"Well, it should be good for a laugh anyway," grinned Barbara. "Especially in *these* shoes."

She was wearing impossibly high winkle-pickers, which I would not even be able to walk in, never mind march. Most of us were wearing casuals, some were in high heels, and then there were Barbara's – in a class of their own.

We left our cups and eating irons in the cloakroom of the Mess and Corporal Payne marched us off to the parade ground. It seemed that even the birds were singing a tune in sympathy with us and she was enjoying every minute. We were already forming the opinion that she was a 'sadist'. However, it was on the parade ground that we could see at a glance how long each flight had been at Wilmslow and really get the feel of the place!

In the centre of the square were a flight of recruits looking very smart in full uniform. They were obviously practising for their Passing Out Parade, which was to be during the following week. Over in the far corner another flight were marching up and down with only two of the girls not wearing uniform and yet another flight looked extremely funny wearing battle dress tops and shirts (despite the heat) with civilian skirts and service shoes. Their efforts to look smart doing their drill and the screams of their corporal were a dead 'give away' that they were not far ahead of us with their training.

Just marching onto the parade ground in front of us were C Flight, who had only been here a week. Long enough, however, for them to have been issued with their lace-up shoes and stockings, the shoes looking like football boots when worn with summer dresses, but infinitely more practical than Barbara's stilettos.

Then, of course, there was us, D Flight, all of us doing our best and trying not to giggle every time we stumbled over each other when our corporal yelled 'Halt!' Most of us wore huge 'circular skirts' puffed out with layers of muslin petticoats. Needless to say, every time we turned to the right or left, there was a clash of frothy skirt and muslin in myriads of colours. It was like the 'ballroom' section of 'Come Dancing'!

I glanced at the flight in the middle of the square and wondered how on earth I would be as smart as that in six weeks. It didn't take me long, however, to be in *no* doubt whatsoever that Corporal Payne had every intention that not only would we be that smart but, if she had anything to do with it, we would be even better! Her reputation depended upon it.

We were kept marching and then standing to attention for what seemed like hours without a break. She told us not to dare move an inch, no matter what happened, and every time someone did so we all had to stand still for a bit longer. Once a bee hovered in front of me and I prayed it would go away, for I did not dare do anything but roll my eyes at it.

The flight who were forced to wear lace-up service shoes with their summer dresses may have looked peculiar but we were soon all wishing that we were dressed the same. Thank God we were getting ours tomorrow – and if this was Corporal Payne's way of convincing us, then she had succeeded!

Suddenly Barbara kicked her shoes off and they went whizzing past my ear as she threw them across the parade ground out of the way. They missed Corporal Payne by a matter of inches. Without batting an eyelid, she slowly strolled towards them and gave the girl a withering look before picking them up between her thumb and forefinger and putting them neatly together on the nearby path.

"You can't aim very straight, can you Brown?" she snarled.

Barbara continued to march in her stockings.

Up and down we trooped, in the heat, and I began to feel very sorry for those other flights on the parade ground who were wearing thick uniform skirts. I came to the conclusion that no matter what it looked like, summer dresses and 'beetle-crushers' were the ideal combination for drill in this weather.

"Swing your arms D Flight..." the little Corporal roared at us. "Dig your heels in – keep your chins up – for crying out loud, when I said keep your chins up, I did not mean you to stop swinging your bloody arms!" And so it went on, for what seemed like an eternity, as, bit by bit, the other flights left and the parade ground emptied.

"Turning to the right – ri-ight *turn* – one-pause-two – McIntyre, don't you know your right from your left? Right I said, right, right, RIGHT!"

Of course, it was impossible for Barbara with no shoes on.

"Brown, fall out and come and put your shoes back on." She indicated to her to stay put at the side of the parade ground and watch. Then, a few minutes later, she brought the rest of us to a halt. Much more of this and I was convinced that I would be 'passing out', literally, six weeks before I was due to do so!

"The next time we do drill it will be with your proper footwear," said Corporal Payne. "Then you will *really* appreciate them!"

We formed up in threes and were marched away from the square. The sound of Cliff Richard getting louder was an indication that we were going to the NAAFI at last.

"Bugger this," swore Big Haggis as we were dismissed and Corporal Payne disappeared in the direction of the Corporals' Club. "Ma shins feel as though they're fallin awa frae ma ankles!" I didn't even bother to ask for a translation as I was soon to discover that Big Haggis's accent and her language became stronger the more stressed she became – and at the moment she was very stressed indeed.

The NAAFI (Navy, Army and Air Force Institute) was like a large canteen – red Formica-topped tables, a counter at one end and (holy of holies) a jukebox, which at the moment was rocking with the latest hit tune, 'Lipstick on your Collar'. This and 'Living Doll' seemed to be the only records, played over and over again.

We queued up behind some of the smart A Flight girls to buy some sticky doughnuts and lemonade. Barbara got talking to one of the airwomen and she and I and Big Haggis joined them at their table. It wasn't until many weeks afterwards that we realised how very honoured we were! There was, though, an ulterior motive for allowing us 'lowly mortals' to be in their presence – after all *they* had all but finished their training and they could enjoy showing-off to us 'babies'. The airwomen in A Flight, although patronising, gave us some confidence though.

"Don't worry," smiled a small blonde girl, as she swilled down her cooling drink. She spoke with all the knowledge of one who had been in the Women's Royal Air Force for five whole weeks.

"You haven't seen the worst yet, but you'll get used to it and it is worth it in the end!"

"Well," went on one of the others. "Think about it. Take a look at the permanent staff. They are not treated like you are and they have their own NAAFI and don't mix with trainees at all!"

"She has a point," said Barbara.

The girls went on to tell us about what we would likely be doing in the next weeks and said that they were getting posted to their Trade Training Stations after their passing out parade. One or two of this top flight were even sorry to be leaving Wilmslow and they all said it had been a 'good laugh!'

I was not totally convinced!

"A Flight!" yelled somebody in the distance. "On Parade!"

They leapt to their feet and gulped down the last of their drinks.

"That's us!" said one importantly. "Duty calls. See you sometime!"

"Well there's hope yet then," said Barbara.

"Oh they must be right," I replied. "After all, if every RAF station were like this one, nobody would stay in, and then there would be no RAF – and then where would we all be?"

"Tucked up in my own little bed at home," wailed Pat. "That's where I would be, at any rate!"

"Me too!" muttered Haggis into her doughnut. "Bonnie Scotland will dae me!"

"D Flight!" Corporal Payne had appeared out of nowhere. "On Parade!"

Haggis nearly choked as we rushed out of the NAAFI, leaving Cliff to finish his song without us.

"Wonder what we are in for this time?" said Maureen as she caught up with us. "Nothing would surprise me any more".

We formed up in our ranks of three outside the NAAFI and I was surprised to note that it was still only 10 o'clock. I couldn't believe it. I felt as though I had been up for hours!

"D Flight, by the left, quick *march!*" she bellowed.

It was a lost cause but we did our best and, to my great satisfaction, we did not stop at the parade ground this time. She was keeping her promise – no more marching until we had got our shoes.

In fact, we were taken to a classroom, where we were to receive our first lecture, all about Badges of Rank and the history of the Royal Air Force. This lecture was given by a WRAF officer, the first I had seen since leaving the Recruiting Centre in London! She was kindly and motherly and actually made her talk very interesting. Apart from anything else, it was a treat to be able to sit down and relax.

She spoke about the formation of the RAF after the First World War and about the exploits of RAF men who became household names, like Wing Commander Guy Gibson and Douglas Bader and it was the start of feeling as though we were about to belong to something very special.

And so the morning wore into the afternoon and before we knew it, the days ran into a week and the six weeks had already dwindled to five. The first week had gone on much the same as the first day, with rising early in the morning to hours of drill, and then evenings of cleaning.

Corporal Payne had been true to her word too, and we did no more drill until we received our footwear. Then, of course, we had to wear suspender belts and stockings, with the heavy lace up shoes, known as 'beetle crushers', How 'glamorous' they looked with our summer skirts and petticoats! However, by now we were past caring – all we wanted was something comfortable on our feet.

Then we were taken for a uniform fitting. It was boiling hot, but there was no let-up as we spent the day in the stifling clothing stores, trying on raincoats, greatcoats, slacks, P.T. kit and even long, silky grey knickers, like bloomers, nicknamed 'passion killers'. What didn't fit was given back and replaced, or we had to have a 'chitty' to show that we were excused for the time being.

A variety of underclothes were thrown along the counter at us – bras, suspender belts, stockings, even sanitary towels with 'Government Issue' written on the packet.

"They surely dinna expect us to wear these?" cried Haggis, holding her passion killers aloft.

"They are to wear with your P.T. skirt," said the Senior Aircraftswoman who was dishing out the clothing.

I held up the short skirt that she passed to me and agreed that you could not wear a pair of frilly Marks and Spark's knickers with *that* – not unless you wanted to be arrested!

Despite the length of time taken to fit us out, we were still like that other flight we had seen on the parade ground – excused skirts. Those of us who were not a standard size were having them made to measure.

As far as our best uniform was concerned, we would have a long wait for that. The whole thing was to be tailored and not to be worn until our Passing Out Parade, which at that moment in time seemed a very long way off indeed.

Ironically, it was 4th July, Independence Day, and just over a week past my eighteenth birthday, when we signed on the dotted line, promising to serve four years for her Majesty. I wondered if her Majesty was fully aware of what she was getting! We were each told our numbers and now we could address an NCO properly as we had been taught. I was able to say my number, rank and name now – and thus, on Independence Day, I became a number!

Even though it had been hard work during the first week, I now came to realise that we had been having it quite easy really in comparison with what was to come. What followed next was the hard work and the discipline that became part of our daily lives in Recruit Training and was going to, hopefully, turn us into 'plus-types'. At this stage I was not confident that it was ever going to happen.

During the evening we had to polish and clean the billet, whether it needed it or not. This was the hardest, and yet sometimes, the funniest, part of the day, especially when Big Haggis got 'stressed'.

It was an unwritten rule that the floor had to be so shiny that we could see as far as our knees in the reflection. Consequently everyone was responsible for their own bed space and we vied with each other to see who could polish the floor to see the furthest up our skirts in the image!

"One of these days it will be polished so much old Payne will be able to see her own knickers!" said Pat.

"That's if she wears any," muttered Haggis.

No-one was permitted to wear shoes and there was hell to pay if the corporal even caught us trying to wear slippers! Yet we were *not* allowed to go in stockinged feet to the washrooms! This meant that piles of 'beetle crushers' were kept in the broom cupboard at the entrance to the billet, and every time someone wanted water for cleaning, we had to go through the ritual of putting our shoes on at the billet door, getting our water, and then removing them on the way back, with one hand, whilst balancing the bucket in the other. It was like some sort of circus act but it certainly tested our character and patience to the limit!

Nobody dreamt of walking over another's bed space in case they left a mark and everyone did the most amazing contortions across beds and lockers to get to the other end of the billet without touching the floor. If we had no choice but to walk on the floor then we slid across it, with our feet wrapped in dusters, thus risking the chance of ending up on our backsides amid peals of wicked laughter.

One evening, early in our training, Big Haggis was down on her hands and knees, furiously polishing away at her 'flair', as she called it, totally oblivious to all around her, when a pair of feet appeared about two inches away from her hand. All of us stared in horror as she let rip before anybody could warn her who the feet belonged to.

"Get your bloody great shins affa me flair!" she roared.

The shoes did not move. Haggis's head slowly crept up, her eyes fell upon the flawless service stockings, the knife-edged pleats in the skirt, the beautifully pressed battledress and eventually found herself staring up into the beady eyes of Corporal Payne. We all stood stock still, trying desperately hard not to laugh. Poor Haggis turned varying shades of pink, red, purple and back to mottled pink and white again, but to our relief the NCO took it in reasonably good part – for her.

"I am glad to see you are so concerned about your floor Macintyre," she said. "But I should watch your language in future!"

With that comment, she deliberately put her foot right where Haggis had been polishing and twisted it back and forth.

"Oh look there," she smiled sarcastically. "It looks as though you missed a bit." Then she about-turned on a highly polished shoe and was gone from the billet, leaving Haggis staring after her!

"Cow!" muttered Pat.

When the billet gleamed to our corporal's satisfaction, we had to lay our kit out on our beds and stand to attention to await the arrival of the WRAF officer and her entourage of sergeant and corporal. Each item had to be in a certain place on the bed – and woe-betide any of us if it had drifted to the wrong place or if we had anything missing.

Maureen was horrified to find that she had mislaid a pair of her passion killers, but Little Haggis came to the rescue. She waited until her bed-space had been inspected and then grabbed her own knickers and boldly slid them across the polished floor for Maureen to catch with her foot behind the Inspecting Officer's back. She quickly folded them and put them on her bed.

Fortunately, neither the officer nor the NCOs picked up the knickers to check the name tag, otherwise they would have seen they belonged to somebody else.

When the billet was being inspected as well, the WRAF Officer wore white gloves. If any dust appeared on them when she ran them along the edges of the furniture or door, then the corporal would go pink with rage and we were given an extra Bull Night for our sins.

There was one WRAF Flying Officer who had the habit of walking right around the billet, leaving dusty footprints behind her, and then, upon reaching the door, turning round and remarking about the disgusting mess on the floor and that we might have made a better effort before she arrived for inspection in future!

There were many times when the creatures that supplied us so faithfully with milk and had done no harm to anybody had their names taken in vain!

There was one good thing about Recruit Training. The time went by very quickly and before we knew it we were the 'top flight'. None of us really knew how we got there, but somehow we had, and we had to reluctantly admit that it was largely due to Corporal Payne.

Of course, there had been exams, relentless drill and P.T. and even Field Day, when we were dropped in the middle of the Cheshire countryside and told to find our way back to camp. It was all hard work, often funny and any ideas that we would pack it in and go back home were fast disappearing – not that we had much choice once we had signed on.

How the Permanent Staff must have chuckled at us as we grew in confidence! The numbers on our Identity Cards were barely dry but we felt like 'old soldiers' compared to the new ones that we saw hobbling around in their civilian clothes. We had uniforms that fitted and shoes that were comfortable and that alone made us feel better.

"You know, it hasn't been too bad," said Pat one day.

"Nah," said Big Haggis. "It is just the lack of men that is the problem."

"Do you know, I hadn't even thought about that," I replied, as I sat polishing my shoes for the umpteenth time.

It was true, our lives were so active that the fact that we were on a camp that consisted almost entirely of females didn't seem in the least bit incongruous. Practically everybody, from the Commanding Officer down, were WRAF. The only men that we saw were a few members of the

Permanent Staff, including the cooks and the Snowdrops – probably no more than a couple of dozen all told.

It really hadn't been all bad either. We had a lot of good times and often dissolved into fits of giggles during the most arduous of tasks.

In no time at all we were the 'top flight' at Pay Parade. This meant standing at the back of the NAAFI, with all the tables and chairs pushed to one side, while the newer recruits were nearer to the front. It all seemed a bit of a farce for a measly few bob a week, but Pay Parade was considered to be a very hallowed occasion. Almost like being in Church. We all had to stand in our Flights with the Paying Out Officer (or Poo, as we called her) and a sergeant sitting at a table in front of us. Each airwoman's name was called in turn and each time we had to stand to attention and say our 'last three' before marching to collect our money from the officer. Then we had to salute before signing for it and again afterwards. It was all a bit complicated, especially for the newest of recruits, but we got the hang of it eventually. If you didn't get it right you were sent back to do it again, so it could all become a very lengthy business. Eventually my name was read out.

"Ratcliff!"

"Ma'am 747 Ma'am!"

I marched up to the desk, saluted, took the money and saluted again, at the same time trying very hard to keep a smile from crossing my face. It wasn't easy.

There was a story doing the rounds at the time that in the Pay Parade for the men at the RAF Recruit Training at Bridgenorth, one particular bloke *deliberately* failed to salute. He was immediately called back by the sergeant.

"What happened to your salute airman?" the Senior NCO had barked on behalf of his affronted officer. "Don't you salute an RAF Officer any more?"

Then came the immortal reply that would go down in RAF legend. "What do you want for sixteen bob Sarge? A bloody March Past?"

He got a 'march past' of course – straight to the Guard Room – and in due course found out what being up in front of 'the beak' and 'going to the glasshouse' was all about!

One pair of shoes had been saved and polished every day for our Passing Out Parade – and on no account had we been allowed to wear them until that final day, although at every opportunity Corporal Payne had inspected them.

Our best uniforms had finally arrived from Clothing Store, where they had been professionally pressed and brushed so that they were worthy of the big occasion. Our best hat, which for the past six weeks had been kept in a box on top of each of our tall lockers, would finally get an airing.

Even a special detachable collar had been put to one side and had been sent to be 'Chinese laundered' – a procedure which resulted in them being turned into something resembling a piece of plywood. It was a skill in itself to get the collar stud through the buttonhole and even to get the tie inside the stiffened and shiny material and it took ages.

We couldn't believe it, but the big day had arrived and we set about putting the uniform on that had been so cared for all these weeks and trying to pack the rest of it and our civilian clothes into a kitbag.

"I'm determined to get these up a flagpole," said Pat, holding up her passion killers.

We all ignored her but I did notice that she very quickly and deftly cut out her name tag before pushing them into her WRAF handbag.

"You wouldn't?" I whispered.

"I would," she grinned.

"No she wouldn't," said Jenny.

I was distracted by Little Haggis as she gazed into her mirror and struggled, like me, with the plywood collar. They really were a nightmare to put on but the end result was worthwhile. I fought with my collar studs and eventually won. I still didn't think I felt like a 'plus-type girl' – though I had to admit that Clothing Store had done their best.

"I wonder what we have got in store for us after today Haggis?" I said. "Pat and I are off to Hereford to learn shorthand and typing, and with you going off to Compton Bassett to learn about communications, we probably won't see each other again after today."

"I hope they don't put her on the telephones," giggled Taffy. "Nobody will understand a bloody word she is on about!"

"You can shout," retorted Big Haggis on her friend's behalf.

We continued to get ready, all the time nattering about our futures and wondering if we would meet with our corporal's approval when she saw what *her* Flight looked like now that they were in their Best Blues. I glanced down at my toecaps and could see my reflection in them and was satisfied.

Tomorrow the World!

"And now, as the sun sinks slowly in the west, we bid farewell to the Savoy Hotel..." mimicked Barbara, as she adjusted her peaked cap with its shiny cap badge on her dark curls.

"I don't think we'll come across anything worse, that's for sure," I replied.

"D Flight! Stand by your beds!" The immortal words rang down the billet and cut short any more joking.

Here was one aspect of RAF Wilmslow that I would miss like a hole in the head. At least the chances of meeting up with that little Hitler again were very slim! Or so I thought...

She marched in, like a little toy soldier, probably glad to see the back of us, if the truth be known. She straightened a button there, altered the angle of a cap there, checked our shoes, brushed our uniforms and then stood back to survey her handiwork.

"Well D Flight," she said. "I told you that I would make airwomen of you in six weeks."

She said it as if it was a compliment to herself rather than to us, which it was really, if we were honest! Then she decided to give us a little lecture.

"You have four years in front of you. Some of you may decide to stay in – some may get married (much laughter from around the room) but I have only one piece of advice to offer you and it's this – remember that your last station is always your best!"

That sounded like double Dutch to me, but it was all she was going to say.

"D Flight – on Parade!"

The moment of truth had come.

I glanced around at the empty billet as we began to file out onto the road – the beds with their neat bed stacks and all our kit packed ready for our departure. Six weeks ago 20 girls had ambled into this billet but, true to her word, Corporal Payne had ensured that *airwomen* would march out of it. You couldn't say fairer than that.

"All ready for the next lot of poor buggers," grinned Maureen as she went past me. She had changed so much in six weeks and was now much more outgoing and seemed happier.

We formed up in threes outside the billet and marched to the parade ground. I felt nine feet tall as we strode on to the centre to the wonderful marches played by the Central Band of the Royal Air Force. As somebody once wisely said, 'you had to be there.'

Suddenly, those weeks of hard work had been worthwhile. Here we were, marching smartly – no more falling over each other – and being a civilian suddenly seemed a very long way away. The 18.07 train from Waterloo might as well have been on the moon.

Crowds of parents were sitting on wooden stands that had been erected overnight along two sides of the parade ground and the Royal Air Force ensign fluttered in the light breeze on the tall flagpole. I wished that my parents could have been there, but it was too difficult for them with two small boys who should be at school. I still wished they were there though, if only to take a photo. I felt tears prick at the back of my eyes.

I managed to steal a glance across at Pat as we left-wheeled onto the area in front of WRAF officers and was surprised to see that her eyes were already glistening with tears. But she was not the only one – the emotion of the occasion was too much for most of us as we marched past the WRAF Director and did a smart 'eyes right' in her direction and she saluted back.

The RAF Central Band played the *General Salute*, followed by the *Royal Air Force March* and then was momentarily drowned out by the roar of three Vulcan bombers zooming low overhead. They showed up majestically, like three white triangles, in perfect formation, against the blue sky. Then they sharply climbed vertically and were quickly out of sight above the clouds. The roar of their engines gradually faded and the sound of the Central Band returned.

Tears flowed down my cheeks as I burst with pride and then, before I knew where I was, it was all over. We had somehow marched from the square to the tune of the *Dambusters March* and had been dismissed. Any embarrassment that I might have had at my wet cheeks soon disappeared as I looked around. There was not a dry eye in the Flight.

"Wasna' it great!?" whispered Big Haggis, who for once was completely subdued.

"Oh go on," laughed Pat as she wiped a tear from her eye. "I know why we are crying, don't *you*?"

I looked at her in puzzlement.

"It's tears of happiness," she grinned, "because at last we shall be able to mix with the men!" And with that she ran down the road towards the billet and I suddenly remembered the knickers that she had put in her handbag.

She wouldn't – would she?

"She's right," laughed Maureen, as we followed on behind, "but mine are tears of joy because this is the last we shall see of Corporal bloody Payne!"

We walked off to our billets, collected our things and went to the bus, while those whose parents had attended went to join their folks. By this time the parade ground was deserted and the Central Band were probably downing some beers in the Permanent Staff NAAFI.

I hadn't seen Pat for ages but soon she came running up, and, panting for breath, scrambled onto the service bus with the rest of us.

"You didn't?" I whispered.

"I did," she said. "But not the parade ground flagpole – I have done better than that … look!"

The bus pulled away towards the camp gates and past the Officers' Mess and my eye followed her gaze.

"I have left a souvenir for the officers!" she chortled.

I nearly choked and the rest of the girls roared with laughter when we caught sight of Pat's passion-killers, swinging merrily from the pristine white flagpole in the garden outside the Officers' Mess.

"Oh my God!" laughed Barbara. "She *did!*"

"How did you manage it?" I asked.

"Well, you know I told you that my brother was doing his National Service?"

"Yes…" I was beginning to get the picture.

"Well, he has a friend who has just got posted to Wilmslow as permanent staff in there." She nodded in the direction of the Mess. "I just had to do a bit of chatting up, that's all."

"I am glad you took your name tag out," I grinned.

"So am I," she laughed.

And that's how D Flight departed from Royal Air Force Wilmslow one summer's day in 1959!

3. *The Sixties Begin*

Pat Seymour and I sat in the Air Force bus, speeding towards RAF Hereford, lost in our own private thoughts. We had both had a couple of days leave after our departure from Wilmslow and had gone home to our families to show off our new uniforms. I was very proud to walk down the road to our house in mine and I had taken great pleasure in collecting my ten shillings from my Dad.

"It was worth every penny of it," he said, with a twinkle in his eye. I was not quite sure whether that was because he had got rid of me or because he was proud of me. As I got older and wiser I realised, of course, that really it was the second of the two.

Now, having met up with my friend at Hereford station, together with some airmen who were going in the same direction, we were on our way again, this time to our Trade Training. I began to realise already that what Corporal Payne had said was true – you do tend to forget all the horrible things about your last station and remember it as being the best. 'Rose-tinted glasses' I think they call it!

The leaves on the trees were just beginning to get that orange tint which heralds the coming of autumn and in the fields, on either side of the road, the farmers had hastily gathered in the last of the corn, leaving behind acres of brown stubble. I occasionally cast a glance at the leaden sky, hoping that it wouldn't rain before we got there. It was a very pretty part of the country.

"Look!" one of the airmen suddenly said, "that must be RAF Hereford!"

The sun was disappearing over the horizon and, across to our left, we could see the roofs of dozens of billets silhouetted, against the reds and oranges of the sky. It made them appear to be much more 'magical' than they really were!

"Doesn't look that much different from Wilmslow does it Ratty?" muttered Pat, bringing us all back down to earth.

"It's a bit bigger" I replied, as I began to gather my luggage together, "we'll soon see though."

The coach pulled up at the Guard room and, lugging our kitbags, we reported to the Duty Sergeant, who directed us to the WRAF quarters. The boys, all of whom were very subdued, disappeared in a different direction. It was almost as if having some airwomen on the bus had taken them by surprise!

WRAF Admin was a small wooden building opposite the WRAF billets. This was the place where the staff looked after our personal matters, sorted out our problems and disciplined where necessary. Well, that's what they told us at any rate!

We were shown to a small office and told to wait. We both let go of our kitbags and gratefully sat down on them, but hastily jumped back up to attention when the door opened to reveal the tiniest little Flight Sergeant I had ever seen. Her name was Flight Sergeant Stephens and she looked just like a garden gnome in uniform! A uniform that had its fair share of medal ribbons adorning it.

I learned later that she was quite capable of putting the fear of God into any airwoman, or airman for that matter, who did not toe the line! She was of indefinite age and stared up at us over the top of rimless glasses. It didn't take me long to gather that she was a Scottish lady!

"Welcome tae Hereford lassies," she smiled. "I'll tak ye awa tae ye billet in a wee while but fust ye must sign this wee book. Noo, ye ken, ye'll find it different here from Wilmslow," she said, in what was, to us, totally unintelligible dialect. "Nae mare marching, nae much onyway, and bull night twa times a week." We sighed with relief as she shuffled around some papers on her untidy desk. "Noo, lets find oot which course you will be on…"

She picked up the telephone and gabbled away to someone on the other end, who obviously could understand her.

"Aye, aye, it's the new lassies, och aye, aye, bye the noo!"

She put the phone down again as we gazed at her in continued awe, whilst I thought that we could have done with one of the Haggis's for some translation.

"That was your Sergeant in charge of the typing course," she informed us, in her sing-song voice. "He has a full course the noo, so your lessons willna be starting for a wee while yet."

Pat and I exchanged looks.

"Dinna ye worry now though," said the NCO. "Ye'll haf tae spend some time on Pool Flight – it willna hurt ye – ye can report here the mons morning and I'll tell ye what ye haf tae do, but I expect ye tired the noo, so lets awa tae ye billet."

We followed her across the road to the line of WRAF billets, which turned out to be exactly like the ones at our last station.

"The rest of the lassies will still be awa at the school," she went on, "but nae doot they will mak ye feel at hame as they come in – dinna forget the noo, I'll see ye the mons morning!"

She waved us a cheery goodbye and toddled off.

We sunk down on to the two obviously unoccupied beds and kicked our shoes off. It had been a long day already.

"Whew!" exclaimed Pat. "I could hardly understand a word of what she was saying."

"Nice though wasn't she?" I replied.

"Mmm," mused Pat, as she roused herself up and started to unpack, "but I bet she can be a right little whatsit if she caught anybody with their hair on their collar or slinging their 'pashers' up the flagpole!"

Then I noticed the black stove in the middle of the room.

"I thought we'd seen the last of those blessed things," I said. "If there's one fatigue I hate more than any other its black leading those things."

"I don't think either of us would make good housewives," muttered Pat into her suitcase.

At the mention of 'housewives' I thought of Maureen. She would be a housewife and mother now if her boyfriend had done the decent thing and married her.

"That was a turn-up, about old Maureen," I said. "It must be awful to go through all that pain and aggravation only to have your baby taken away."

"I know," said Pat seriously. "I hope she will be OK at her new station – poor old Grannie."

I had liked Maureen. She had seemed such a nice girl and I couldn't help thinking that it was her baby's loss not to have her as a mother. I just hoped that the mother who the child ended up with was as nice.

We continued our unpacking in silence and then lay down on our beds in the quiet and empty billet. However, the peace was soon shattered by the most unholy sound of shrieking girls and doors bursting open along the lines of billets. Ours flew open and in raced dozens of airwomen, all in uniform, with files of papers under their arms.

A small freckle-faced girl, wearing glasses, dropped her books on her bed and stared at us.

"Oh hello," she said, "have you just come from Wilmslow?"

"Yes," I answered. "I'm Joan, but she calls me Ratty, and this is Pat Seymour – I havn't worked out what to call *her* yet."

Soon they were all standing around and introducing themselves whilst consoling with us for having to be on Pool Flight.

"Ugh," grunted the freckle-faced girl, who was called Janet. "Pool Flight is just like Wilmslow, only more boring."

"Oh bloody hell!" exclaimed Pat. "Are you sure?"

"What's the food like?" I questioned. "It was foul at Recruit Training."

"Same here," said Janet brightly. "It's just the same, we live on tea and toast."

"Oh ker-riste!" exclaimed Pat.

That evening we were able to have our first taste of NAAFI life in mixed company and without forever being under the watchful eye of a corporal and without ever hearing those dreadful words "D Flight on Parade!" It was like being let out of jail!

The NAAFI was similar to the one at Wilmslow, with the inevitable jukebox in the corner. The only difference was the tune. This one seemed perpetually to play "Why am I so

Starry Eyed" by Michael Holliday and "Travellin' Light" by Cliff Richard. Cliff was everywhere.

It was very strange, but at the same time pleasant, to be able to mix and talk with everyone and to actually be asked to jive by some of the boys sitting around. It certainly made a change from jiving with girls all the time!

Pat and Janet and I soon got talking to three Scots boys who had arrived at Hereford on the same day as us, and who were all very miserable as they had not asked to come into the Air Force as we had. They were National Servicemen. What made it even worse, in their eyes, was that they knew National Service would be coming to an end soon and they had just been 'caught'!

Stuart was a dumpy little chap with straight black hair and was absolutely convinced that the butchery trade, that he had been an apprentice to, would be lost without him for the next two years. He did not want to be here and that was that!

Wally was tall and lean, with a pale, thin face, surmounted by a mop of wavy red hair. He also was quite sure that the Air Force could manage just as well without him as with him, and was still suffering from the shock he had been given when he was told that he was going to be trained as a typist. It was all too much to cope with! He had just finished an apprenticeship as a carpenter, and considered it daft that now that he was qualified and a craftsman he still had to do his National Service. There was no getting out of it though. It was that or jail!

Finally there was Tommy. He was the joker of the three and I took to him immediately. He had dark hair and a craggy face with a continuous expression of a hurt spaniel. He also came from just outside Glasgow. There seemed to be a lot of Scots in this Air Force!

Tommy's one and only passion in his life was his jazz music. He was sure that the RAF had done him out of a worthwhile career and had, at the same time, deprived the world of the best guitarist and string bass player that ever lived. He had no time for Rock and Roll, be it Bill Haley or Cliff Richard, and was totally faithful to his Jazz and to Folk music and was convinced that one day he would be famous.

He was so mortified at being a National Serviceman that it was almost entertaining to listen to him complaining! All three had thought they would get away with it by being 'deferred' until after their respective apprenticeships. They were all wrong and so here they were.

Wally and Stuart tormented Tommy without mercy.

We were to become firm friends with this trio and I was soon to learn that Tommy could, when he chose, be the life and soul of the party, despite his hatred of the Royal Air Force and his objection to officers in particular and all things Air Force blue.

They too were going to be on a Pool Flight whilst waiting for the Typing Course to start, but to them, even this fate was not as bad as becoming a 'poofy' typist!

"A typist!" Tommy exclaimed. "That's girls' work!"

We were disappointed to find out though, that in its continued quest to keep the sexes apart, WRAF Admin made sure that our Pool Flight and the boys' Pool Flight did not mix! The boys seemed very familiar with it all though.

"They'll soon have us leaping around, painting the coal white and black-leading the dustbins," said Wally.

"I can't wait!" grumbled Tommy.

"You have got to get up early in the morning too," said Stuart, sensing an opportunity to wind him up. "That won't please you, will it, my old mate? You can sleep through a hurricane."

"Rubbish!" he retorted. "Of course I can get up in the morning."

"Oh yes?" laughed Stuart. "What about at Recruit Training then, when you woke up and found yourself on the football pitch?"

"Aw shut up will you!" He went bright red, but Stuart needed no pressing to relate the story for our benefit.

It seemed that it had not taken them long to discover that he could sleep through anything, particularly after a few beers, and so one night several of the boys had gently lifted his bed while he was sound asleep and carried it several hundred yards to the football pitch and then placed it carefully by the goal mouth. Tommy had slept through it all and as he was some distance away from the billets, and therefore the Tannoy system, he even slept through reveille! He eventually awoke and found himself staring into the eyes of a very irate Physical Training Instructor and his trainees.

Fortunately, everyone had seen the funny side and he did not get put on a charge. The trouble was, we were never quite sure who to believe half the time – Stuart's stories seemed just as plausible as Tommy's denials!

We could have sat and listened to these boys and their stories for hours, but we still had to be in by 11pm, even here. Soon we were soon back in the billet and tucked up in our beds. I was so tired that I had a dreadful horror somebody might carry mine away and leave it on the football pitch, for I felt sure I would not wake up at the correct time in the morning.

How utterly wrong can anyone be? My eardrums were shattered with a terrific shrieking noise, followed by some unearthly fiendish laughter, and then...

"Ape call – doodily ub ah! Ape Call – doodily up ah! If you wanna gerra man – go Ape!"

The tune pierced through my head so that I almost saw stars. I rolled out of bed and onto the floor as the Tannoy shook above my bed.

"Right, wakey-wakey, rise and shine you 'orrible lot! Get up and out of bed ... and you in the corner ... out, out, OUT!"

This was followed by another rendering of the ape call, a scream like Tarzan, and lots of loud cackling laughter.

I thought that this sort of thing only happened in American movies, but we were soon informed that this was the Station Radio System, that the camp had its own disc jockey and that this was his idea of a joke *every* morning, aimed specifically at the trainees. Permanent Staff could turn their Tannoys off – we couldn't.

Well, it was certainly different to Corporal Payne giving the underneath of our beds a kick and yelling 'the sun is burning your eyes out' anyway!

I was to be subjected to this form of early morning torture for the rest of my time at Trade Training, and gradually got used to it, but I wished that somebody had warned us beforehand.

The Tannoy had its uses, though, for we could send records to each other. The favourite one for the boys to send to the girls for a joke was 'Fanlight Fanny the Frousy Nightclub Queen.'

One could always keep up to date with the gossip on camp because often a lovesick airman would send a record to one of the airwomen entitled 'Take me Back Baby' together with a suitable message such as 'meet me round the back of the NAAFI at 8.30pm on Tuesday after Bull Night' – and there he would wait in vain.

We would listen and roar with laughter every time we heard these messages, which were so obviously embroidered upon by the DJ, who, thankfully, was only allowed to use it for an hour a night.

When we started our work on Pool Flight we very soon learnt our first RAF slang word and that was 'skive'. Skiving was a 'skill'. The point was that in order to keep you occupied for the period of waiting for your Course, WRAF Admin would dream up anything for you to do from, as Wally had put it, 'painting the coal white and black leading the dustbins' down to scrubbing passages over and over again.

That was the WRAF Admin side of the game. Ours was to try all sorts of idiotic pranks, or to make ourselves scarce, in order to get out of doing these jobs, or at least to take as long as possible in carrying them out (although often it was harder to get out of doing the job than to just get on and do it!)

Our favourite hiding place became the Ironing Room, where it was nice and warm and we could read magazines without interruption. Also very successful, but less comfortable, was our method of cleaning out the Rest Room. We had one billet with easy chairs in it and a radio and record player, the idea being that airwomen could relax here instead of going to the NAAFI, where the boys were. Consequently it was never used!

We were often given the Rest Room for a fatigue and we could lie on our stomachs on the floor with a book in front of us and a duster in one hand. If anyone came into the room we would hastily place the duster over the book and be feverishly polishing the floor as if our lives depended upon it! Thus, we thought we were pulling the wool over the eyes of the Senior NCOs, but of course they had all done it before us when they were airwomen and I doubted whether there was a skive going that had not already been well tested before us!

The trouble with Pool Flight was that nobody wanted us. WRAF Admin did not want us, because we had come to learn a trade and they didn't want to keep dreaming up jobs to keep us occupied and out from under their feet. Our Instructors did not want us yet because we had arrived before the course was due to start. Really we were just a nuisance to everybody, particularly on the occasions of Commanding Officers Inspections. WRAF Admin just did not want us around when the Commanding Officer came by, because we made the place look untidy! Yet we were not allowed to go in the NAAFI, we were not allowed to go off camp and we certainly were not allowed in the billets he would inspect on his rounds. Neither could we skive in the ironing rooms, which were also on the CO's itinerary. It was all very complicated.

"Just disappear airwoman," an NCO would say, "just disappear."

More often than not we would 'disappear' over to the sports fields and just sit on the grass and wait until the inspection was over, which was miserable as it was already autumn. It was too ridiculous for words.

One of the girls on our Pool Flight, a very pretty eighteen-year-old called Wendy, decided that the only way to 'disappear' effectively was to change into civvies and go for a walk! She thought she would be able to get in and out of the billet before the Commanding Officer appeared. Sadly, it was not to be and Wendy had one of her most embarrassing moments. So did the CO...

She was down to her 'bra and pants' when they all strode in, unannounced – the CO, his Adjutant, the Station Warrant Officer and Flight Sergeant Stephens.

She stood, speechless, in the doorway, while the whole entourage strolled around the room, trying to ignore the hapless girl. However, being a true airwoman with air force blue blood in her veins, Wendy drew herself up to her full five foot height and saluted!

"Carry on airwoman," said the CO, with a totally straight face.

Wendy said afterwards that this was one occasion when she wished she had been wearing her passion killers and not frilly red undies from Marks and Sparks! But she had done us all a favour and had changed policy at RAF Hereford. We were never told to 'disappear' again.

Happy skivers.

So, the days dragged into weeks, lightened by the occasional high spirits, and still we were on Pool Flight, with no word about starting our course. I went home for a long weekend and, just for once, I did *not* look forward to coming back to camp!

The warm summer sun had disappeared for good and was replaced by early morning fogs and frosts. It was dark by 5.30 in the evening. We were beginning to think that we would be on Pool Flight all over Christmas and I was ready to re-think all my earlier eagerness.

Then, one evening, after yet another day of moping around the drying room and cleaning the Rest Room for the umpteenth time, Flight Sergeant Stephens gave us the news that our course was to start and we were to report to the classrooms on the other side of the camp in the morning. I couldn't believe it! At last the moment had come. No more cleaning and polishing all day and every day, and no more skiving. We were going to be trained to do a job of work at long last.

Wendy, Pat and I trudged up the road to the classrooms with a new spring in our step the following morning. The cold air nipped at our noses and our breath made smoke signals in front of us, but all our optimism had returned.

We were the first to arrive at the classroom, which was in a billet similar to our accommodation, except that it had rows of desks, upon which sat the poor, defenceless typewriters that were going to receive such a hammering in the near future. Over each of the keyboards was a shield that you put your hands underneath, so that you could not see the keys.

Facing the desks there was a large screen, about six feet wide and four feet high. It looked like a huge television screen, but the 'picture' was of a typewriter keyboard, with each of the letters lighting up in turn. It was our Instructor's pride and joy!

The stove, which no RAF billet would be without, was in the middle of the room, with its tall chimney reaching out through the roof. I noticed that the aperture in the ceiling for the pipe to go through was far larger than the chimney itself and that there was a gap of about one foot all around, through which we could see the grey sky and feel the cold air.

"Seeing Wally and Tommy trying to work a typewriter is going to be good for a laugh," giggled Wendy, who, like me, had done some typing before.

"Oh it's a shame," smiled Pat. "Fancy making them be typists! They don't even *look* like typists."

Before I could ask her what she thought a typist looked like, the boys began to reluctantly turn up, along with another two girls who I had not met before. They were Mo and Betty and had been in E Flight, a week behind us.

Then we met Sergeant Oliver, who was yet another Scotsman, which put him in the good books of Stuart, Tommy and Wally straight away. He had a round, moony face, almost babyish, and wisps of dark hair, receding rapidly at the front. He had, quite clearly, been around in the RAF for a while, as he had a number of medal ribbons on his tunic, including World War Two ones.

He actually treated us five girls like young ladies and made it a pleasure to go to classes and learn. He had us eating out of his hand in minutes. This attitude earned him undying respect from his class and, although the lads were always ready to play their jokes, they never knowingly did anything to upset the sergeant and, grudgingly, learned to type.

"Will you look at that?" moaned Tommy. "These fingers are turning to bananas. I'll never be a touch-typist!"

But even he worked at it and, painfully slowly, learned enough to be an effective typist, despite the embarrassment of having to do it in the first place. He knew that once he left the RAF he would be unlikely to touch a typewriter ever again! The world of jazz was waiting for him – and he was right.

As we moved further towards the winter, the weather really turned cold and the freezing air came down at us through the hole in the roof. I even began to wear gloves for typing, but it was the last straw when snow began to fall and came drifting into the classroom. Out came the gloves, the scarf and the greatcoat and we all felt like Bob Cratchet in 'A Christmas Carol' as we huddled over our typewriters.

It often got so cold both in the classroom and in the billet that icicles, sometimes three feet long or more, would form along the top edge of the windows and hang down like prison bars.

"Ker-riste!" exclaimed Pat, as she pulled one off. "Look at that!"

Wally pulled off another one and the lesson ended with an icicle sword-fight. There was never a dull moment.

There was, however, plenty of homework to do, for we not only had to learn our typing without looking at the keys, but also had to study how an office in the Air Force is managed.

And, of course, recent RAF History. Sergeant Oliver was very particular in telling us about the latter, especially when it came round to Remembrance Day. Most of what he said fell on 'stony ground' but he persevered and showed us pictures of the War Graves in the Netherlands.

"If you get the chance, you should visit them one day," he said quietly. "Then you will understand."

We smiled politely. If the truth were known, we were far more interested in Elvis Presley, but we were only eighteen. In any case, I couldn't see any chance of me ever going to Holland.

"You may not be at the 'sharp end'," he said, looking at our blank faces, "but you will help to make the 'sharp end' function and you need to understand what it is all about."

We smiled sweetly and looked forward to our NAAFI Break, but we knew he meant well and he *was* a lovely man – and, as it turned out, very prophetic!

Any ideas that we might have harboured, in our dreams, that any of the boys would ever become actual *boyfriends* were very quickly forgotten. They were interested in two things only – football and how soon they could be demobbed.

"Roll on death," muttered Wally. "Demob is too far away."

They were friends who happened to be boys – and that's all – much to our bitter disappointment!

I knew that we would miss them when they got posted to their permanent stations and the girls stayed on to do the Shorthand Course. There was absolutely no way that they were going to stay to do shorthand! Not for anybody.

My first Christmas in the Air Force arrived and we all went home, with strict instructions that we had to be back on 28th December. The train journey back from London to Hereford seemed longer and darker and more miserable than it ever had before, especially after being home with the family and all the trappings of the festive season.

For the Scottish boys it was even worse – not only had they had a much longer journey but, to add insult to the injury, they were to miss their traditional New Year.

"Jeez!" said Stuart. "You can tell that the folk who make the rules up are English. Don't they have New Year in this part of the World?"

"Sassenachs!" grumbled Wally.

They were so miserable that even Sergeant Oliver felt sorry for them, and he was Scottish himself and had to be back too.

On New Year's Eve, Wendy, Pat and I met them in the NAAFI and tried our best to cheer them up. Somebody put 'Rock Around the Clock' on the Jukebox. The girls could not resist jiving to that one, even if it *was* with each other, as the airmen looked on. Very few of them jived, but those that did were very popular, sometimes dancing with two and even three girls at once. Tommy, Stuart and Wally preferred to watch.

"There's a dance down the town you know," said Wendy, as she sat down, puffed out after jiving. "Why don't we go? We can see the New Year in there."

"You must be joking hen," moaned Tommy. "On twenty-nine shillings a week?"

"We'll pay for ourselves," I replied, knowing that our wages were twice as much as theirs.

"We still can't afford it," said Tommy. He put his hand in his pocket and pulled out some change.

"Look, that's all I have got until payday – and just think, I could be getting a fortune as a civilian with my jazz band."

"Oh no, see, you've done it now," joked Wally. "He won't stop now, moaning on about what he thinks he is missing and his bloody jazz band."

"Let's gatecrash the dance then," said Wendy, still not to be put off on this, the last day of 1959.

"Airwoman!" I exclaimed "We'd get killed if anyone found out."

"Oh rubbish – we won't get caught." She took another bite out of her cheese roll and rummaged around in her purse for a sixpence for the jukebox.

"Listen," she said. "How can anybody be expected to do anything on twenty nine shillings a week? I bet prisoners in jail get more than that for fag and booze money."

"Well I dunno," I replied, agreeing with her sentiments, "but how can they gatecrash?"

"I'll tell you what," said Wendy, now getting quite carried away with her plan. "We girls can afford tickets, so we'll go in and then we'll open a window or something and let them in. How about that?"

"It's a good idea," said Tommy. "Let's try it!"

"Oh, OK then," said Stuart, who was always game for anything. "I'm damned if I'm going to sit around here on New Year's Eve anyway. I'd rather just go to bed."

Normally the WRAF had to be in and bed-checked by eleven o'clock, but there was a special dispensation for New Year and we all had passes until 1am. Nobody wanted to waste them, so we needed no more persuasion. A few minutes later and we were all striding arm-in-arm past the Guardroom to get the bus into town.

I didn't own a watch but Pat did – she looked at it in the light of the street lamp as we got off the bus.

"It's ten o'clock already," she said. "We don't have that long."

The three boys didn't hear her, as they had already disappeared around the back of the dance hall.

There were plenty of windows in the building and, despite the cold, many were open and rock and roll music filled the air. The place was heaving with revellers and we were lucky to get in, even *with* money,

"Come on," said Pat, "we had better hurry or they'll be in before we can help them."

We paid for our tickets and pushed our way through to find the back windows. Unfortunately though, the only really accessible way in was through the Ladies Toilet.

"Oh my gawd, that's torn it!" cried Wendy.

"You and your bright ideas," I chided, as we pushed our way round through the crowd.

"Shut-up!" Pat hissed. "Let's go in and open the window and have done with it. They will have to take pot luck."

We waited until there was nobody in any of the cubicles and then opened one of the windows, though the timing could not have been worse.

Just as the boys were pushing each other through, the door to the Ladies opened and a girl came rushing in, hitching her skirts up en-route, to go to the very cubicle that they had just scrambled into from outside.

"Oh shit!" she exclaimed, quickly straightening her skirt.

"Not yet!" laughed Wally. "Let me get out first."

The boys stumbled about as their eyes became accustomed to the light and they rushed towards the main door out into the dance hall.

"Sorry about that," giggled Pat. "National Servicemen, you know – no money," as if that explained everything.

We didn't feel too guilty though. After all, we girls had paid the full of five shillings to get in when the dance was nearly over anyway.

Having recovered from their experience, the boys soon got over the initial guilt of gate-crashing and started to enjoy themselves. Tommy was his usual irrepressible self, with his dry sense of humour and, of course, full of criticism for the band, especially the guitarist!

It felt as though we had not been there for more than five minutes when the band and the dancing stopped and, on the loudspeakers, we heard Big Ben heralding in the New Year. There were cheers as everybody bid farewell to 1959 and said hello to the sixties and a whole new era. *Auld Lang Syne* was played and we all clasped hands of friendship. The old year was shaken off like an old coat and now we had a whole new decade to look forward to.

It was a clear, starry night, but we did not feel the cold as we strolled down the road to get the bus back to camp, whilst Tommy mimicked playing the guitar and sang his Scottish folk songs to whoever wanted to listen. We probably looked drunk, but nobody was. We couldn't afford to be and we had managed with one drink between two for most of the evening. We were inebriated by the occasion.

A policeman sliding down the icy road on his bicycle gave us a hostile look and so we quietened down until we were out of his sight, but not for long, for then Tommy gave us a lovely rendering of 'Button up Your Overcoat' ,whilst mockingly trying to button up mine.

"Take good care of yourself, you belong to me," he sang.

I wished so much that the words he was singing would come true, but I knew I had as much chance of that as having an eighteen inch waist! I was trying to forget that, in a very short time, our typing class would finish and we would all be parting company, probably for good. There was even a kiss or two, but not the kiss of a lover, but of warm friends wishing each other a Happy New Year.

The sixties had begun.

Three weeks after the New Year the boys got their postings. We met them in the NAAFI and Tommy's grim face said it all.

"Where are you going?" I said.

"Don't ask him," laughed Stuart. The tears were falling down his face with laughter.

"Shut up!" grimaced Tommy. "It's not bloody funny."

"Oh it can't be that bad," said Wendy. "Not back to square bashing, surely?"

"Not quite that bad, but nearly... RAF Cranwell."

Wally slapped him on the back. "You will love it there mate!"

"Oh dear," I replied, trying hard to suppress my own laughter. Somebody at Record Office had an eye for a joke.

"Bloody RAF Cranwell, the Officers Training School! Just imagine, as if we didna see enough officers, they post me to where they *train* the little buggers."

Oh dear, poor Tommy, how he hated the officers! He hated them as a matter of principle, as if it was entirely their fault that he had got clobbered for National Service! It was a standing joke how much he hated them. Now he was going to where there were hundreds of them and he really looked as though he was about to explode.

"Well *you* won't be mixing with them anyway," I said.

"That's not the point," he grumbled. "Think of all that saluting I shall have to do."

We all did our best to keep straight faces but it was very difficult.

We said our goodbyes to the boys that evening in the NAAFI and then later outside the WRAF Billet. There was no romance involved, but the way Tommy called me 'hen' made me wish there was.

Within no time at all, people were going indoors, because it was 'bed check' time for the airwomen. I saw two Station Policemen heading our way, shining their torches in the bushes and round the back of the billets to make sure that there wasn't any hanky-panky going on, and I realised that this was another chapter closing.

"Bye hen," said Tommy, and gave me a light kiss on the cheek. I watched him as he trudged down the road in the snow and joined up with Wally and Stuart as they waved back to the crestfallen Wendy and Pat. We watched until they were mere specks in the distance.

We didn't get much opportunity to miss the lads because we girls started on the shorthand course straight away and had only a short time to study this new subject, which was much more difficult than typing and involved plenty of homework to master the little squiggles and dots. I thought I would never get the hang of it, but when you know that if you fail your test at the end of the week you will have to stay longer at Hereford until you do pass, it does tend to focus the mind!

I received a letter from Tommy, who took pleasure in informing me that he had been right all along and the place was crawling with bloody officers and worse, much worse, in his opinion, the place did not even have a decent Jazz Club! It was totally uncivilised and he was just crossing the dates off the calendar. Demob could not come soon enough for him, especially as it had been announced on the News that National Service was, indeed, finishing – it was like adding salt to the wound.

"I was born two bloody years too early!" he grumbled.

Meanwhile, I slowly got used to the mysteries of Pitman's shorthand and eventually our course did come to an end. We were given our exam, which would, if we passed, give us the rank of Leading Aircraftswomen, two steps up from the lowest of the low!

March had lived up to the proverb – it had come in like a lion and now the weather had calmed down, and in fact we caught the first rays of a watery sun as we walked down to our classroom to receive our results and to be told where we would be posted to.

Thank goodness our studies had been worthwhile, for all five of us passed our shorthand course at 100 words per minute. All done in six weeks! We couldn't have done that in Civvy Street!

I even surprised myself and couldn't wait to sew my brand new propellers on my sleeve. Now I knew what Corporal Payne must have felt like with her new corporal's stripes! I reckoned if I had a spare pair of propeller badges I'd have sewn them on to my pyjamas too, even though it took ages (and a lot of swearing) to get them stitched on straight.

We were all beginning to feel like 'plus-type girls', whether we were or not...

We sat in our classroom waiting for Sergeant Oliver to announce out postings. Fleetingly, I thought what a laugh it would be if I got Cranwell, but in actual fact my main wish was to have a station near to home.

"Of course, some of you might go abroad one day," said the NCO. He was obviously in one of his 'nattering' moods.

Abroad! I had never even *thought* of abroad!

"Oh, I don't think so Sarge," I laughed. To me, the Isle of Wight was abroad.

"If you take a tip from me," he said, "you will volunteer after about two years – otherwise they will send you anyway and probably to somewhere that you don't want to go."

He had a point – but *abroad*? Strange though it may seem, the possibility had hardly crossed my mind before.

"I wouldn't mind going to Cyprus," said Mo. "Lovely and hot."

"Germany is nice," said Sergeant Oliver. "You can do the Nijmegen Marches if you get posted to Germany."

I did not have a clue what he was talking about and was more concerned with him opening the blessed envelope that he had on his desk and telling us where we were going next week! I was sure he was doing it deliberately! Besides, the very idea of Germany was a bit alien. After all, my dad had been fighting them only twenty years previously.

He started to finger the envelope and then took out the foolscap sheet of paper with our future typed on it. I crossed my fingers and hoped that I would not get posted to the Outer Hebrides.

Pat and I sat side-by-side, staring unseeingly at the blackboard as he started to read out, in alphabetical order, where the members of the class were being sent. I stared straight ahead and listened to names I had never heard of being read out.

"Benson, Abingdon, Shinfield Park, Lossiemouth…"

"Lossiemouth? That's Scotland isn't it Ratty?" whispered Pat.

"Oh please don't send me to the Outer Hebrides," I prayed. "All I want is to be down South, so that I can go home occasionally."

His voice droned on, amid cheers from some and groans from others.

"LACW Ratcliff," he finally said. "RAF Medmenham." He looked across at me. "Oh, aren't you the lucky one?" he grinned. "You have got *God's Little Acre.*"

For a moment I shuddered. Where on earth was Medmenham and where were Pat and Wendy going? Within a few minutes I got the answer to both my questions. Medmenham was in Buckinghamshire and not too far away from my home, and Pat and Wendy were going to be posted to Brampton. For the first time since we had joined up, Pat and I were going our separate ways.

"Why is it 'God's Little Acre' Sarge?" I queried.

"You'll see," he answered mysteriously. "You'll see…"

We all ambled back to the billets and packed in silence, for there was nothing really left to say. We were well and truly airwomen now. We had got over the euphoria of our Passing Out Parade and had been trained to do a job of work, which hopefully we would do well. We made promises to keep in touch, knowing that we might with some and probably wouldn't with others. There would be no more Pool Flights and – please god – no more station Tannoy to wake us up with that bloody 'ape call' in the morning! If I had heard that damn disc jockey and his 'ape call' just one more time I think I would have shoved his microphone right up his backside!

"I know…" said Pat, breaking the silence, "let's go over to the NAAFI."

"OK," I agreed. "I'll give the others a shout."

I went to the billet next door and called Mo, Wendy and Betty.

"Come on," I said. "We are going for a last look at the NAAFI!"

The five of us strolled across the road, bought our usual Pepsi and studied the latest additions to the jukebox.

"It's about time they got some Elvis Presley on here," said Wendy. "They have only got 'All Shook Up'."

She put her sixpence in and the NAAFI came alive to the sound of the great man, who few of us had seen yet. At best, we had seen some still photos. As far as Pat was concerned he could have had two heads – the voice said it all.

"Oh my God!" she said. "Did you see him in *Love Me Tender*?"

I had missed it. It had been on at our local cinema just after I had joined up, and once it had been, that was it. A film rarely did the rounds again. It certainly was unlikely to be on television, even if we had one to watch – which we didn't. All we could do was look at photos or wait for him to make another film.

"Oh my God," Pat repeated, as if the record was stuck. "He was just *gorgeous* and I cried all the way home. He died in the end, you know."

"Thanks for that," said Wendy. "We don't need to see it now."

Pat wasn't listening; she was almost in a swoon at the very thought.

"I once saw Bill Haley on Waterloo Station," I volunteered.

"What, in real life?" exclaimed Wendy.

The conversation came to a halt as Pat pointed meaningfully at her watch. We could put off the inevitable as long as possible by talking about Elvis and drinking our Pepsi Colas but we *were* posted and we did have to go.

We took a last look round – it had never been the same since the Scots boys had left – and then we walked to the billets to collect our bags and get on the RAF bus that would be taking us to Hereford train station. Another chapter was nearly over.

The station was full of commuters used to seeing a motley array of uniformed Air Force personnel going off in all directions. Carrying our heavy luggage we struggled off to our respective platforms, some of us Northbound and some Southbound, some to be seen again in the near future, some not.

The Northbound train arrived first and swallowed up Betty and Mo. We waved frantically as it pulled away, and soon they were gone leaving the rest of us. Mine arrived next and the girls almost had to push me aboard in order to get me on before it moved away again. They flung my kitbag in after me and I leaned precariously out of the carriage as it chugged away from the station, leaving my friends to wait a further half an hour. In no time at all they were just small dots in the distance.

I was sorry to say goodbye to them and I had a hard job to fight back the tears as I settled down with the other passengers. I suddenly felt very alone in a compartment full of civilians.

Well, how could they know that I had been with my friends for nearly ten months, that we had always been together and that now I was completely on my own, again, trundling towards an unknown RAF Station, to an unknown boss, and an unknown job and, as yet, unknown new friends?

4. *God's Little Acre*

"Marlow Station, you are at Marlow Station."

I climbed stiffly out of the train and stretched my limbs. The bus that would take me from Marlow to Medmenham was already waiting outside the station and, as I pushed my luggage onto it, I wondered whether they had discovered telephones or running water in this out-of-the-way backwoods place. Although it was not far from the town of High Wycombe, and indeed London, it was all very rural and I half expected the bus to be held up by a herd of cows at any minute.

The discovery of a squashed and beaten-up cheese sandwich amongst my luggage calmed my nerves. I'd almost forgotten that I'd bothered to buy it, but I sat back and ate this hungrily, admiring the picturesque scenery as the bus took me to my destination.

It was a beautiful day. The meadows on either side of the road were a lush green and bright with the freshness of yesterday's rain, and the trees were beginning to show the first sign of young leaves. Here and there I could see splashes of colour, purple and yellow, probably crocuses, and great clumps of daffodils growing wild in the hedgerows.

There was no doubt that the residents of Marlow were quite used to airmen and airwomen arriving in full uniform and lugging kitbags, so I hardly got a second glance from the people on the bus as I sat there in my 'best blue'. Ten minutes later I was standing outside the gates that led to Royal Air Force Medmenham and I realised immediately that it was very different from anything I had known before.

Gone were the wooden billets with hoards of airwomen all over the place and the uninviting guardroom with the aeroplane outside and the 'Snowdrop' who didn't want to be there. Here was a station that was clearly loved and I too fell in love with it the minute I stepped off the bus. I could see immediately why it had the nickname 'God's Little Acre'.

The main entrance consisted of two huge gates of twisted and decorated wrought iron, flanked on either side by white stone pillars. They were wide open as if in welcome and revealed carefully tended borders of daffodils and tulips along the side of the drive, which was edged with whitewashed stone kerbs. The window frames on the little guardroom, on the right hand side, just inside the gate, were also painted a brilliant white and there were small window boxes overflowing with flowers.

To the left, there was a large sports field and situated on three sides of this were the Blocks, one for the men, one for the airwomen, and one for the male NCOs. I learned later that the WRAF Senior NCOs were accommodated in the WRAF Block but separated from us riff-raff by a locked and bolted door.

There were no billets, except for a few used as offices, and the Blocks looked well kept and neat after the horrible wooden billets with their stinking coke stoves I had so far come across. It would be central heating from now on! Each building was surrounded with carefully tended gardens and, as far as I could see, there was not even a parade ground.

This was 'putting to bed' the theory that 'your last station is always your best'! This showed that there were some exceptions, surely.

"Hello lass! Here, let me take your kit bag and suitcase for you." A handsome young 'Snowdrop' took them from me before I could argue. That did it – I didn't need to see any more. I was won over!

I walked beside him down the narrow gravel road to the WRAF Block and I noticed how convenient things were, with the NAAFI located immediately opposite and the Mess next to it. Everything that was important in a young airwoman's life was a dozen yards from our accommodation!

"Welcome to Medmenham," he said, as he pushed my luggage in through the doorway of 'Salmon Block'. "Hang about there a minute and I'll go and find the sergeant."

The swing doors that led inside slammed shut behind me and I was standing in the large entrance hall, alone. On the table beside me was a large bowl of beautifully arranged spring flowers that reflected themselves in the highly polished floor.

My thoughts were soon interrupted by the return of the SP with the WRAF sergeant. I took a liking to her straight away. She was short and dumpy and her uniform looked as though it was really straining to meet around her. She looked about fifty and her round, rosy face was wreathed in smiles as she bounded up to me and took my hand, shaking it furiously. I'd never had an NCO do that in my life – not even Sergeant Oliver!

"Hello there," she beamed. "I expect you are tired, so we won't bother with any formalities this evening – we can sort you out in the morning. Did you have a nice journey down dear?"

"Not bad Sergeant," I whispered, totally taken aback at the friendliness shown.

"Good." She picked up one of my cases and started up the stairs, leaving me gaping like an idiot at the vision of a Senior NCO picking up the suitcase of a mere airwoman!

"Come along lass," she fussed. "Come along now and I'll show you to your room and the young women up there will look after you. Scots girls, you know, nice girls – when they are behaving themselves that is!"

I was beginning to think that the Royal Air Force was formed purely for the benefit of the Scots, but I followed her up the wide staircase and along the gleaming corridor that had doors leading off on either side of it. It was, incidentally, the first corridor I had seen with polish on! Until now, we'd had stone ones that we had to scrub!

She stopped at the door at the very end of the corridor, marked with the legend 'Room 15'.

"Here you are then. Young Laird should be in there and she'll look after you."

She pushed open the door to reveal accommodation undreamed of at Wilmslow and Hereford. It was a large room with one bed in each corner and a highly-polished table and two chairs in the centre of the room. At the side of each bed were built-in wardrobes and dressing tables, painted pink, very far removed from the prison-style lockers I had been used to. At the head of each bed was a small reading light and above that a larger, more powerful light. The windows, which filled the wall facing me, looked out over the sports field and the trees beyond.

Sitting cross-legged on one of the beds was an elfin girl with short dark hair, wearing a pair of faded blue jeans and a white shirt. She looked up and jumped off the bed as we came into the room.

"Here you are Laird," said the Sergeant kindly. "Somebody for you to look after."

"Aye Sarge," said the girl.

The NCO glanced around the room and she caught sight of the inside of one of the spare wardrobes, its door swinging wide open. This, presumably, would end up being mine.

"And Laird," she barked. "Will you *stop* hoarding all the bloody cleaning materials in the spare wardrobe and put them back in the broom cupboard for others to use."

LACW Laird blushed and ran to the spare cupboard and removed the offending brooms, as the Sergeant took her leave of us and left us to ourselves.

"Sorry about this hen," she grinned. "I was just keeping them because I want to get the room cleaned early tonight and get down the NAAFI – it's Domestic Night."

"Sorry to have mucked up your plans," I said. "Anyway, I'm Joan, but some call me Ratty."

"Oh don't worry," she said, in her broad Scottish accent, as she resumed her position on the bed. "Domestic night is no great panic here – and in any case I've done most of it."

"That's a new word," I said. "We called it 'Bull Night' at Hereford and we were not allowed to go out until after the rooms had been inspected."

"That was Hereford," she laughed. "Here we have Domestic Night and you can do it when you want as long as it gets done.... I'm June," she continued, "but everyone calls me Lairdie – and that bed over there with all the rubbish all over it is Jan's – and everyone calls her anything. Those two beds are spare, so take your pick."

I lifted my cases onto the bed nearest to the wardrobe from where June had moved the offending brooms and began to unpack.

"Only three in a room?" I said. "I've been used to 23!"

"Haven't we all," said June, getting up from her bed and combing her hair. "Jan and I only came here a few weeks ago from Compton Bassett."

"Compton Bassett?" I exclaimed. "Some of our flight went there. Did you meet Big Haggis?"

"We had lots of Haggises at Compton," grinned June. "Some big ones and some little ones."

"She was in D Flight," I persevered, "big girl with a very freckly face and *very* nosy."

"Not that twerp that wanted to know if we were all virgins?" grinned June.

"That's the one!" I laughed.

"We all got an extra Bull Night because of her – we laughed so much our NCO went potty – I think she got posted back up to Scotland after our course."

She resumed her position on her bed. She looked more like a young boy than a girl.

"I'll show you around later on," she went on, "and you can see why they call it God's Little Acre."

"You must have a lot of cleaning and polishing to do though," I remarked, as I pushed the last of my underclothes into a drawer. "That hall downstairs and the corridors are immaculate."

"Hell no!" June laughed. "We have cleaners to do all that – We do have to do the corridors on domestic night though, but we have an electric polisher."

"Don't you use bumpers here then?" I cried, absolutely aghast at this new revelation. I was starting to think I had come to a Holiday Camp. Bumpers were a sort of swinging brick – a very heavy weight on the end of a pole, and you put a soft cloth underneath, usually a pair of 'passion killers' and pushed them back and forth until the floor shone like glass and you ended up with aching muscles where you never knew you had them! Having seen the hall downstairs I was convinced it could only have been done with bumpers.

"Bumpers!" cried June. "You've seen the last you are ever likely to see of bumpers."

Having been forced to use a bumper and black lead stoves for the past ten months, it really made you appreciate not having to do it anymore .

"I can't believe it!" I exclaimed. "You'll be telling me next that you can put your feet up and watch the telly as well."

"Three, to be precise," giggled June. "There are two in the NAAFI – one for ITV and one for BBC in another room – so that there are no arguments about which channel to have on, and we have our own television in the WRAF Block in the downstairs rest room."

I gaped at her open mouthed.

"You mean I shall be able to pick up on Wagon Train where I left off ten months ago?"

"Oh yes," she grinned. "Robert Horton is still riding across the prairie, and what is more you can curl up in front of the telly in your undies and nobody worries – after all, we have to have the curtains pulled shut otherwise you wouldn't be able to see the screen, of course.

She leaned out of the window, grabbed a bottle of milk that had been keeping cool on the outside windowsill and switched on a kettle that, until now, I had not noticed.

"Coffee?" she laughed. "Sugar madam?"

"Now," she went on, "take that blessed uniform off and put some civvies on and we'll go to the Mess when we have had our coffee."

"Oh yes, that reminds me," I said, as I took up her suggestion and struggled out of my sweaty uniform. "What's the food like in the Mess. It's not the usual tea and toast all the time is it? Because if it is, I would rather go to the NAAFI."

June looked quite hurt. "I'll have you know that we won the Command Catering competition last year!"

She was not exaggerating. The food was delicious. It was beautifully presented and we had a selection of almost everything. It was the first really good meal I'd had in the Air Force and I happily settled down to a big plateful of egg, chips and sausage, followed by ice cream and jelly, and a cup of piping-hot tea. Of course there was a selection of other, healthier foods, like an array of salads and fish, but the egg and chips would do for me!

I later wrote to Tommy and said, "Guess what? We even have a choice of tea, coffee, lemon, orange or lime squash," to which he ruefully replied, "Guess what? *We* have a choice too – cold tea out of the urn or nothing!"

We finished our meal and then, as promised, June showed me over the camp.

"I won't take you to the NAAFI yet," she said, "it's too early, but I'll show you The Monastery first."

I wondered what she meant by 'The Monastery' and the mysterious way she said it. I thought it might be a nickname for a local building, but all was soon explained. There was, indeed, a Monastery. How long ago the Monks had lived in it I do not know, but now it was part of the Headquarters building and some of it was used as the Officers Mess. I had not seen it before because of the way it lay, down a slope, partially shielded by large fir trees. However, as we walked along the roadway from the WRAF Block and followed the curvature of the road, the tall and beautiful building came fully into view.

It had large square windows and turrets on either side of the main entrance, one of which formed the clock tower. It looked sturdy and strong, as if it had been there for a very long time indeed and could stand up to any invasion. To one side there were gardens and lawns – to the other, the single storey extension that had been incongruously added to house the scores of offices now used on a daily basis.

The nearby yew trees and cypresses added to the mystery of the old building and I would have had the full impression of stepping back in time, but for the uniformed airmen and airwomen pouring out of the side of the place at the end of their day's work.

"Isn't it lovely," I said, as I gazed up at it in awe.

"Mmm," my friend replied. "It's floodlit when it gets dark and the officers are having a 'do' but it's pretty eerie when they don't light it up."

I looked at the tall building and its dark towers and could imagine she was right, especially when there was nobody working in the offices.

We walked across the lawns and into the woods that surrounded the far side of the building. June led me down a narrow path, just a track through the trees that had been trodden through years of use, and soon I found myself standing on the quiet bank of a river. She pointed to rows of canoes moored to the side.

"Those belong to us and we are allowed to come here and canoe if there is a PTI present," she informed me. I'd run out of superlatives now and just stood and gaped.

"Close your mouth, there's a train coming," June laughed. She was enjoying being my guide.

"Come on," she giggled, "we had better be going back, it's getting dark and I, for one, do not like being out here at night because we also have a ghost."

"A ghost?"

"Aye, now whoever heard of a monastery without a ghost," giggled June, as we walked up the little track through the woods.

So this was Medmenham, Headquarters Signals Command. All this in not much more than a couple of acres of land. It was God's Little Acre all right. But God's Little Acre boasted a ghost as well did it?

'Oh well,' I thought, as I followed June back to the WRAF Block, 'We'll soon see...'

But as we passed the Monastery, with its towers showing black against the setting sun and the offices at the side now empty and silent, I realised that this was indeed the perfect spot for a ghost, if there was one. It looked like a setting for a film with Peter Cushing or Christopher Lee.

We got back to the block and got ready for bed in our 'very fetching' blue and white striped 'issue' pyjamas. Everyone wore them. They were practical and warm and, after all, there were no men around to impress with sexy 'baby doll' frillies!

We both settled down and left Jan's bed light on for her, and I briefly wondered if I would meet her before I nodded off. I knew she would be in when she had finished her shift in the Comm Centre but I was also tired. It had been a long day.

I did not have to wait long though. The door burst open and there was a thump as a WRAF handbag was thrown onto the floor.

"Where's the swear box, I am going to have sixpence worth of swears!!" I heard the clink of money as it dropped.

"Now here goes...." There was a deep breath and then a tirade of six juicy swear words, some of which were new to me. That was my introduction to Jan.

Joan, June and Jan.

June and I sat up in our beds and switched our lights on to see what her rage was all about. She was plumper than June, though not fat, with a round, freckled face and curly brown hair which, at the moment, was sticking out in all directions under her beret. She began to pull off her uniform, completely disregarding where it landed, and continued her speech.

"That bloody Corporal," she growled. "I am not kidding Lairdie, he thinks he owns that damn section when we are on evenings."

"He does," said June patiently.

Jan stopped in her tracks, her shirt collar dangling from her hand, and looked across at me.

"Oh hello, I'm sorry hen! You must think I am terrible!"

"Huh!" scoffed June, who actually liked the corporal in the Comm Centre. "Well, at least the money in the swear box is mounting up. What's he been up to now?"

"Oh everything," groaned Jan. "He drives me mad. He's a right big-head. Do you know, tonight he wouldn't even let us cook our supper until we were sure all the signals had come in! Now, honestly, how can we tell that when we are on 'lates'? – Answer me that?"

"The cheek of the man!" said June sarcastically.

"Don't tell me that you do cooking when you are working?" I smiled.

"Only on late shift, because we always bloody well miss tea," replied Jan. "Besides which," she continued without even pausing for breath, "it gets spooky down there at night and a good meal helps to calm our shattered nerves!"

She sat in front of her mirror, festooned her hair with rollers and then slapped her face all over with a gooey cream. When she had finished she looked like something from the 'Black and White Minstrels'!

"I don't know how you can sleep in those things," giggled June.

"Ah well Lairdie," she said, "it's all in the cause of beauty you see. If I want to have the men falling about me like flies then I have got to make the effort and suffer for it."

"The trouble is," retorted June, "we never see if your efforts have any effect."

"Give me time, give me time. The men just have not realised what they are missing yet."

"If the truth be known," laughed June, "they probably *have* realised what they are missing and this is why they are staying away."

"Any more of your cheek, young June Laird, and I'll de-bed you," scowled Jan. "And don't think I wouldn't, tired as I am."

"Oh no not that, not tonight," cried June in mock panic. "I promise I'll say no more – honest!"

"You'd better not, or you and your bedding will be going on the floor."

I turned out my light and left Jan wrestling with her rollers and arguing with Lairdie. The last I remember seeing of her before my eyes closed with sleep, was the sight of her doing strange contortions with her pillow so that her head would hang over the edge of the bed, thereby avoiding the rollers digging into her skull. It was all in the name of beauty.

If anybody had walked into our room they would have thought that the Medmenham ghost was visiting us already, for the sight of Jan's round face covered in cream, plus her rollers, was a sight to behold.

The following morning I dressed in my working blue uniform and beret and reported to the sergeant in WRAF Admin as requested. I signed for my bedding and then went direct to the Unit Headquarters, which was a small insignificant little building just inside the entrance to the station. I opened a white door labelled 'General Office' and this revealed the large Registry with dozens of airmen and airwomen deeply immersed in mountains of paperwork. A counter ran along the side of the office, rather like a shop, and behind this was a corporal, again surrounded by papers.

"Ah yes, a new arrival," he looked up at me. "Fill in this form and I will tell you where you will be working, so that you can enter it under paragraph four."

I dutifully filled in the long form and when I arrived at paragraph four I waited patiently.

"P Staff," said the NCO. "Looks like you will be working in P Staff – just fill it in – there." He pointed to paragraph four. Quite clearly I had not paid sufficient attention when we had our lessons on RAF abbreviations at Hereford, so very carefully I wrote 'Pee Staff', much to everyone's amusement.

The Corporal took one look and burst into peals of laughter. Apparently, I had at least started *his* morning off with a smile!

"P Staff means Personnel," he grinned, "and you write it like this…"

"You will be working for Group Captain Peters down at P Staff," the still chuckling Corporal told me. "He is the Senior

Personnel Staff Officer and you are a lucky girl because he is a really nice chap."

Granted, Sergeant Oliver at Hereford had been a very nice chap too, but a Group Captain – a Senior Officer – that was something different again. I had visions of saluting every five minutes and being afraid to speak. It was an awesome thought. The idea that I, an eighteen-year-old would be doing shorthand for a Group Captain, was quite nerve-racking.

The NCO stood up and pulled his beret onto his head.

"I'll take you across to Headquarters," he said cheerily, "then you can start work."

The Monastery was still an impressive sight as we approached it. However, as I suspected, we didn't actually go into the place, but in through the offices to one side of it. To our left, as we went past the Duty 'Snowdrop', was a communicating door into the 'old' side of the building but the NCO quite clearly knew where he was taking me and we continued straight on.

A row of white painted doors lined the corridor we walked down and each one had some initials painted on them in black letters. Suddenly we were there.

The legend 'P' Staff Registry was written on the door. He knocked and we went straight in.

"Here you are Flight," he said, "all yours."

It was a large office where two airwomen were already busy typing furiously. Further down the room a tall, slim, fair haired corporal was filing some papers away and sitting opposite him was a short, dumpy man in civilian clothes, of indefinite age. He could have been anything between sixty and ninety, for he was like a little dumpy gnome. He reminded me of Tweedledum or Tweedledee. His name was Mr Lee.

The Flight Sergeant in charge of the Registry, who had been sitting at his desk behind the corporal, rose to his feet when he saw us. All faces turned towards me curiously as he shook my hand. He was a stocky man with a red face and grey hair, and he was puffing away on a large pipe.

"Welcome to the sweatshop!" he said. "I'm Flight Sergeant James. Come and meet my girls." He introduced me to SACW's Marshall and Ruston.

Apparently 'Rusty' had been doing most of the Groupy's work and I would be working mainly for the more junior officers, although I would be expected to help out with the Group Captain when needed. As for SACW Marshall, I wouldn't be seeing her again after today. She was off to Germany and I was her replacement.

"Follow me…" said Flight, "you might as well meet the riff-raff." By that, he actually meant the officers. I briefly thought of Tommy with hundreds of them at Cranwell as I followed my new boss down the corridor. First one door opened and then the next, where an officer looked up from his desk, smiled, and then got on with his work. Then, last of all, I was taken in to see the Group Captain.

I saluted smartly and realised straight away that I had no cause to worry. One look at his kind eyes and warm smile was enough to tell me that he lived up to his reputation. He was tall with greying hair, his face was brown and weather-beaten and he had undoubtedly been handsome in his day – indeed, he was still pretty handsome *now*. His medal ribbons and flying wings on his tunic showed that he hadn't always been sitting behind a desk either. Very far from it. He had been a pilot in the war and in 1940 had been one of 'the Few' that had defended us over the skies of London.

He leapt to his feet, like the true gentleman he was, a smile lighting up his face. In a strange way he reminded me of my Dad.

"Good morning young lady," he grinned. "So you are coming to do my work for me are you? And what do you think of our Station?" He said it as though it was his personal pride and joy.

"Oh I think it is lovely Sir!" I told him truthfully.

"Not bad is it? Have you ever been flying?"

"No Sir!"

"You havn't?" he exclaimed. He threw his arms up in the air in mock horror. "Well we will have to put that right, won't we?" Then he turned to the Flight Sergeant. "Flight, remind me to take this airwoman for a flip with me sometime will you – you can't be an airwoman without going in the *air!*"

"Certainly Sir," said the Flight Sergeant, while I just stood there, bereft of speech. I didn't know whether to be pleased or scared. I hadn't thought about going flying any more than I had thought about going abroad! I'd only joined the Air Force to be a 'plus-type' and to win my ten bob bet – but that agenda had changed at my Passing Out Parade.

We left the Group Captain to his work and went back to the Registry. Within the hour I was seated in front of him with my shorthand pad, taking down his letters, while he spoke clearly and slowly for me. He knew it was my first time and he was 'treating me gently'.

After only a day or two in the Section I was to discover just what a comical little character Mr. Lee really was. Sometimes we could not work because we were laughing so much at him, and often Flight would get impatient and then dissolve into giggles himself.

He was the sort of little man who only had to 'stand there' and he had you in hysterics and anyone coming into our Registry would have thought our little fat civilian was a case for the nearest Mental Asylum. Quite often, especially if he could not find a particular file he wanted, he would suddenly make for a large pipe that ran down the wall in the corner of the Registry and climb up it as if it were a drainpipe.

"You are all sending me up the wall!" he would exclaim, from his vantage point high up in the corner, near the ceiling.

The Officers were totally unfazed by him and just carried on as if he wasn't there, as if it was quite usual to have your civilian clerk dangling from a pipe in the corner of the office. We could come back from lunch and find the little chap pretending to be asleep, stretched out along the top of the filing cabinets. At least we *hoped* he was pretending. If he had actually dozed off and rolled over he could have broken his bones. He was always full of stories and we were never totally sure whether he was pulling our legs or not.

He told us that he had a baby alligator called Doris! He, allegedly, kept it in his garden, which backed on to the River

Thames and when he wasn't creeping around corridors or climbing up water pipes he was extolling her virtues!

"Oh Doris comes to me just like a faithful dog," he said one day. "You can come and see her if you like."

We declined the offer.

Then one day he came into the office looking very downcast and forlorn. Apparently Doris had made good her escape and had swum off down the river! Far from being concerned about any poor canoeist or rower that might find themselves face to nose with a baby alligator, Mr Lee was much more concerned about what might happen to her in the great outdoors and away from her special tank. We were never really sure about her existence. In fact, at Medmenham, we were never very sure about the existence of anything! At a time when there was talk on the radio and in the newspapers of sputniks landing on the moon, we were ready to believe whatever we were told.

On the 16th July, when I had been in the WRAF just over a year, Jan and June began talking about ghosts. We were sitting in the NAAFI after tea and they were sharing their last cigarette before pay day.

"Hey, I've just had a thought," said June. "It's the 16th – y'ken what that means."

"Mm!" Jan choked on the cork tip of the cigarette as she finally reached the end. "Shall we go and look for it?"

"Look for what?" I inquired. "Oh Jan, put that damn thing out, you've reached the end of it, honest!"

"The camp ghost," replied Jan patiently. "She is called the Grey Lady and the story is that she comes up the river and walks the Monastery on the 16th of every month, looking for her baby that was born out of wedlock!"

"Oh, so I heard!" I retorted. "There's no such thing as ghosts though, and in any case why should a Nun be looking in a Monastery?"

"I didn't think there would be men going to the moon but it looks like there *will* be one day!" Jan exclaimed. There was some logic in that!.

"She is looking in the Monastery because the Monks took her baby away," said June, as if it made total sense.

"We'll go out tonight," said Jan. "We can all creep out of one of the downstairs windows after the Block has been locked up – it's time we had a bit of fun."

"Do we dare?" I wasn't very sure about this plan at all. I was nineteen now, and the oldest, and trying to be sensible.

"We won't get caught if we are quick about it," replied Jan. She finally accepted the fact that there was no more puff left in her cigarette and put the cork tip in the ash tray.

I reluctantly agreed, at the same time wondering what I was letting myself in for.

It seemed like ages before the Duty Airwoman came round and did her bed check. On a permanent station, if you were under twenty-one, you had to be in by 2359 and there was always somebody there to make sure you were. We also had another 'hazard' in that our room was right next door to the Senior NCO's part of the block, separated only by a bolted door, so we had to be particularly quiet.

June poked her head out of the door and watched the Duty Airwoman disappear down the corridor and then, when we thought she had been given long enough to settle down out of the way, we crept down the stairs, in our pyjamas, to the ground floor wash room, carrying our WRAF raincoats over our arms. Jan got out first.

"Come on you two," she whispered, "the coast is clear."

We covered our pyjamas with our raincoats and climbed out at the back of the Block. There was a full moon shining fitfully through the clouds.

"Run!" called June, who was much more athletic than Jan and I were.

"How the devil can I run when my pyjama legs keep coming down below my coat?" I whispered.

"Shh!" hissed Jan, "nobody's going to see you, come on!"

"Except the ghost," retorted June.

We tiptoed down the road, away from the Block, and then ran helter skelter for the trees that surrounded the Monastery. I quickly rolled my pyjama legs up again and we crept towards the building that showed a darker shade of black against the starless sky.

"Ugh, doesn't it look spooky!?" I whispered.

"I thought you said there was no such thing as spooks!" said Jan.

"I did," I replied, "and I don't think there are. It just looks spooky, that's all!"

We crept behind the large hedge and silently waited. Once an owl hooted and shattered the silence and my flesh crawled. We waited a while longer and still nothing happened.

The Monastery.

"Oh, nothing is going to happen," said June. "We could stay here all night and not see anything."

"Let's go back then," I whispered. "I'd sooner be in bed anyway!"

Then, at that precise moment, a terrible howling sound came from the direction of the gardens. The three of us clung together in fright, our hair standing on end, our feet rooted to the spot! The howl came again – long and drawn out – like a howl of pain.

"Oh shit!" exclaimed Jan, "just let's go!"

We ran as if the devil himself were after us, and this time I did not care about my pyjama bottoms showing below my coat! We tore up the road to the WRAF Block and poured ourselves in through the open window to safety, arriving breathless and shaken in Room 15. We spent the rest of the night making cups of coffee, with powdered milk, and trying to work out what it had been, all of us firmly convinced, for a while anyway, that we had been the first three people to actually see – or rather hear – anything of the infamous Grey Lady.

To our complete disappointment and shame, we learnt later that the night howler had simply been one of the stewards that had been working late in the Officers Mess! He had spotted us lurking in the shadows and had decided to give us a fright by doing a bit of 'lurking' himself in one of the darkened upstairs rooms and howling from the window. We could cheerfully have killed him but we didn't have the courage to tell him that the three people he saw were us!

"I have never been so mortified in all my life!" exclaimed Jan, when she found out. "What an embarrassment."

However, the following month, she came much closer to seeing the ghost and, for the life of us, we couldn't see how *this* could have been caused by the pranks of stewards.

It was Jan's turn to be on night duty on the 16th and although she always had a fear of working on that date, she had no choice in the matter. On these night duties there would be one teleprinter operator and one telephonist working together in that part of the Monastery that had once been the stables.

All the entrances to the building were locked at night, with the exception of the back entrance, which was guarded by two 'Snowdrops' and it was impossible for the stewards to get into that part of the building at all. The teleprinter room itself was a small office. In one corner of the room an iron staircase led up to the rest room, which, presumably in the olden days, had been either a hay loft or the stable boys quarters.

It was 1am on this particular night and the two airwomen had received most of the signals and had decided to have a game of cards to pass the time. Suddenly Jan heard a noise coming from the Rest Room – it sounded like footsteps.

"Who's up there?" shouted Silvia.

The footsteps changed and this time it sounded as though somebody was walking down the iron steps from the Rest Room to where the girls were. The noise echoed through the office and the steps seemed to vibrate. Now they were really frightened.

"Who can it be?" whispered Jan, as she clung onto Sylvia. "Bloody hell, I'm scared!"

"It's the 16th today," Sylvia reminded her unnecessarily.

They knew that the date was tailor-made for pranksters and Jan had not forgotten her experiences the previous month. Nevertheless, she shuddered and grabbed hold of the nearest heavy object, which happened to be the sellotape holder. Then the noise stopped and the girls breathed a sigh of relief.

"I'm going up there," said Sylvia.

"Oh no, don't" cried Jan. "Don't leave me."

"Don't be silly! The ghost is up in the Rest Room, not down here."

Sylvia ran up the stairs and Jan sat still, listening to her poking about. A few minutes later and she reappeared.

"Well, honestly, there is nothing up there. Let's carry on with our game of cards," she said.

The girls continued playing cards for about fifteen minutes, and then the noise sounded again. Definitely like someone walking down the stairs.

"But ghosts are supposed to be supernatural," whispered Jan. "You wouldn't hear the sound of their bloody feet!"

"Well, we bloody well are with this one," replied Sylvia. "I'm going to phone for the Station Police to come down here. I can't cope with this any longer."

She dialled the number and within seconds the Duty Policeman arrived.

He laughed when they told him their story, but fortunately for them, the sound came again while he was with them. After getting over the initial shock, he too went up to have a look around the Rest Room – and found nothing.

"Perhaps it's the wind!" he offered, unconvincingly.

"Maybe the IRA!" said Sylvia, even less convincingly.

"Don't be silly," replied Jan. "What would the IRA want with us?"

The SP went right round and checked all the windows, which were bolted and barred, and then he stayed with them for the rest of the Night Shift. Of course, the Officers' Mess was in the Monastery as well, but there was no way that anyone could have got through and into the upstairs Rest Room without being seen. It was very scary.

Nobody could come up with a valid explanation and Sylvia and Jan were so convinced that there had been 'something' that they were never put on duty again on the 16th.

However, if we thought that was the last time the Grey Lady would 'appear' we were mistaken...

5. *"You don't blow – you spit!"*

Not long after Jan's experience with the camp ghost we lost our use of the spare bed and cupboards. These were to be occupied by one Jessie Reynolds from Preston, who was slim, blonde and drop-dead gorgeous.

She also annoyed everyone because she just managed to keep her hair off her collar, without actually getting it cut. It almost defied the laws of gravity as she carefully rolled it underneath in a sort of page-boy style. If it was combed out it was way beyond regulation length but somehow she got away with it.

With the addition of Jessie we soon became known throughout the camp as The Four J's and it was because of this that our 'brilliant idea' for the NAAFI dance came into being. It was to be a Tramps Ball and the four of us thought we would try to be different and original.

"I know," said Jan, "let's go down to the farm at the back of the Dog and Badger and see if we can have some farm sacks, and then we could make them into sack dresses."

"Oh that will be really trendy," said Jessie.

The idea had hardly had a chance to formulate before Jan and June ran down to the farm and returned with sacks that stank of farmyard.

"We can't wear those!" I cried, "Ugh, they stink to high heaven."

"Yes we can," retorted Jessie. "We'll boil them."

There was no stopping her when she got a 'bee in her bonnet' and the laundry room was filled with steam as she boiled the things and eventually produced something that passed as clean. Then we cut holes in them for our head and arms to go through, little realising that we had made the, already flimsy material, even flimsier! By now it was like muslin.

Not to be put off and fired with enthusiasm, we used lipstick and scrawled across the back and front of our sacks the legends' J No.1', 'J No.2', 'J No.3' and 'J No.4'.

"That's not good enough," said Jess. "We need something funny, to catch the eye." She thought for a minute.

"I know," she laughed. "How about the four bags of Room 15?"

"Do you mind!" replied Jan, quite shocked, "I'm not a bag, I can't walk around with *that* on me."

"If I can, you can," said Jess, and she changed the J's to the word 'Bag'.

We finished off the whole ensemble with brightly coloured woollen stockings and fixed some pieces of straw in our hair and we looked as common as the muck that, until recently, had been in the sacks.

Jan surveyed her handiwork in front of the mirror.

"Oh yes definitely," she laughed. "Aren't we fashionable?"

"I reckon this bit about the four bags is asking for trouble" I said.

"Hooray!" everyone chorused.

As it turned out, I was right. We made quite a hit at the dance, in more ways than one. What with the continual jiving, and boys trying to treat themselves to a piece of sack for a souvenir, we were soon having to hot foot it back to the Block to save our modesty and change into something more respectable that would not tear so easily. Once we had changed into our normal clothing, we jived until bed-check time. The camp was so small that by now I knew everyone and so we were never at a loss for jive partners, and if the boys didn't want to dance then the girls would dance together. We didn't care!

We were able to drink cider, but didn't tackle anything else, so by midnight we were very merry, but not drunk. Unlike the boys, the airwomen lived a bit too near the WRAF Senior NCO's to take too many chances! The boys, on the other hand, had no such restrictions to their behaviour. They made several efforts to walk straight lines, but failed. Inevitably, it was us that were pointing them in the direction of their accommodation and not the other way round!

The combination of the fresh air and the cider began to do its work as we made our way unsteadily back up the road. My eyes felt as though they were coming out on organ stops, and my legs felt like rubber as Jan and June decided that they would sing to the Senior NCO end of our block!

"Stop it!" cried Jessie. "You'll get put on jankers – come away!"

I couldn't sing for laughing, but eventually we decided that perhaps it was, indeed, a bit unwise to serenade the sergeants at bed check time, especially with 'Bless 'em All' and we reluctantly tottered off back to our own end of the Block.

"I don't care if you don't appreciate my singing," carried on Jan, as she fell flat on her bed, kicking off her shoes as she landed and ignoring the mound of clothes underneath her. "I shall show you that I am musical. I shall join the Band."

Where this sudden idea to join the Signals Command Band had come from is anybody's guess, but it was totally out of the blue.

"Let's all join!" laughed June, as she entered into the spirit of things. "It will be a good skive!"

"But none of us can play any instruments," I reminded them gently. "That could be a set-back before we start."

Jessie was peering into the mirror, trying to see straight as she put her hair in rollers. She wasn't very successful and rollers dropped to the floor as she gave it up as a bad job.

"Well, they will teach us won't they!?" she said. It was logic to her.

"Course they will teach us," said June. "They should be highly honoured that we are offering our services. They want more girls in the Band, it says so in Station Routine Orders."

"So it does," I laughed, "but I do think they might be hoping for people who can play an instrument!"

"I want to play the drums!" announced Jan, as she started to sort out her bed.

"OK then, I'll play the trumpet," I replied. "I just fancy playing the trumpet like Eddie Calvert."

"Even Eddie Calvert had to learn once," said Jessie, helpfully. "Who knows, you may be able to play "The Cherry Pink and Apple Blossom White" one day!"

We all finally settled down for the night, dreaming our own dreams about how the world was just about to reap the benefits of the combined musical talents of the Four J's.

The Signals Command Band was under the proud jurisdiction of 'Bandy', as he was known throughout Medmenham and beyond. He was a Flight Sergeant but everybody called him by his nickname. It consisted of mostly airmen but Bandy was trying to get more airwomen to join. It was voluntary, so all practices were to be in our spare time, other than during Commander-in-Chief's Inspections, when we were allowed time off work to go away on various engagements around the country. This, of course, was the main attraction. However, Lairdie's idea that it might be 'a good skive' was dispelled very quickly!

It was a good band, but of course not as professional as the Central Band of the Royal Air Force that played for our Passing Out Parade, who were in a class all of their own. After all, the musicians in the Central Band were full-time. The Signals Command Band did have some very talented musicians too, but they now also had the Four 'J's, who were not, which was a bit of a handicap for them!

The four of us strolled across the sports field to the large gym hall where Bandy had his practice sessions to ask if we could join. I was convinced that I was going to be the greatest thing since Satchmo or Eddie Calvert, even though I could not read a note of music! I reasoned that if I could learn shorthand in six weeks then learning to read music ought to be a piece of cake.

The other three were quite sure that they were doing the Band the ultimate in favours in offering their services as drummers, though they had never seen a drum in their lives! I was not so sure.

When we first set eyes on Bandy, his tall, lean form was bent over a bass drum and we deduced that he was whitewashing the ropes. The long, skinny figure straightened up and looked down on us over a pair of rimless glasses. He had a pointed nose and the glasses kept slipping down over it, causing him to be forever hoisting them up again with one hand, while he scratched his balding head with the other. He reminded me of Robert Donat in 'Goodbye Mr. Chips!'

"Well!" he exclaimed, looking vaguely in our direction, "what can I do for you young ladies?"

"We'd like to join the Band," I informed him brightly.

"I see!" he started rummaging through some sheet music. "Do you know what these notes mean?" he asked, pointing to the dog-eared music score.

"No!" I told him honestly.

"Right, you'll do!" he said, keeping a totally straight face. "What do you want to play?"

Like most Senior NCO's at Medmenham, he was completely unfazed by anything.

"The trumpet please."

"Ah well now, it just so happens that I need some trumpeters for the Commander-in-Chief's Inspections this year – it doesn't really matter if you can't play very well, it will make the numbers up and look good with more airwomen in the Band!"

"Charming!" I thought to myself, my hopes of replacing Satchmo rapidly disappearing.

"We want to be drummers!" announced Jessie.

"All right, I will get you fixed up with some drums in a minute and you can start having a practice."

He started rummaging around in another pile of music and from somewhere beneath it he extracted a mouthpiece and attached it to what I thought was a 'squashed up' trumpet.

"This is not a trumpet, it is a cornet" he informed me. "It's all the same – take it into one of the end rooms and start trying to get some noise from it". Then he turned to the other three and began looking for some drums.

I wandered into the spare room at the end of the Gym, sat myself on a chair, and tried to blow into the instrument. Nothing happened. I tried again, still nothing. My dreams of fame were now completely disintegrated. Now I was blowing until I was blue in the face and all I could get out of it was a very rude raspberry sound. Eddie Calvert and Satchmo were quite safe!

I could hear the bang, bang, bang of the drums as the other three J's started to bash the life out of some poor defenceless instruments, and then Bandy appeared at the door.

"Good gracious airwoman!" he exclaimed. "You look like a bloody Victoria plum, girl! You don't blow, you spit."

"Spit!" I cried. "What, you mean like when we spit and polish our shoes?!"

"Exactly like that", he took the cornet from me, replaced the mouthpiece with another one, puckered his lips up and poked his tongue between them, cutting a comical figure as his glasses slipped down even more.

"This is how you do it, like this… see!"

I replaced my mouthpiece and copied him and the note I got made me jump about three inches from my chair! It sounded like an animal in pain! Bandy then took great pains to show me how to read the C scale and carefully wrote on the blackboard, underneath each note, the number of the valve I should press down to get a particular tone. He left me then, and I continued to practice for all I was worth.

My efforts were rewarded and I thought I was brilliant, when after about half an hour, I managed to play it all through both up and down the scale. However, our dreams of glory were shattered again, when we got back to the Block.

Norma, an Irish girl, from the room opposite us, came in carrying mugs of steaming coffee. She shared her room with Sylvia, the telephonist who had been on duty with Jan on the 16th.

"Oh you little love Norma," said Jan. "I was dying for that."

"What was that terrible row coming from the Gym?" asked Norma, knowing perfectly well what it was. "There was this dreadful banging noise and above it all there was a sound like the mooing of a cow in pain."

"Oh, don't be rotten!" I exclaimed. "That was their drums and my cornet and I thought we were doing very well!"

Sylvia poked her head through the door behind her.

"Don't tell me they have let *you* join the Band," she laughed. "You skiving old rogues."

"Why don't *you* both join?" said Jan. "It's a laugh and Bandy wants more people – and we can skive off work for twelve weeks in the autumn."

"Well, that would be just great," chuckled Norma. "Can you imagine it? Whoever heard of a band with six people in it who can't play their bloody instruments?"

"We would have learnt by then!" I told her patiently. "I can play the C Scale already."

"Correction," shouted Sylvia from out in the corridor. "You *think* you can play the C Scale!"

We did, however, manage to persuade Norma and Sylvia to join the band and pretty soon Bandy had the unenviable task of teaching four drummers, one trumpeter and a cymbals player, none of whom could read a note of music! He was a glutton for punishment!

We did work hard though and my first great breakthrough into the realms of music was a very imperfect rendering of 'Land of Hope and Glory'. I was so elated with my success that I played the tune over and over again. At the time I did not know any other melodies except the 'Last Post' and the C Scale.

The girls in the WRAF Block stuffed their ears with cotton wool each time they saw us leave with band equipment, and accompanied by remarks of "Oh no, not Land of Hope and Glory again – please!" we trudged across the sports field. I resolved to myself that *this* time would be the time when I would learn the Air Force March. (It was odd how the Air Force March always managed to sound like Land of Hope and Glory when I played it!)

By the autumn, as the C-in-C's Inspections became imminent, we were at least able to march along without putting a note in the wrong place, and if we did, well we were covered by the real experts in the Band.

"If in doubt, don't play it," said Bandy, "especially if you are trying to see where you are marching – we don't want you going arse over head do we?"

You need a lot of coordination to read music and watch where you are going at the same time!

It was no skive really. We actually did have our work cut out in those weeks before we went away, although we did have many light-hearted moments too.

During the week before our first performance Bandy had all us novices sitting in a circle in the Gym Hall, practising for all the marches we would play. I felt a complete cheat with all the fingering written down on my music, but at least I managed to get some sort of tune that way, as a background for those that were really playing the melodies!

He had his own unique way of conducting. If we could not get a sequence right he made his own words up to it.

"Come on!" he yelled, pushing his glasses back up his long nose. "Get some swing into it! Remember you all know this march...." and then he sang.

"Have you ever, no I've never, but I'd like to..." or

"Never, never shoot a duck, for it may be-e some-body's Uncle,

Never, never shoot a duck, for it might be some-one's Aunt..."

Most of the time he had us in hysterics. During one musical piece called 'Three Little Maids' Bandy just could not get us to play it right, no matter how hard he tried. Then he really lost his temper.

"Oh, for goodness sake!" he shouted, throwing down his baton. "It should be fairylike and you are playing it like a load of bloody elephants! Look, you play it like this..."

He picked up the nearest trumpet and played the notes, at the same time doing the 'dance of the little cygnets' from Swan Lake across the Gym Hall. This was all too much for any of us. The sight of tall, gangly Bandy tripping sideways across the room like Rudolf Nureyev, his glasses slipping further and further down his nose and a trumpet to his mouth, caused us to fall about with shrieks of laughter. He looked like the King of the Fairies. In fact, some of the boys were beginning to wonder whether he *was* one!

And so yet another rehearsal ended with tears of laughter streaming down our cheeks!

I pushed my way through all the Best Blue uniforms hanging from the rail in the centre of the bus and tried to find my seat next to Jessie. Our bus was an RAF one and we had utilised the hand rail for our best uniforms so that they did not get creased. Our cases were in the back of the vehicle and our instruments were strewn over the back seat.

"Blimey!" I exclaimed. "I hope the driver can see where we are going, because I can't."

"By the way," said Jessie. "Where *are* we going?"

"I've no idea," I replied.

Jan leaned over from her seat behind us.

"We are going to Thorney Island," she said. "It's on the South Coast."

"Oh thanks," replied Jessie. "It's nice to know."

The bus trundled out of camp, with few of us giving any thought to those that we had left behind having to do double the work to cover for our absence. Groupy hadn't been very concerned though.

"Don't you worry," he had smiled. "Enjoy yourself and you can make up for it when you get back."

Before we had travelled very far, a group of the boys, who could play really well, resurrected their instruments and were playing jazz tunes in the back of the vehicle. It was, therefore, a merry journey down to the South Coast and our bus and its musicians looked like Satchmo's jazz band in the introduction to 'High Society'. We must have appeared a comical sight to passing motorists, with the boys playing the latest jazz tunes and the girls sitting in the front of the coach, busily whitening webbing belts and polishing instruments.

It was late afternoon when we arrived and, after dropping off the boys, our bus drove us straight to the Officers Mess, where we would be staying the night.

There were no airwomen at this station, so therefore no WRAF Block. It was the first, and likely to be the only time I had ever been in such an establishment.

"This is definitely the life!" said Jan, as we walked up the carpeted stairs to the Officers quarters. "I should have been an officer."

"They wouldn't have you!" laughed Jessie.

"You never know." I said. "We might get a cup of tea brought to us in the morning!"

"You must be joking!" exclaimed Jan. "If some old steward comes in and sees me with my hair in rollers, I'll just die."

"Wonder what sort of a hash we will make of it tomorrow?" muttered Sylvia. "I hope I don't clash me cymbals in the wrong place!"

I looked at her fairly ample bust and hoped she didn't either. It could be nasty.

Sadly, we were only allowed to *sleep* in the Officers Quarters. Any ideas we might have had about eating there were soon dispelled as we were shown the way to the Airmen's Mess for tea. As it was predominately a male station, it was an unusual sight for the airmen to see airwomen in their Mess, so they stared at us as if we were Martians that had just landed in their midst.

The following morning was lovely and sunny and soon after rehearsals we were putting on our best uniforms and white webbing belts ready for the parade. We also wore white braiding with tassels on over our shoulders and really felt like the 'bees-knees'.

The large concrete runway at Thorney Island was being used as a Parade Square and the aeroplanes were side by side behind us, facing in from the sea. Despite the hot summer sun, the sea breezes tore across the open surface of the runway and we had a job to keep our hats on securely and play at the same time!

The signal was given for the parade to begin. The job of Mace Bearer had been taken over by a WRAF Flight Sergeant, which was quite unusual at the time, but was the only way that airwomen would have been allowed to go off camp in a mixed group. She quite clearly had some previous experience, but she had also been practicing without our knowledge, which we thought was a bit underhand! We had believed we had got away with being able to go away without a Senior NCO being present until *she* suddenly turned up.

We thought it was a complete pain in the neck to have a WRAF Senior NCO with us, but it was gallant of her to have spent so much time learning so that airwomen could be in the Band.

"Signals Command Band, by the left, quick march!"

She lifted the colourful mace in front of us and we immediately struck up the Air Force March.

Well, ninety percent of the Band did. There were one or two of us that just played the bottom notes to keep the beat for those playing the melody.

We halted in the centre and to the front of the aeroplanes and the airmen marched past in front of us. Then everything went silent while we waited for the C-in-C's car to arrive.

Suddenly the order came, "Parade attention – Colour Party present arms!" and we played the General Salute.

The large form of the C-in-C Signals Command unravelled itself from the Staff Car and we played a selection of tunes as he walked around, inspecting the airmen.

Not so long ago I had been at another parade, my first, at Royal Air Force Wilmslow. I had seen the RAF flag hoisted in front of me and had watched a group of Vulcans zooming across the sky as the General Salute was played by the Central Band of the Royal Air Force. We weren't in the same league as them, but we were not doing so badly and I was doing my bit, even though it was a very minor part.

The parade was over as quickly as it had begun and the C-in-C congratulated Bandy on the turn out of his Band. Little did he know that he had five airwomen, one in particular, who only played a very limited number of notes!

The same sequence of events took place on every station we visited over the next few weeks. Consequently I was working two or three days in the section and then two or even three days throughout the Command, from Thorney Island and Tangmere in the South, to Haydock in the North, and many other RAF Stations in between.

There was one final duty in the year for the Band and that was Battle of Britain Parade in early September, when most the inhabitants of RAF Medmenham had to march through Marlow town headed by the Band finishing with the Church Service. It was a splendid occasion with the mace carried by the WRAF Flight Sergeant again. This time my parents were able to attend and they stood at the side of the road and watched us go past, along with the crowds of onlookers. They looked proud and, just for once, I *did* feel like a 'plus-type girl' as I caught sight of them grinning in my direction.

"Told you it would be good for a skive!" said Jessie, when we handed in our white webbing belts and braids for the last time.

"Well it wasn't what *I* would call a skive," I replied. "That was damned hard work."

I was quite glad to get back to my typewriter.

Medmenham wasn't far from where I came from, so I usually managed to get home once a month and bring Mum and Dad up to date on most of our exploits, although not all!

By now, Dad had a car and he would happily do the double journey to drive me back to camp on the Sunday evening and compare notes between Medmenham and his own days in the Air Force. He and Mum also had the dubious pleasure of meeting the three other J's, and Mum actually got to see inside the WRAF Block. However, men were still not allowed within shooting distance, not even my Dad, so he had to wait outside.

The trees surrounding the Monastery at Headquarters Signals Command began to take on that golden and red colour of autumn, while the dark evergreens made a sombre background for the brilliant red, yellow and orange chrysanthemums, which had now replaced the crocuses colouring the lawns on my first day at the camp. And then, for some reason best known to ourselves, the autumn suddenly became the 'silly season' – the season for practical jokes, getting into scrapes and doing daft things.

"Look at all this clutter on my bed!" moaned June. "It all belongs to Jan. I'm not kidding. Anyone would think she hadn't got any cupboards."

"I've got all her rollers on *my* bed!" said Jessie.

I looked around the room; she had certainly left her mark when she got ready to go out this evening – Jan always did when she was in a rush – and it looked as if a bulldozer had been through the place. Her own bed was heaped with clothes, June's bed was covered in make-up and shoes. Jessie seemed to have acquired Jan's rollers and I, because my bed happened to be near the long mirror, had got her brush and comb.

"She gets worse by the minute," wailed June. "I think we should teach her a lesson."

"Let's hide all her clothes," suggested Jessie.

"Good idea," grinned June impishly. "Oh, I forgot, she's on evenings."

"Oh, maybe we should not do it if she is working then," said Jessie.

"Rot!" exclaimed June, as she began to gather up all Jan's clothes. "She's always a couple of hours nattering when she comes in, and besides that, she's got tomorrow morning off to straighten everything out. In any case," she added as an afterthought, "we'll help her."

We began collecting up all her clothes, including everything in her cupboards and drawers.

"Lets stick them all in the bath and lock the door from the inside," said June. "I can easily climb over the top of the adjoining wall and into the other bathroom next door."

We made frequent trips to the bathroom with piles of Jan's clothes, laying them carefully in the empty bath. We even removed all her bedding, including mattress, until all she had left to call her own were the bed springs.

June locked the door of the bathroom from the inside and then scrambled like a little monkey over the wall that separated it from the one next door (all the baths were divided by walls that finished about a foot from the ceiling).

We then waited patiently for Jan to return from her evening duty. It wasn't long before we heard the familiar sound of her footsteps in the corridor.

"Quick, she's coming!" cried June, as she dived into bed. "Turn the lights out!"

It was uncanny how this just *had* to be the evening when our friend decided that she would be considerate and not turn on the big light and wake us all up! Instead she crept into the room and felt her way in the dark over to her bed.

I already felt awful.

"I'm dead beat!" I heard her yawn. "I wish they would post that little fat corporal."

She sat down on bed springs.

"What the bloody hell is this!?" she cried, switching her small light on. "Oh shit! Where's my bloody bedding?"

We could not stop ourselves from giggling under the sheets. We were like eleven-year-olds at Guide camp!

"Oh come on you lot, wake up, I know you are not asleep," cried Jan. "What have you done with my bloody bedding!?"

"I think you owe fourpence to the swear box," said June.

"Bugger the swear box!" exclaimed a furious Jan. "Where's my bedding Lairdie?"

She tore June's bed-covering away from her and pulled her onto the floor.

"Come on Lairdie, you rotten little sod, I want to go to bed." She strode back to her bed space and then caught sight of her empty cupboards.

"Oh sod it, you've taken away all my clothes too – where are they Ratty?"

She sat down on her bed, or what was left of it, quite failing to see the funny side of it.

"Oh come on you lot – a joke's a joke, but this is too much. Where are all my clothes?"

"Didn't you leave them on my bed?" said Jessie, trying to smother her laughter.

Jan was completely oblivious to the veiled sarcasm.

"Not *all* of them!" she cried. "Tere were some in my cupboards... Oh, I give up! I'll sleep in my uniform then, on the bare springs. I don't care."

We were just about to give in and tell Jan what we had done with all her things when she found out for herself where they were from a different source altogether, and one we had not bargained for!

It seemed that the Duty Airwoman, whose job it was to see that the Block was properly secure for the night, had found a bathroom door locked and yet no sounds coming from within. She thought that somebody had fainted, and because she did not have the wit to look over the top, she had telephoned the Guardroom. It was just our luck to have the thickest female in our Block as Duty Airwoman that night!

Along came an RAF Policeman, feeling very privileged to be allowed in the hallowed portals of our accommodation. Only he, of course, was not as daft as the wretched girl that had phoned him up. He hoisted her up so that she could look over, and of course she recognised Jan's clothes neatly placed in the bath.

Wondering how thick anyone could get, he hastened back to the safety of his Guardroom.

Once she had recovered from her embarrassment, the Duty Airwoman was soon knocking on our door to tell Jan where she could find her belongings, and June had to do her climbing routine all over again to unlock the door.

Jan never altered though, and I really don't think the place would have been the same if she had!

On Friday nights it was the habit of some of the boys to go down to the pub in the village to do some serious drinking. The Dog and Badger could be reached by a short walk down the main road outside the camp or a 'short cut' through the trees at the back of the camp and a quick hop over a wire fence.

The D & B specialised in some particularly strong cider, and it was the boys' duty to test it out on pay day! Often they would come back quite late and then stand outside the WRAF Block and sing to Jessie. There was something about cider that always seemed to make people want to sing and all the boys were totally and hopelessly in love with the girl.

Usually the singing did not last too long and was perfectly harmless fun and even the WRAF Senior NCOs tended to ignore it. However, on one particular Friday they were worse than usual.

"They are not in tune tonight!" laughed Jessie, who was completely unmoved by their adoration.

"It must have been somebody's birthday," said Jan. "Oh my god, listen to them!"

Sure enough, the two boys under our window were singing "We want Jessie for a sunbeam, we want Jessie for a sunbeam."

Jessie giggled and made ready with a basin of water to throw over them. She was already interested in the corporal in her section and certainly not these two reprobates.

"Shh listen," whispered Jan. The singing had stopped and we could hear them talking.

"I dare you," said one, "to go up into that room and see Jessie."

"Don't dare me," said the other one, "cos I love Jessie!"

Jessie giggled. She really was a very attractive girl.

"Come on," said the first boy, dissolving into whispers and giggles, "let's go and see the girls. Let's see if we can get in the back door and go and see Jessie."

She raced to the window and leaned out.

"I can't see anything," she whispered, "they seem to have gone."

"They wouldn't come up here would they?" gasped Jan. "They would get put on jankers if they got caught."

"I hope they don't come in," I said, as I clambered out of bed and pushed the door tight shut. "I have got my hair in rollers!"

We lay for a long time under the covers in the darkness but nothing happened.

"I didn't think they would pluck up the courage," announced Jessie, as she sat up in bed and switched on her light.

"Och, they are all mouth and troosers," said June, with a hint of disappointment in her voice!

She had hardly finished speaking when we heard a commotion in the outside corridor, the door flew open and the two boys fell in, landing on the floor in front of us.

"Get out you fools!" cried Jan. "Supposing the sergeants hear you!"

"We love Jessie!" drawled the first boy, who everyone called Scouse.

We all grabbed our housecoats to make ourselves respectable and then attempted to push the boys back from whence they came, whilst I tried, and failed, to get the rollers out of my hair without them noticing. Little did any of us know that a generation later they would have been openly invited in and nobody would have batted an eyelid. However, in 1960 it could get them thrown out of the RAF.

"We want Jessie for a sunbeam!" sang Bobby.

"I'm thirsty," slurred Scouse, and he ambled over to our table where we kept 'Len', our goldfish, who was swimming around in his bowl, doing no harm to anybody. Scouse lifted the bowl and tried to drink Len's water, ignoring the fish swimming around, minding his own business amongst the weeds.

That was enough for June, who had recently won him at the local fair. He was named after the very corporal that was getting on Jan's nerves in the Communications Centre. But it was June who had named him, not Jan, for June quite fancied Len, though none of us could understand why.

"Do you mind?" she cried, rushing over to him. "That is Len. You can't drink Len!

In the meantime Bobby was reeling round the room, bumping into everything in sight. It was the sound of the heavy door to the Senior NCOs quarters being opened that caused us all to stop dead in our tracks for a split second. Then, in unison, we moved at such a speed that it would be a credit to any situation comedy.

Jan and I found brute strength from somewhere and forcibly man-handled Bobby down the corridor and into the drying room. It was a bit hot in there but it served the purpose.

We rushed back along the corridor and into the room just at the very moment that the door started to open at the end of the corridor. In fact it was like a scene from a Whitehall farce as the door from the NCO's quarters opened at exactly the same time as ours closed behind me. It was a very near thing!

I flung myself onto my bed without even thinking about Scouse! Jessie and June were already under their covers, pretending to be asleep, with the room in darkness.

Our door was opened and the light was switched on. I screwed up my eyes as if I was not used to the sudden light after an hour or so of darkness, but this did not fool the WRAF NCO who was standing, hands on hips, wearing a long green dressing gown and staring at us in rage.

It was none other than Flight Sergeant Howard, the 'mace carrier' for the Band.

"What the devil is going on in here?" she scowled. "What's all the noise about?"

"Nothing Flight Sergeant," said Jan meekly.

"Nothing? NOTHING!" she glared. "What was it then, the camp ghost? Do you know it is past midnight? I charge you all with causing a disturbance!"

I stared frantically around the room, wondering what had happened to Scouse, and even toyed with the idea of agreeing with her that it could have been the camp ghost!

"You haven't had *men* in your room have you airwomen?"

She said the word 'men' as if she were talking about something she had just wiped off her shoe!

"Oh *no* Flight," cried Jessie, sounding quite shocked at the mere suggestion of such a dreadful and unladylike thing.

I was still wondering what on earth had happened to Scouse. There was no way he could have got out of the room and we were on the first floor, so he could hardly have gone out of the window. I thought maybe he was hiding under one of the beds.

"Are you *sure* you have not had men in here?"

"Certainly not Flight," I replied.

"You had better not," said the Flight Sergeant. "Anyway, you can report to me at 8.30 in the morning," and with that she flounced out through the door.

"Whew!" signed Jan. "That was close. It'll be jankers for us now!"

I waited until I heard the bolt slide back on the other side of the door in the Senior NCO's quarters.

"What happened to the other chap?" I asked.

"My God!" gasped Jessie. "I shoved him out of the window!"

We all rushed and peered out into the darkness. I had visions of finding the poor lad with a broken neck on the grass below, but instead he was hanging by his hands from our windowsill. His feet were swinging backwards and forwards past the window below. He had been there all the time, silently hanging from the ledge until the sergeant had gone. We helped him back into the room and then he sheepishly walked down the corridor to where his friend was waiting and the two of them crept out of the Block the way they had got in.

"That's us in dead lumber now," said Jessie. "Jan is right, we'll be on a charge for sure."

"It's Saturday tomorrow," said June. "I reckon that she meant that we were to report to her on Monday. After all, supposing we were going home for the weekend?"

"She knows we are not going home for the weekend," pointed out Jessie. "None of us have filled our 48-hour passes in."

"How can she know that without checking?" said Jan. "I think June is right, let's wait and report to her on Monday. I don't want to get into any more trouble for waking her up on a Saturday morning."

"OK," yawned Jessie, as she snuggled down into her bed, "but I hope you are right!"

I hoped she was too, but I had a suspicion that she wasn't!

It was 9am on Saturday and we were enjoying our breakfast in bed. It was a day off for all of us and we each took turns on Saturday mornings in going over to the Mess and bringing back cups of tea and bacon sandwiches. I had just sunk my teeth into a particularly delicious bacon sandwich that June had made, when our door flew open to reveal the irate form of the Flight Sergeant, now wearing uniform instead of the green dressing gown! I stopped eating, the roll hovering in mid-air, while the butter oozed down my chin.

"What is the meaning of this?" she yelled. "I thought I told you to report to me at 8.30. Get dressed this instant! I shall expect to see you outside my door in less than five minutes."

She slammed the door behind her.

For a minute all four of us stood in silence like statutes, and then all hell broke loose as we threw our sandwiches to the winds and clambered into our uniforms. We were in such a hurry that none of us even attempted to speak, and in less than five minutes we were knocking on the door to her private room. The door opened.

"Thank you!" she said sarcastically. "I have been fully dressed and waiting for you since 8.30 this morning, and this is *my* day off."

"Sorry Flight!" I muttered. She ignored me.

"You are charged," she carried on, "with causing a disturbance and failing to carry out an order. You will report to the WRAF Admin Office at 08.30 hours on Monday."

The door closed and we strolled dejectedly back to our room, to find Liz, who was in the room beneath us, waiting outside our door.

"Do you know anyone with mauve socks!" she said brightly, "cos they were swinging past our window last night!"

"Don't you say anything," snapped June. "We are in enough trouble already."

"I only asked!" laughed Liz.

On the Monday morning I found out what 'being up in front of the beak' was like.

At 08.30 we lined up outside the WRAF Admin, our best blue uniforms pressed and our shoes highly polished, and all of us feeling totally mortified.

Oh my God, my first charge in the Air Force, what a disgrace! I thought.

Two corporals marched the four of us into the office, without our hats, and told us to stand to attention in front of the desk. It was all very solemn.

Borrowing the WRAF Admin Flight Sergeant's desk for the duration of the 'charge' was the Squadron Officer. Next to her stood Flight Sergeant Howard, whom we had upset in the first place, and hovering in the back of the room was the WRAF Admin Flight Sergeant herself. She was not very happy that there had been such 'goings on' in her WRAF Block.

"I might have known," she muttered under her breath, "that it would be *you* lot!"

"Cheek!" I thought. "Anyone would think we were always up to no good."

"Attention!" yelled one of the corporals.

The Squadron Officer looked up from the paper on the desk that obviously contained the details of our misdemeanour then looked down again. She reminded me a bit of Tessie O'Shea, with a huge bust that could hardly be contained inside her tight-fitting jacket. Her hat was balanced precariously on top of thick bleached blonde curls that were having a struggle to keep off her collar. She looked at us again as if she hadn't been sure of what she saw the first time and then down at her notes.

"You are charged," she read, "with causing a disturbance and failing to carry out an order." She looked across at the other NCO. "Read them their rights corporal."

The corporal stared straight ahead and recited our rights as if she had a record inside her and had just been wound up.

"You have the right to remain silent," she chanted, "you have the right to bring witnesses in your defence, or you have the right to make a statement."

We all stared straight ahead at a spot on the wall opposite.

"Well!" cried the officer. "What do you wish to do? If you remain silent you must accept the punishment, as you know."

"We'll make a statement." I said hastily.

I could feel Jan bristle next to me. She was rightfully annoyed. Now we would have to give some sort of explanation. We knew if we told the truth we would really drop the boys in hot water, so we had to dream up something.

"Well airwomen?" she said, getting really impatient by now. "Did you cause a disturbance?"

We fixed our eyes on the wall about a foot above her head and glared at it.

"All right," she signed, exasperation in her voice. "Then I have to take it that you *did*."

I carried on staring at the wall.

"What about the second charge then?" said the now extremely angry officer, looking in my direction. "*You* tell me airwoman. Why did you fail to report to the Flight Sergeant on Saturday morning when you were ordered to do so?"

No answer.

"You will answer me or I will have a separate and further charge for you!"

"I don't know Ma'am," I muttered.

She gave up with me and turned to Jan.

"Alright, *you* explain it for me!"

"We thought that she had made a mistake Ma'am," said Jan. "We thought that she had meant today, Monday".

This was, quite clearly, the wrong thing to say.

The Squadron Officer turned a violent shade of purple, while the two corporals that had marched us in fought to hide their laughter.

"You thought what?" she cried. "Since when has it been the custom for airwomen to *think* for Senior NCOs? If you had been required to report on Monday I am sure that the Flight Sergeant would have said Monday and not Saturday, isn't that so Flight?"

"Yes Ma'am," replied our accuser.

The WRAF Officer was really getting quite angry, and in the background our Admin Flight Sergeant started to look uncomfortable at the thought of her airwomen behaving in such a thick manner!

"I sentence you to seven days restrictions." She rose majestically from the chair and nodded to the corporals to march us out of the office.

"Left turn – quick march!"

We marched out, closely followed by the WRAF Admin Flight Sergeant. The corporals collapsed into peals of laughter now that they were out of sight of the WRAF Officer.

"It's not funny corporal!" scowled Flight. "This sort of thing gives my Block a bad name."

"Sorry Flight," I muttered ashamedly.

"You *will* be young lady!" replied Flight. "You will report to the Guardroom in the morning at 7.30am in your working uniform, and then again in the evening at 22.00 hours in your best uniform. You will not be allowed off camp at any time during the seven days and you will also have two hours of fatigues each evening."

"Oh lord!" I thought. "Shades of RAF Wilmslow again!"

We were still standing to attention, holding our berets.

"Alright, replace your berets and dismiss," growled Flight. She stalked off, leaving us to reflect on our sins and the corporals to go off to work.

That evening, as promised, the Flight Sergeant saw to it that we each had two hours fatigues. June and Jan were sent to the kitchens in the Mess, where the Camp Catering Sergeant found them a few tables to scrub. Jessie and I were banished to the bathrooms and ironing rooms, which by the end of the week were surely the most scrubbed and polished in the Air Force!

Norma and Sylvia thought that the whole thing was hilarious, and Scouse and Bobby were very sheepish for a long time. They were, however, very grateful to us for not splitting on them and we did quite well for ciders in the NAAFI for a while.

As for Liz, as far as I know she is still trying to find out who owned the mauve socks!

6.   Per Ardua...

Our sessions of cleaning the bathrooms and scrubbing tables in the Mess whilst on Restrictions – or *jankers* as it was commonly known – calmed our high spirits for a while. Christmas drew near without any untoward events to upset the WRAF Block or our Flight Sergeant.

It wasn't all socialising, anyway. We were still expected to do a good days work in our Sections and the others had just sat their exams to be Senior Aircraftswomen. They passed and took great pleasure in tearing off the badges with two propellers from the sleeves of their uniforms and replacing them with a badge with three propellers, like mine.

Now we were *all* three steps from the common riff-raff – and we had been in the WRAF for just eighteen months. The next rank would be corporal, but we needed more education for that.

Fired with a new enthusiasm, Jan and I started to go to evening classes to see if we could get our GCE 'O' levels. In this subdued 'academic' atmosphere, Christmas passed by almost without being noticed (and I did not tell my Dad that I had been 'up in front of the beak'!)

Whilst I went home for the festive season, Jan and June stayed on camp. For one thing, being Scots, they wanted to go home for New Year instead, but for another, they wanted to have Christmas Dinner in the Mess. I realised why soon enough.

It was a tradition in all three Services that at Christmas the officers should serve the other ranks with the meal and that idea appealed to the two girls. They were not going to pass up on the spectacle of the officers in charge of the Signals Section serving them with their turkey and mince pies! On the other hand, I was not going to miss my Mum's cooking for anyone and neither was Jessie! So, for a while, we all went our separate ways.

By the time I got back to camp there had been much partying and June had a steady boyfriend. We weren't all that impressed, however, because he was the little Corporal from the Comm Centre. We wondered, between ourselves, what the attraction was.

"Don't ask me?" said Jan, who was as surprised as me. "I do not have a clue what she sees in him!"

It was too cold to go ghost hunting and the novelty had gone out of being in the Band, so during the winter we left it to the experts. There were few distractions from our routine of going to work in the morning, like everyone else in the country, and then coming back to the Block at night, in the dark. Many evenings most of us were quite happy to put on our dressing gowns and sit in the Rest Room, watching the WRAF Block television, although, more often than not we crossed the road to the NAAFI and jived until we dropped. In the meantime, both June and Jessie were courting – June with her Len and Jessie with a handsome corporal called Tony.

Thus the winter passed by uneventfully.

I had been at Medmenham for exactly a year and the crocuses were beginning to show their heads again when Norma and Sylvia moved on and things began to change. They had decided to apply for an overseas posting and suddenly received notice that they were to go to Germany. Of course, they were excited, but filled with trepidation as well. None of us had ever been abroad before and, after all, Germany! It wasn't all that long ago that we had been at war with them. 'Abroad' was still a big adventure, only afforded to the rich, and Germany seemed like a very long way off.

I was sorry to see them go, for we had been a happy little gang but, as Sylvia pointed out, she and Norma had been at Medmenham for longer than the rest of us. They had better volunteer or get sent! I remembered Sergeant Oliver telling us the same thing.

Bandy would be losing a drummer and a cymbals player but I don't think he shed any tears!

We helped them to pack their things.

"I am *not* taking these," said Silvie, holding up her passion killers. "I think I'll find somewhere good to put them before we leave."

"You might need them," I joked. "They say it's cold in Germany."

"Then I'll get a cold bum," she grunted. "There's no way these are ever going on my backside again!"

"Actually," said Jessie, "you don't have to put them or any other underclothes out for a kit inspection any more, didn't you know?"

"Hooray!" shouted Norma, and threw hers in the air.

It took the four of us a long time to assist Sylvia and Norma with their kit amid the laughter and chasing each other with the infamous passion killers. Eventually, though, both of them, plus kitbags and cases (but minus the dreaded bloomers) were safely boarded and with final hugs and a few tears they were on their way. We waved until their bus was out of sight and then slowly walked back down the road to the NAAFI.

"Look at that," said Jan, as we reached the main door. "She managed it – look!"

The grey silk passion killers had been thrown up and caught on the outside security lamp.

"That's my girl!" laughed Jessie.

"Well, at least the four J's are together still," said Jan as she picked up a handful of fast-melting snow and threw it at an airman who had stopped to look at Silvia's passion killers high up on the lamp, "Well, almost anyway."

We went into the warm NAAFI and Jan bought the snacks while Jessie went and put a record on the jukebox and for a while we sat and listened to Cliff Richard, who was still one of our favourites. Eventually, though, she was joined by Tony and they walked off together arm in arm.

"Have you heard from Tommy lately?" June suddenly said.

"No, he'll be demobbed now and chasing his dream of being a jazz musician I expect."

"Oh well," sighed June. "Never mind. Plenty more fish in the sea, eh?"

"Plenty!" I agreed. "But they are not swimming *my* way."

"Sylvia and Norma will be alright," said Jan, "because the men outnumber the women something rotten overseas!"

"It's not fair," she continued. "All the nicest ones are married. I never find anybody single!"

Poor Jan was fated, it was true. Every time she 'fancied' someone it always turned out that 'somebody had got there before her'. National Service was finishing and the blokes that were in the RAF now were older and career-minded, and if they came across as mature and worldly-wise they were usually married. Then there were the regulars who were just out of training, who Jan considered to be 'much too immature' anyway.

"Never mind Jan," I said. "Perhaps we'll have better luck in Germany, if we get it."

"Oh, knowing my luck, I'll end up in Hong Kong," she grumbled.

If Germany was 'the moon' to us, then Hong Kong might just as well have been in another galaxy. However, it *was* time we volunteered for overseas service before we were posted somewhere we didn't want to go. Besides, we knew that things could not stay the same forever.

There had also been a letter from Tommy – he was a civilian now and had just been accepted for a career with a famous jazz band. Any delusions that I had that *he* might end up being my boyfriend were swiftly put to rest.

It was time to move on.

I had been busy typing letters in the Section and Mr Lee was in the middle of one of his usual tricks of trying to climb up the central heating pipe when Station Routine Orders were delivered to the office. I read them through and then passed them to Rusty to read.

"Airwomen in the Secretarial Trade groups are invited to apply for postings to Headquarters 2nd Tactical Air Force, Royal Air Force Germany," read Rusty. "Any airwoman holding the rank of SACW and who has completed at least eighteen months service may apply to Unit Headquarters for the relevant form."

"What do you think?" I asked her.

"Dunno," she replied, "but it is a fact that we can't stay here forever."

"Germany is a good posting," said Flight. "You might get to do the Nijmegen Marches."

"No they won't," said the corporal. "They don't let the WRAF do that.

I hadn't a clue what they were talking about and let them carry on arguing while I carefully used pink correcting fluid to put right an error on a stencil I was typing.

"They could post us to somewhere horrible, or even worse..." I froze as the thought entered my head for the first time. "Oh my dear good god – permanent staff at Wilmslow!"

"Hell, I never thought of that!" cried Rusty in panic. "Lets put in for Germany immediately – I'd die if I got sent back to Wilmslow – I would honestly!" She had turned quite pale at the very thought!

"Imagine meeting up with Corporal Payne again!" I shuddered.

"I'll go and get the forms straight away!" cried Rusty and was through the open door without a backward glance.

"What's the Nijmegen March?" I asked Flight as she disappeared down the corridor.

"Oh, it's just a one hundred mile route march!" he laughed. "But it doesn't matter, the corporal says that airwomen don't do it, so he must be right."

"Just as well," I replied. "I'm not marching one hundred miles for anyone."

We were still waiting for our postings when June announced that she was going to marry her corporal. The union had not met with universal approval, including, sadly, her parents, so it was a very subdued wedding, with about half a dozen people in the local church. The NCO in charge of her Section at work 'gave her away' and another NCO was best man. Jan acted as bridesmaid and it had all been over in a jiffy. There wasn't a wedding dress – just a little tailored suit and neat hat. Soon she had moved out to live with her new husband in rented accommodation and there was an empty bed in our room. It had all happened very quickly and all we could do was wish her well.

"Three down, three to go," Jan mumbled, as she looked miserably at the corner of the room that her friend had occupied for nearly two years and nodded across to the room opposite where Norma and Silvia had been. We felt very sad and decided to go and drown our sorrows with some cider in the NAAFI.

Autumn had come to God's Little Acre by the time Rusty and I received our instructions to go for medicals and eye tests before our posting.

"Have you heard anything yet?" I asked Jan.

"Not a peep," she replied. "They should get a move on. I could do with some duty-free fags."

She put down the cigarette that for the last five minutes she'd had attached to a hair grip whilst trying to get the most out of it.

"I think that's had it!" she said, "and I only have two pennies left. Thank God it's pay day tomorrow."

"I've got sixpence," I laughed, "but it is holding up my stocking."

"What!" she gasped, "can't you find something else to hold up your stocking?"

I searched around and finally cut a button off an old blouse and rescued the sixpence.

"I bet if we went round this WRAF block there would be a fortune in sixpences holding stockings up," she grumbled.

It was true, the rubber 'buttons' that the loop of the suspender went over in order to grip the top of the stocking were always breaking off. Sixpences usually fitted the bill.

"Anyway," I said, with your two pennies and my sixpence we may have enough for the girl in the NAAFI shop to split a packet of five between us."

Jan pulled her beret on and buttoned up her battledress top. "Do you ken?" she growled. "It's three and sixpence now for a packet of twenty fags – three and bloody sixpence for twenty Nelson – it's robbery – I'm going to have to give up!"

We made our way down the stairs and crossed the road to the shop, where the NAAFI girl sold us five between us for eight pence.

"Well that's that!" sighed Jan. "I'm skint now until tomorrow."

We pulled our jackets around us as we walked down the road and I hoped that the button holding my stocking up would not pop out, leaving the back suspender to do the job all by itself. That would be far too much of a strain on it!

Every time the sixteenth of the month came round, especially now that the nights were getting darker, there was the usual talk of the Grey Lady and somebody always willing to creep undetected out of the Block after hours to try and establish whether or not she existed.

We chose the night of the Officers Mess Ball to go on another hunt for the Camp Ghost, even though the memory of our efforts last year were still fresh in our mind. Jan was very wary about the whole thing, for after her experiences on Night Duty in her own Section she needed a lot more convincing that there was no such thing.

"I don't believe in it anyway," I said, as I pulled on my WRAF raincoat over my pyjamas. "We know it's only the officers mucking about and they have their 'do' on tonight anyway."

"You can believe what you like Joan," said Jan, "but I heard what I heard that night and so did Sylvie – there is definitely something very funny about that Monastery."

"Oh don't be a wet blanket!" giggled Jessie. "Let's go for a laugh!"

We crept downstairs in the darkness, undid the catch on the Drying Room window and climbed out. It was a starry night with a bright moon and we could hear music coming from the Officers Mess as we crept along the side of the Block, taking care to keep in the shadows.

"Now I know we are mad!" whispered Jan.

"Shhh."

We stole down the road and crouched down behind a yew tree in the darkness. The faint sound of water lapping against the sides of the canoes moored by the riverbank mingled with the jollity coming from the Officers' quarters. Jessie was determined to make a night of it and had the initiative to buy a few pasties from the NAAFI to turn it into a picnic.

"Pity there isn't a decent bloke here," grumbled Jan. "Fancy sitting eating pasties by moonlight with two bloody women."

Light clouds swept across the moon and if ever there was a night for the Grey Lady to show up this was it. I looked up at the dark turrets of the Monastery and wondered what God's Little Acre had been like when it was first built. I was willing to bet that nobody had bargained for it ever being an RAF station! The monks would revolve in their graves if they could hear the frivolity coming from its old walls. It was a funny old world.

After a while even Jan began to relax. Although we had this niggling feeling that there *could* be a Grey Lady we were really looking to see what the officers got up to.

"I must have a fag," gasped Jan, having made short work of the food. She fumbled in her raincoat pocket for her lighter.

"Well keep your hand over it then," I reminded her. "We don't want anyone to see the glow!"

"Who is likely to see the glow?" whispered Jan.

"I dunno, maybe the Grey Lady!" I joked, as we dissolved into giggles again.

Suddenly the expression on Jan's face changed. Her face went still and ashen and her eyes stared horrified at something over my left shoulder.

"Shit!" she gasped.

"Oh stop larking about!" I whispered, but I gradually turned round to see what she was looking at.

I can only describe what met my eyes as an 'apparition', for there, in the full light of the moon, was a tall figure in long flowing robes, just standing there, motionless. We could clearly see the nun's habit as the figure strolled across the lawns. We couldn't run; we just stood there transfixed behind our tree.

"Oh I just don't believe this!" I cried. "I bet it's one of the officers mucking about.

"I told you!" whispered Jan. "There is definitely something not right about this place."

Jessie was already shaking with laughter at the sight before us. The figure slowly but unsteadily, moved across the lawn, pushing aside some of the garden chairs that were scattered about. I thought for a moment that it was coming towards us and my skin turned stone-cold, more in case we got caught than because I was as convinced as Jan was. However, fortunately for us, the apparition turned and strolled towards the rose bushes at the side of the Monastery. Then, leaving us in absolutely no doubt any more, the 'ghost' stopped at a large tree and turned to face it, completely shattering all Jan's illusions by lifting its robes and peeing against it!

We stared in disbelief and then started to giggle again as we realised that it must have been a Fancy Dress Ball in the Officer's Mess that night!

"That's the funniest looking Nun I've ever seen," laughed Jessie.

"Shh," I giggled. "She – I mean *he* – will hear you!"

The apparition finished his business and then continued his walk around the garden, while we shook with laughter in our hiding place, although Jan was determined not to be completely convinced.

"It could be one of the Monks *dressed up* as the Grey Lady!" she volunteered.

"Oh rubbish Jan!" laughed Jessie. "Ghosts don't piddle against trees!"

"Why would he?" Jan went on. "Don't they have toilets in the Mess?"

"Perhaps he couldn't wait," I giggled.

Then, just as I spoke, another apparition appeared from round the back of the Monastery.

"Be quiet," tittered Jessie. "Lets watch."

Apparently Grey Lady No.2 had no idea that Grey Lady No.1 was in the garden, for when they caught sight of each other's flowing robes in the moonlight they ran in the opposite direction from each other, having frightened themselves to death, and the words they both used were even more colourful than any heard in the WRAF Block!

By now the tears were rolling down our cheeks as we laughed uncontrollably and I was dying to spend a penny myself, though I had no intention of going behind any bush or tree!

"Come on," I laughed. "That's our ghost-hunting over for *this* 16th of the month."

We walked back to the WRAF Block in the shadows and climbed in through the rear window, none the worse for our experiences. If the Duty WRAF heard us, she did the decent thing and kept quiet about it. As it was, I couldn't get up the stairs fast enough, for my bladder was bursting. Besides, it was way past midnight and in the morning I was due to have a medical for my posting overseas.

We had been passed fit for overseas service and each day Rusty and I studied the Preliminary Warning Roll to see if our names appeared on them, to tell us the date our posting would be.

My Dad and Granddad thought I had gone totally barmy. They had fought the Germans in two separate generations.

"All that time I spent in muck and bloody bullets on the Somme fighting them, and now you go and have tea with them!" my Granddad had grumbled, irritably.

It seemed to take ages for things to get moving but suddenly the moment had come and we only had two weeks left at God's Little Acre.

Rusty shrieked at me to stop typing and look at PWR's.

"Look!" she said. "Our names are here!"

I grabbed them out of her hand and read our names again.

"Posted to RAF Germany with effect from 28th October."

But Rusty had already disappeared down the corridor to tell everybody in the Section.

I was summoned to the Group Captain's Office but, this time, not for shorthand.

"I didn't realise the time had gone so quickly," he said, as I sat down, ready to take dictation, "and I haven't even taken you flying yet!"

I was hoping he had forgotten all about that!

"That's OK Sir," I replied, truthfully.

I had never been flying in my life and I wasn't that anxious to start now. I had tried to shut out the notion of the flight to

Germany and, like Vivienne Leigh in 'Gone with the Wind', I would 'think about *that* tomorrow."

"A promise is a promise," he grinned. He picked up the phone on his desk and spoke to the operator.

"White Waltham please."

Then there was a slight pause while he waited to be put through and he looked back at me and smiled.

"We shall go and do some aerobatics, OK? – You can put your shorthand pad away for today."

I thought he was joking, but he obviously got through to where he wanted because he spoke briefly into the telephone again.

"Get my aircraft ready for me, there's a good man."

Within half an hour we were leaving to go to RAF White Waltham. The 'Snowdrops' looked on at the unusual sight of a Group Captain driving with a mere airwoman in his passenger seat and waved us through.

At White Waltham they weren't so shocked. They were used to him. It was only a few miles from our station and he went there often. They saluted as we went past them and Groupy drove across to where the training aeroplanes were all lined up. It didn't take me long to realise that one of these had been prepared for the officer..

"This is a Chipmunk," he informed me, "and you *will* be wearing a parachute!"

"I wouldn't have the nerve to use it even if I had to Sir," I said.

"Bet you would!" he laughed.

I followed him to a large black shed and, once inside, I found it was like a 'rest home' for inactive pilots. The young officers were leaning back in chairs, their feet on the table, reading the latest cricket scores. They looked like they really fancied themselves in their flying jackets and white scarves. Most of them were leaning against the weather charts, smoking pipes, and another was stretched out in an armchair, studying 'Playboy'.

I felt as though I had stepped into the film set of 'Reach for the Sky' and they were all waiting to 'scramble' – except that there was no 'scrambling' to be done any more. They were nearly twenty years too late.

"Busy are you?" said Groupy quietly.

To a man, they all leapt to attention.

"It's all right," he grinned. "I'm just here to give my typist a spin. Make sure I get the cricket results won't you?"

Once again, I thought he was joking.

We left the shed and, feeling like a trussed chicken, I climbed into the little Chipmunk behind my boss. The engines began to roar and we were soon speeding across the tarmac for my first flight in an aeroplane. There was a final thrust and the ground sank away beneath us. Not that I saw it – I had my eyes tight shut and pretended I was at the fair.

I opened them again as the cricket results came over the radio and into the headphones.

"...and now the teams come out of the Pavilion to resume the afternoon's play..." Radio control had been true to their word. There were no instructions coming over the RT, no weather warnings or aerodrome messages, just the bloody cricket scores!

"...and Dexter scores a magnificent boundary..."

"Hooray!" yelled Groupy. "Hold tight!"

He promptly turned the plane into a loop.

When my internal organs had lodged themselves together in their correct places again, he calmly asked me to take control.

"What!?" I yelled.

"Go on, take control," he shouted. "All you do is hold the stick and guide it so the green line on the dial in front of you is level with the line across the screen."

I adjusted my headphones to make sure I was hearing right. It sounded simple enough, but when you are rigid with fear it is not so easy.

"No, tilt the bugger the other way, we are going into a dive!" he yelled.

I pulled back the stick.

"Not as much as that – or we will be able to say hello to the Russian Sputnik!"

I knew that the RAF Motto was 'Through Endeavour to the Stars' but this was ridiculous! I thought of Tony Hancock and his Wing Commander sketch where he said "don't open the hangar door – I'll go through the skylight!" Now I knew where it came from!

Gradually, I got used to it and soon we were soaring around the sky looking down on the minute objects on the ground beneath. I don't think that the Groupy's hand actually left his controls though, and I didn't blame him!

"I'll take over now," he said. "I don't think we'll let you land it today!"

"No fear!" I yelled over the sound of the engines. "*Ha, bloody ha ha,*" I said under my breath.

He smoothly brought the plane down on the ground, while I closed my eyes and gritted my teeth again.

"...oh lovely bowling by the Australians, Dexter is out!"

The little aeroplane lurched forward and stopped just short of the hangars. The word he used rhymed with 'duck'.

Following my adventures with Groupy, I went home for the weekend with tales of my exploits and, less than two weeks later, both Rusty and I received notifications that all our paperwork was ready. We were to leave for Germany the following Monday.

"What's RAF Germany like?" I asked our Flight Sergeant one day.

He came and perched on my desk while Mr Lee caused much amusement by pretending he was 'hiding' behind the stationery cupboard. All we could see of him was his belly sticking out.

"Well, it is huge," he said. "You can fit Medmenham on the sports field there, and you are bound to meet up with people that you knew in Recruit Training, they always seem to meet up again in Germany."

"Oh well, as long as I don't meet anyone that I don't want to meet," I replied.

"Like Corporal Payne," Rusty shuddered.

"You can't fit Mr Lee into your suitcase can you?" smiled Flight, nodding in the direction of the round tummy. "I'm sure he thinks we can't see him."

"Come on Mr Lee, out you come," called Rusty. "We have to go now."

The belly moved, followed by the rest of the body and he looked genuinely upset.

"It won't be the same without you two," he muttered. The bell rang over his desk. It was a summons from one of the young officers.

"Oh damn it! I wonder what he wants now?" he moaned as he toddled off.

Thank God for the person who invented tights! Since we had joined up we had struggled with stockings and suspender belts, or corsets if we were overweight. Now, some angel from heaven had invented tights and another, even higher deity, had decided that we could buy our own and the dreaded suspender belts could be thrown away. Along with passion killers, they were 'history'. From now on we would get an allowance for tights, which were becoming commonplace in the shops and, because we were using our own underwear, it did not have to be included in the kit list anymore and therefore did not need to be put out for kit inspections.

Things indeed were changing, but little did we know that we were on the threshold of a decade that would see more changes in our lives, both civilian and military, than we could ever begin to imagine! However, just at the moment, my main concern was that, from now on we would be able to jive in the NAAFI without all and sundry seeing our suspenders and we would not have that constant fear of them snapping and sixpences or buttons rolling across the dance floor any more.

On our last morning Rusty and I went down to the Section. There were already two new airwomen due to be posted into our jobs that very day and Flight was busy making sure that we hadn't totally wrecked the typewriters for them!

"Can't you tell us anything more about Germany Flight?" said Rusty. "I'd love to know what we have let ourselves in for."

"Well, you'll know tonight!" grinned Flight, "because you'll be there."

"You will just have to wait and see," said Mr Lee. "Are you going to miss me?"

"Of course," I smiled. "Nobody could climb a hot water pipe as well as you do!"

"Well I don't want to get rid of you both..." said Flight, looking at his watch, "but time marches on and your bus goes in half an hour."

"Oh lord, we'll have to go!" cried Rusty. "Goodbye Flight, Mr Lee, and thanks for everything."

"Goodbye both of you and good luck," said Flight.

Groupy poked his head out of his office just as we began to walk down the corridor.

"Well, isn't anybody going to say goodbye to me then?"

"Oh sorry Sir," we came to attention. "We thought you would be busy," said Rusty.

"Goodbye Sir," I said and saluted.

"Goodbye girls and good luck in Germany."

He was such a lovely man.

"I am going to miss him," said Rusty, as we hurried down the corridor, wiping the tears from our eyes that were already welling up. He was old enough to be our father but he was our hero.

We ran helter-skelter along the road, away from the Monastery and met Jessie and Jan, who were dragging our kitbags onto the bus.

"I think they want rid of us," I panted. "Just look at them both helping us on our way."

I hugged them both. "Good luck Jess!" I said. "I hope that everything goes all right for you and Tony."

"Bye everyone!" cried Jessie.

"Cheerio Jan!" I shouted. "Hope to see you soon."

"So do I!" she shouted back.

Rusty and I sat down in our seats just as the bus began to pull away and the tears were, by now, streaming down our faces. Our roommates had been joined by a little knot of other airwomen who had also come to see us off.

"Good luck!" they all shouted. "Don't do anything we wouldn't do..."

The little group of girls, and some boys, all frantically waving to us, disappeared out of sight, as the bus turned the corner that led out onto the main road. I looked back at the Monastery, its towers just visible through the trees.

My eyes moved to the fast disappearing WRAF Block, the Sports Field and the Gym Hall where we used to practice in the Band and where Bandy was, no doubt, trying to teach some other poor souls. I saw the profusion of flowers splashing around the edges of all the buildings and I looked up at the grey sky that foretold of snow.

I glanced across at Rusty, who was pressing her face to the window to take her last view of the camp, the tears now streaming down her face unchecked. We were leaving an RAF Station that was undoubtedly loved.

"Goodbye God's Little Acre," she whispered.

The bus drove out of the camp and the last glimpse I had was of a smart airman shutting the decorative iron gates behind us.

"Well, we've done it now," I said.

It had been our home for the past eighteen months but now we had an aeroplane to catch – an RAF Viscount Air Trooping aircraft, bound for Dusseldorf Airport in Germany.

It was going to be a huge adventure for us both.

7. If you can't take a joke, you shouldn't have joined!

"All personnel posted in from the United Kingdom should change their money at the desk and then make their way to the RAF transport on the left hand side of the Arrival Bay."

The voice on the Tannoy bawled out instructions continuously while a general bustle of activity went on around us. Airmen were busy issuing orders to dozens of men who were wearing dark green, ill-fitting 'uniforms' and who, even in the cold, were sweating under the weight of the kitbags and cases they were carrying on behalf of ourselves and the families to the waiting coach. It passed through my mind that those very men could well have been Nazi sympathisers a few years ago!

"Schnell, schnell!" the airmen shouted to the Germans, and they never argued back.

"Guess that means 'hurry up'," confided Rusty, intelligently, as we walked over to the cash desk to exchange our money.

We had left the UK on a grey, miserable day in the early afternoon and spent the 1½ hour journey trying to see the sea, and then the land, through the clouds, while talking about what we expected to find when we arrived. We were, by now, too excited to be nervous. By the time the aeroplane was due to touch down, darkness was beginning to loom up and everywhere was covered with a fine dusting of snow, so we saw very little!

Besides, I was in a daze most of the time, not sure whether I was dreaming all this or not! It was an experience that I never thought would come my way.

As soon as our luggage had appeared on the moving belt in the arrival lounge, it was gathered up by the men in the green uniforms and bundled onto the coach. We didn't have to touch it at all.

"This isn't money!" wailed Rusty. "It doesn't mean anything to me."

"I'll never get the hang of this," I agreed, looking at the strange coins and notes. "Give me pounds, shillings and pence any day of the week."

"Of course you will," butted in an airman who had been waiting behind us. "It seems odd at first, but if you remember that a mark is just slightly under two shillings you won't go far wrong!"

'Know-it-all!' I thought. "Thanks!" I said "are you going to RAF Germany?"

"Two Taf you mean!" he smiled. "Yes, I'm just back from leave."

"Doesn't it snow early here?" said Rusty, shivering. "I'm quite cold."

"Oh it's not too bad!" he replied. "The weather isn't much different from the UK really."

We meekly followed one of the 'green men' – as we were calling them by now – to the bus. Even the driver was wearing the rough-looking outfit.

"What's the significance of the uniform?" I asked the airman, as he had sat down behind us and seemed to know everything. "It's horrible, anyway."

"Oh, they are the German civilians who work on the camp," he informed us. "Mostly drivers and odd-job men."

Rusty and I exchanged glances.

"Oh don't worry," he whispered. "They are uniform mad in this country. Wait until you see a German copper! They look as though they have just dropped off the top of the Christmas tree with all their braid and badges."

"They look like very rough old uniforms," I said.

"Serve 'em right," he replied gruffly, as if our poor driver was personally responsible for the Second World War. We carried on peering out of the window.

"Talk of the devil!" said 'Mr Know-it-all. "There's a copper now ... See what I mean?"

I followed his stare and saw an imposing-looking gentleman in navy blue riding breeches and black, shiny boots, a royal blue jacket completely covered in gold braid, and a peaked cap surmounted by the same gold braid. On his hip he carried a leather holster containing a large gun.

"Whew!" whistled Rusty. "I wouldn't like to cross that chap's path."

"By the way," I remarked as an afterthought. "I'm Joan and this is Rusty."

"I'm Brian," said the airman. "Oh, and here comes Ann, last as usual"

An airwoman scrambled onto the bus and made her way towards us, sitting down next to Brian. She was short and dumpy with a mop of flaming red hair.

"I'm not kidding," she panted. "I got stuck behind all those families and I thought I would miss the bus back to camp. I don't fancy walking."

"Good leave?" said Brian.

"Smashing, but it was spoilt with the idea of having to come back to this rotten dump."

We spun round to look at her.

"Don't you like Rheindahlen?" I asked.

"No I don't," she replied. "It's too bloody big! You can walk miles and never get off camp."

"Oh take no notice," laughed Brian, seeing our apprehensive looks. "She's never happy unless she is moaning."

"Honestly," said Rusty, beginning to lose patience. "I have *yet* to find anyone who can talk intelligently about this place. It's like Marmite, either they love it or they hate it, or they can't remember anything worth telling, or won't, one or the other. We don't know the first thing about it even now!"

"Perhaps people want you to be surprised," said Ann. She was still trying to get her breath back after her exertions. "And you *will* be. Anyway, you shouldn't have joined if you can't take a joke!"

Before I could reply, the bus started up and soon we were speeding out of Dusseldorf airport and onto the road to Rheindahlen – home of Headquarters 2nd Tactical Air Force and the British Army of the Rhine.

"I can't say as I like this driving on the right lark," growled Rusty. "I feel that everything coming the other way is heading straight for us!" She turned round to Ann and Brian again.

"Do tell us what it is like, really," she said. "And if you tell us its big we'll personally throw you off into the road."

"Well, it's difficult to describe," giggled Brian, "without saying it's big, because it *is* big."

I grabbed Rusty's arm as she turned round and tried to strangle him.

"You'll find out soon enough, but we mix with the German Army and Air Force, the Dutch, Belgians and Americans, and its part Royal Air Force but mostly Army." He turned to Ann. "What else can I tell them?"

"The food is terrible," she said. "Even worse than at Wilmslow!"

"Oh my gawd!" I sighed.

"But we have two cinemas and a swimming pool," laughed Brian, "and a Theatre, three Churches a YMCA and a YWCA, a Malcolm Club and two NAAFIs – and there are *miles* of corridors in the Big House, where you most probably will be working – it is said to have over 2,000 offices…"

"Wow!" I gasped, interrupting him. "It *must* be big!"

The conversation ended in laughter and we settled down and watched what we could see of the scenery as the RAF bus sped through the darkness. From the light of the streetlamps on the snow we could see that we were going through numerous small villages and then back into the countryside again. The trees and fields began to give way to houses this time – not the little German villas we had seen on the journey, but houses standing in long straight rows, like soldiers on parade and all the same. Then we saw a little parade of shops, the lights from their windows shining onto the snow.

"Tell us when we go through the camp gates," I asked Brian. "I can't make it out."

They burst into peals of laughter again.

"We have been inside the camp gates for about quarter of an hour," grinned Brian.

"That's our German shopping centre," said Ann. Then she indicated over to the left. "There's one of the Churches – and just down here – see – the Astra Cinema."

Brian pointed to the right, just in time to show us the welcoming sign of the NAAFI. Seconds later the bus turned a corner and pulled up outside one of three large WRAF Blocks. He and the driver helped us out with our luggage and Ann showed us where WRAF Admin was.

"Oh by the way," she smiled wickedly, "WRAF Admin is a bit crap too – it's straight in the front door of Block 1 and first office on the left."

She gave Brian a kiss on the cheek and lugged her case over to Block 2 and disappeared through the swing doors, giggling as she went.

"I wonder what she meant by that?" said Rusty, as we struggled with our luggage to where she had indicated.

We timidly knocked on the door, bearing the legend 'WRAF Admin Office' and waited in the corridor.

"Come!" The short, sharp command was vaguely familiar. No, it couldn't be! Could it?

"I *know* that voice," I said, almost under my breath.

"So do I," whispered Rusty.

I reluctantly pushed open the door and we went in together. Seated at the desk, with her head bent low over some forms was the sergeant. But it wasn't just *any* old sergeant. There was something familiar about the set of the shoulders, the creases in the jacket. There was something equally familiar about the shape of her beret, even though it wasn't on her head but minding its own business on the corner of the desk. It was a beret that would stay in shape because its owner commanded it to! The sergeants stripes on her arm looked brand new.

A strange sense of foreboding swept over me as I realised that my worst fears were about to be confirmed.

She looked up from her work as if she could read my mind!

"You look pale airwoman!" said Sergeant Payne, "bad journey?"

And there she was – little Hitler herself, Corporal bloody 'Payne by name and pain by nature' – only now she had been promoted! Wilmslow's gain was our loss! She had put on a bit of weight and her short hair had an attempt at a wave in it now, but her face was devoid of make-up and she still looked as though she had swallowed a wasp.

I stared with my mouth agape, like Macbeth seeing the ghost of Banquo. I thought how unjust that the new recruits at Wilmslow should be spared, while we had met up with her *twice!* I thought of Humphrey Bogart in *Casablanca* – "of all the gin joints in all the world... etc, etc."

"Are you alright airwoman?" she persisted, with her usual sarcasm.

"Yes Corporal – er – I mean Sergeant," I whispered hoarsely. "I was just surprised to see you again."

"Ah well, the Air Force is getting smaller," she chuckled.

"Anyway, you both are in Room 102 ... it's upstairs and is the room facing you at the top." She pushed a piece of paper our way. "Sign here and report to Unit Headquarters first thing in the morning. It's signposted all the way, so you can't miss it."

We picked up our cases and kitbags and wearily climbed the stairs to the room she had indicated.

"Bloody hell!" said Rusty. "Fancy us getting the Block that has the WRAF Admin Office in it!"

"Were you at Wilmslow at the same time as her?" I asked, as we climbed the stairs.

"Yes," she replied "but I don't think she remembered me. I wasn't her flight. I was B Flight and we had Corporal Fisher."

"Lucky bugger!" I muttered, as we arrived at Room 102.

The door was 'enhanced' by a clean white sanitary towel with one loop round the outer door handle and the other round the inner, forming a very effective doorstop'.

It was not all that different from the room we had vacated at Medmenham, except it looked as though we were back to the ordinary old-fashioned lockers and beside cabinets that had been so common in Recruit Training. The days of having large spaces to throw our clothes around in were gone. We would have to be a bit tidier now, especially with Madam Payne downstairs.

In one corner of the room, a pale, fair-haired girl was grovelling around on the floor, pulling a plug out of the wall as the steam from the boiling kettle enveloped the area where she was kneeling.

"Oh hi!" she said, as she gave a final tug. "Blast this thing! The kettle always boils its head off while I'm wrestling with this plug... You are just in time for coffee anyway." And then, as an afterthought, "Sorry about the doorstop, it does the job though, don't you think?"

And that was our introduction to Marilyn, or Mal, as most people called her. She was slim, maybe underweight if anything. Her fair hair was, at this moment, curled and brushed back from her pale face. She was only half in uniform – her skirt topped by a bright red jumper.

Hanging from the door of her locker was her working blue top and a cosy white duffle coat. Large hair rollers were festooning her bed but obviously the effort of having put them in was being wasted for the steam from the kettle had caused the front of her hair to come out of curl and hang damply about her forehead.

I sank down on one of the empty beds and Rusty sat down on another.

"Thanks!" I said gratefully, taking the offered mug of steaming coffee. "I'm still quivering from the shock of seeing Corporal – I mean Sergeant – Payne!"

"Oh don't forget the 'Sergeant' bit," laughed Mal. "She is proud of that third stripe, you know!"

"I'll bet," I replied. "I bet she wears it on her jim-jams."

"Oh, she is not so bad really," said our new friend. "In any case, we don't see that much of her."

"That's comforting," I muttered, as I started to unzip my kitbag and my frothy petticoat burst out.

Mal finished changing into civvies but pulled on a pair of sensible warm slacks.

"Get yourselves unpacked," she said, "and then I'll take you to the NAAFI."

We finished putting our clothes in the small lockers and then she showed us the way to the NAAFI. Even at this early stage I could fully appreciate the size of the place. Whereas at

God's Little Acre the main road through the camp had been little more than a tarmac lane, here it was a public highway, with buses going to the nearby town of Munchengladbach and vehicles were whizzing up and down it all the time. I made a mental note that I would have to look left first when crossing the road.

We passed the Unit Headquarters, where we were supposed to report in the morning, and the Station Guardroom, which was in the middle of the camp and not at the gate, like I expected it to be. Not that there were any gates anyway. It was an 'open camp' with seemingly no beginning or end!

"There's our second home," said Mal. She pointed to the large sprawling, grey, single-storey building with the comforting words 'NAAFI' written outside in red neon lights that we had passed in the bus earlier. It was to be the hub of all our lives!

"This is ours," she told us, "but there is another one for the Army on the other side of camp."

"Slightly bigger than what we have been used to eh?" said Rusty.

"I should say!"

"It's pretty large," said Mal, who seemed to be quite enjoying being our guide. "It has the usual cafeteria and Corporal's Club and it has a Beer Bar, Games Room, Television Room for those that can understand German, and the Weavers!"

"Weavers?" I queried.

"Oh W.V.S. Lounge, it's run by the Women's Voluntary Service, so we call it the Weavers."

We strolled into the Cafeteria and ignored all the eyes fixed on the new talent as we went to the counter and ordered a cup of tea and some rolls.

"I don't understand this money," said Rusty. "Here, you had better take your pick," and she put the coins on the counter. The girl took what she needed and Rusty put the rest back in her purse.

"You'll soon get the hang of it," said Marilyn. "Let's take a pew over here!"

"Cor!" I exclaimed. "Just look at all those men!"

She laughed. "This is just a few of them. There are a lot at work and loads in the Beer Bar!"

"Lovely!" grinned Rusty. "That will do me."

I looked up to see three boys walking towards us, all in uniform, as if they had just come off duty.

"Hi Mal!" said a tall, dark, thin-faced boy of about twenty, "How are you doing?"

"OK," she replied. "Johnny, this is Rusty and Joan, they arrived this evening."

"Hello!" said Johnny, who was obviously her boyfriend. "Welcome to Germany – this is Chalky and Trevor!"

Trevor was a rather tubby boy with a round, rosy face and it was soon clear from his accent that he was Welsh. Chalky White looked very young indeed and I wondered if he even shaved yet. All three were 'regulars'. National Service had, by now, all but finished.

We had a pleasant hour with the little group and ate some NAAFI sandwiches while they told us all about this vast station and had a general moan about their own jobs and the food in the Mess. We were also pleased to see that there was a jukebox, with all the latest records on it, many of them American and which we had not heard before. All too soon though, it was time to get back to the WRAF Block. We had already had a long day.

We trudged through the snow and the boys left us a few yards from the door. Any nearer and they would have incurred the wrath of the Duty Airwoman.

"Well!" I said to Rusty, as we got ready for bed. "I wonder what they are all doing back at Medmenham?"

"Don't know," she replied, "but you know how they always say that your last station is always your best – well, I am beginning to think they might be right after all!"

She picked up her washing bag and towel and made for the door, which still had the sanitary towel hanging from the handles.

"And it had better be a good camp chum," she said as she went out into the corridor, "because we have got another two bloody years here, I would like to remind you!"

I didn't need reminding. I settled down in my bed and put out the light and thought of home, and of the three J's left back at Medmenham.

"Goodnight," said Mal.

"Night," I replied in the darkness.

For the first time since leaving Wilmslow, I felt just a little bit homesick.

The air was crisp and the sun shone onto the snow, dazzling our eyes, as we trudged around the camp on our first morning, booking ourselves in. We had already sampled the breakfast in the Mess and had mutually decided that in future we would stick to toast, for the only real use that place had, we agreed, was the fact that it kept the draught off the Parade Ground!

The Unit Orderly Room was much the same as any other Orderly Room, except, like everything else, it was bigger. We could now appreciate the enormity of the place, the biggest non-operational station in the world, and it took us all morning just to get about four signatures on our little blue arrival card.

"Well, Stores know we are here," I said, "and the Orderly Room, and Pay Accounts, and according to this list we have to go to the Main Building now – wherever that is – apparently it is called the Big House."

"Whew!" gasped Rusty. "My feet are killing me. Let's call in at the NAAFI and have a drink, and then maybe somebody can direct us."

We found the place practically deserted, save for a few shift workers who were killing time on their morning off. I went to the counter and tipped my money out and asked the girl to take the price of two cups of coffee, while Rusty walked over to a small knot of airmen who were seated in the far corner of the room, reading the papers from home, which were all about the sputnik and the possibility that it might lead, one day, to men going to the moon. When she returned, her coffee was cold, but at least she had found out where the main building was.

"Honestly, what rubbish they are reading," she said. "Anyway, the Big House is through some buildings at the back of here and then across a golf course. It's quite a walk though."

"Golf course?"

"Yes, it seems they have a golf course, doubles up as a helicopter pad, and it's used as a shortcut to the Headquarters Building," she replied, "otherwise some people go by bus or bike."

"Oh well, I can only follow you," I sighed. "If we get lost I'll know who to blame."

"Don't blame me – blame them." She got up out of her chair and did her jacket up as one of the boys went over and put some money in the jukebox. We heard the familiar sound of Buddy Holly, so we lingered for the three minutes that it took to play "It's Raining in my Heart". It was the only chance we had to hear records from now on.

"Such a shame about him," muttered Rusty, as we put our berets on and waved to the boys.

I nodded my heartfelt agreement and followed her to the back door of the NAAFI.

Sure enough, after we had followed the directions Rusty had got from the boys, we eventually found the snow-covered golf course. It was a huge expanse of white, going slightly uphill and interspersed here and there with fir trees. There was a well-trodden path in the snow, diagonally across it from right to left, but you could quite easily imagine what it would look like in the summer.

After still more walking up the incline, the roof, and then the rest of the 'Big House', came into view. We trudged across the snow, occasionally slipping on parts where it had hardened after being trodden down by other feet, and every so often throwing snowballs at each other. As we got nearer we began to realise just how huge the place was.

"Big House is a good name," said Rusty. "Look at the size of it!"

It had hundreds of windows and was larger than any building either of us had seen before. In front of the building, hanging limp in the windless air, were rows of flags of the nations based at Rheindahlen. It was surrounded by an iron fence and there were a number of cars parked at the front of the place. As we got nearer, we noticed that there were many more Army personnel about, WRAC as well as the men, and just nearby we could see the Army NAAFI and cinema.

A main road separated the golf course from the perimeter of the Big House. We crossed it and went in the first gate we came to, only to be immediately stopped by an Army police sergeant, who insisted on escorting us out again and in through another gate to 'the RAF side', as he called it.

Here he handed us over to one of our own Royal Air Force policemen. The building seemed to be split into roughly half Army and half RAF. We were taken into a small office just inside the door and told to wait. A few moments later a Flight Sergeant materialised in the doorway and began scribbling on a piece of paper.

"Here you are," he said, when he had finished scribbling. "This is your temporary pass. You will get a permanent one later and you must give this in when you leave the building – understand?" We nodded. He then picked up the telephone and dialled a number and a few minutes later we were joined by yet another, older looking, Flight Sergeant.

"Two new airwomen for you," said the first Senior NCO. "All yours Bill!"

We were handed over like a couple of parcels at the main sorting office then followed him dutifully along the maze of corridors.

"This is like Hampton Court Maze," whispered Rusty, "only bigger."

"Yes," I agreed, "but the difference is that you can get *out* of Hampton Court Maze – eventually."

After what seemed like an eternity of walking down the endless corridors, the Flight Sergeant led us into yet another office where he sunk down into a chair behind a desk.

"Whew!" he gasped. "I am getting much too old for this lark. The corridors in this place don't get any shorter." He propped some glasses on his nose and then began to shuffle through his papers.

"Now... to get you fixed up in Sections!"

"About time," I thought. "The day is half over."

I fidgeted nervously, wondering where on earth we would be working. Would we get somewhere like P Staff, where we were used to the work, or would it all be completely new?

"Now, I know we need a new girl in Command Accounts..." said Flight "... and I think – yes – one for P Staff."

Rusty and I exchanged glances, knowing that we both would prefer the job we were used to.

"I expect you both want to work there," said Flight, reading our thoughts. "I see you have both come from P Staff, so you will have to toss for it, say a number each of you, one or two?"

"One!" I said

"All right, two then," said Rusty. He picked up the phone and dialled an internal number.

"Oh hello Sarge! I have a new girl here for you, but say a number, one or two?" There was a pause, "O.K. I'll bring her down, goodbye!" He looked across at Rusty.

"The Sergeant said 'two'," he grinned, "so it's all yours. Which means it's Command Accounts for you, airwoman," he added in my direction.

I felt pleased for Rusty, but sorry for myself, for Command Accounts was completely new to me and I didn't know what to expect. We waited for the NCOs to come and take us to our new Sections.

"They will be quite a while," said the Flight Sergeant. "They both have a long way to walk."

That did not surprise me at all.

"I am sure I shall get lost in this place," I said. "I could never find my way out of here!"

"You'll get used to it!" he replied. "If you follow the signs you can't go far wrong."

"I'd better write to my Mum and tell her that if I go missing not to worry because I'll be just finding my way out of the Big House," said Rusty.

We sat and tried to show an interest in the Air Force News that he offered us to read and then, after what seemed like ages, the two NCOs arrived.

"When you have visited your Sections," said Flight, "get somebody to bring you back here and then I'll take you out of the building. You can start work this afternoon after you have picked up your duffle coats."

I would be glad to get mine – it was really quite cold and our greatcoats were very cumbersome. Again we trudged the corridors, Rusty going in one direction with her NCO and I following mine to Command Accounts. Occasionally, where many corridors met, there was a large signpost. It felt like something out of Alice in Wonderland and I expected any moment to see the Cheshire Cat grinning at me from one of the many doors or the White Rabbit disappearing down yet another corridor crying 'Oh my ears and whiskers!'

"Here we are," said the NCO suddenly. "Come and meet the rabble."

We had come to a halt outside a number of doors bearing the legend *Command Accounts*, The end door in the corridor was marked with 'Command Accounts Registry' and it was into this office that I was led by the young man, who had introduced himself as Corporal White.

"This is "Paddy," said the Corporal, gesturing towards a slightly-built, grey-haired little man, who was surrounded by files.

"Pleased to meet you," said Paddy, with a broad Scots accent (what a surprise!)

He too was a corporal and the 'Paddy' was a result of somebody being 'funny' years ago and it had stuck.

"Come on the noo," he said. "Let's meet everybody!"

We walked around the large Registry. Sitting at a table immediately behind Paddy's desk was a young airman who was introduced to me as Simon, because Paddy maintained that he was the simplest thing in the Air Force! He seemed to take it all in good part.

At a table behind him, an elderly lady was typing envelopes. She was Frau Braum, a German civilian clerk who spoke perfect English. Next, Paddy took me to the end of the Registry, where a fair-haired, middle-aged man was busy filing some papers away. He also was dressed in smart civilian clothes.

"This is Michael," said Paddy. "If you want to know anything, ask him."

"Hi!" said Michael, "pleased to meet you."

"Pleased to meet you too," I replied.

He was also German and not only did he speak English perfectly but he spoke it with a Cockney accent, even though he had never been out of his country of birth.

"Now," said Paddy. "I'll take you to meet *our* Groupy."

He said the 'our' like somebody talking about his own very proud possession ... and I soon learned why.

We left the Registry, walked down the corridor again and found a door marked 'Command Accountant'. Paddy knocked gently on the door and we went inside to meet the Group Captain. I saluted and he stood up and pumped my hand whilst giving me a beaming smile.

"Welcome to Command Accounts my dear," he said. "I'm sure you'll like it here, we'll look after you." He gave Paddy a warm, friendly grin and told him to 'take care of me'.

My Group Captain at God's Little Acre had been a 'dear' and so was this one. There were a few corporals, especially female ones, who I had come across, that could learn a thing or two from the Senior Officers I had met. Group Captain Rogers was an officer and a gentleman from the top of his wavy grey hair right down to his highly-polished black shoes and like the Groupy at Medmenham he had a 'fruit salad' of ribbons and pilot's wings on his tunic that told their own story – but it was a story that, for many of his generation, would only come to light in the future. It was something they didn't talk about just now, and especially not in this place.

"Isn't he nice?" I said to Paddy, as we went back along the corridor once again.

"The best!" said Paddy with fervour. "If only they were all like him."

"I won't bother you with the other officers," said Paddy, dismissing them out of hand as totally unimportant compared to the Groupy. "You'll meet them soon enough, but I'll take you to meet the crowd in the other Registry."

We walked across to the part where the two corridors made a crossroads and, turning to our right, I found that there was yet another section to Command Accounts. In here I met two other sergeants, Corporal White again, and a long, lean SAC who was introduced to me as John. By the time we arrived back at the original office, where we came in, Rusty was already waiting for us.

We handed in our temporary passes and trudged back in the general direction of the Mess. At the highest point of the grass incline Rusty stopped in her tracks.

"Let's have a good look round," she said. "We can see a long way from here."

I looked around me and I could see no ending to this vast camp. As far as the eye could see in any direction were married quarters, blocks, billets and endless buildings of all shapes and sizes. We could see sports fields, the swimming pool, shopping centre, Malcolm clubs and churches.

"It's incredible!" I gasped. "I wonder how big it actually is. I literally cannot see an end – it goes over the horizon."

"The Wing Commander in my office told me that there are over two thousand offices in the Big House, which pretty much confirms what Brian said," replied Rusty. "Only the Pentagon in America is a bigger military office block than this."

"Whew!" I exclaimed. There was little more I could say – I had run out of words.

Having decided to face the Mess, we strode into the large white building at the end of the parade square and joined on the end of the queue for lunch. A horrible concoction was put onto our plates by Belgian cooks and there it stayed, ready to be transported to the waste bucket. It seemed a bit pointless bothering with the 'middle man' – the cooks might just have well have chucked it straight in for themselves, saving us the bother of doing so, although there were many people tucking it away as if it had just come from the Savoy Grill. It was obviously an 'acquired taste'.

"Ugh! I guess it's back to the NAAFI again," I grimaced. "I can see I am going to be broke at this rate!"

Marilyn arrived and poured herself a cup of tea before sitting down beside us.

"Is that all you have?" I said. "No wonder you are slim!"

"Well, they don't muck up the tea too much," she replied, "but actually I saw you come in and I only came to say that I normally go to the Sally Bash for a meal and wondered if you wanted to come with me?"

"Anywhere other than this!" said Rusty, "but what's the Sally Bash?"

"The Salvation Army Restaurant," she answered. "They do some good meals over there and it's a lot cheaper than the NAAFI."

"They need some of the Medmenham cooks over here," I said.

"Well, the pigs are well fed anyway," said Mal, as we put our coats back on and made our way in the direction of the Salvation Army Restaurant.

"How did you get on this morning?" she went on.

"My feet are falling off," I said, "but I think everyone knows we are here now. I'm in Command Accounts and Rusty is in Personnel."

"Oh well done!" cheered Mal. "I work in the Big House too!"

We pushed open the doors to the Salvation Army Restaurant and ordered ourselves egg, chips, sausage and bacon. She had been right; it was delicious. We got the whole lot, including a cup of tea and bread and butter for two marks, and at the time there were twelve marks to the pound, so it was brilliant value. It was our first decent meal since arriving in Germany less than 24 hours ago, but which already seemed like a week. By the time I had finished eating I was ready to face anything, even Sergeant Payne!

We walked back to WRAF Admin where we met our 'dear' sergeant for the second time. She looked at us with those sarcastic eyes of hers as she handed us over our white duffle coats and cigarette coupons as if they were her own personal property. Now we were ready to begin life at RAF Germany, and with my white duffle coat pulled up over my uniform and my fag coupons in my pocket I really began to 'feel the part', even though I hardly smoked! It was just that it was fashionable and, more to the point, I wasn't at home under the disapproving eye of my mother.

We strode out yet again on the trek to the Big House – ready for what the next two years might throw at us.

❖ ❖ ❖

"You have got an interesting new typewriter cover," said Paddy with a smile, as I walked down the corridor into work, after being there a few days.

I didn't know what he was mumbling about, but he was right – I did have a new typewriter cover – a pair of passion killers draped all over it. That was the first clue. The second was the dulcet tones coming from Paddy's office.

"Jee-zus Ker-rist, it's bloody cold this morning!"

"Pat Seymour!"

The mop of blonde curls popped round the side of the door, closely followed by the rest of my friend from training days.

"Hello Ratty! You took your time getting here didn't you?"

"Well I'll be... Where did you come from?" For a minute I was totally taken aback. Then I recovered and threw the knickers in her direction. She dodged out of the way and they sailed straight past her and into the corridor. She dashed out and picked them up before anybody else did.

"Been here ages mate. Just back from leave and I am in Block Two."

"You lucky bugger," I retorted. "I am in Block One with sergeant, *Sergeant* no less, Payne!"

"Sod's law!" she laughed. "Listen, it looks like the officers are starting to come in, so I had better go before I get you in trouble."

"Yes you had better."

"I'll see you later back at the Block," she said. "I'd better get to work too – I'm late already and it's a long walk." With that she was gone, but I knew we would have plenty to chat about later.

Despite the size of the Big House, the office set up was not that much different from Medmenham. John was responsible for running the Coffee Swindle and nobody could do any work until they had their first drink made by him and had eaten the cheese rolls brought from the NAAFI Wagons that were pushed round the corridors all day. It was, all in all, quite civilised! Of course we didn't have Mr Lee to shin up the drainpipes or go to sleep on top of the filing cabinets, but I could live with that.

Often John brought the coffee in to me and then sat on my desk and chatted until one of the Flight Lieutenants shooed him out and I soon settled into the section as if I had been there for years – after all, shorthand is shorthand, no matter where you are.

Despite Rheindahlen being so different, I soon found that the jokes and the humour and the daftness were just the same as anywhere else. Unlike Medmenham, we now had a parade ground and it *did* get used two or three times a year, including Remembrance Day. Everybody who was available had to be on parade and this was where the Station Warrant Officer came into his own.

The SWO was of the 'old school', with a barrel chest, shoulders that looked as though they had a coat hanger permanently under the coat and a large handlebar moustache. He had an uncanny ability to make anyone want to crawl under the tarmac of the parade ground if they could and he made Sergeant Payne look like a novice.

As Remembrance Day fell in the cold of November we all wore greatcoats buttoned up to the neck and gloves. It almost seemed pointless bothering with the rest of the uniform as it was all covered by the all enveloping greatcoat. In fact, one or two of the boys decided that they would save themselves some time in the morning by simply pulling on their RAF trousers over the top of their pyjamas and then buttoning up their coats to the neck, the idea being that they would go straight back to bed after the parade.

They should have known better! The eagle eye of the Warrant Officer doing his pre-inspection before the main parade spotted them in a minute. His eyes lit on the tell tale hint of a blue and white stripe material peeping out over the top of one airman's collar and, first of all, he gave it a gentle tweak with his pace-stick. Then he carefully put the stick on the floor and, using two hands, he gave, that which offended his eyes, an almighty tug.

"What on earth is *this* airman!?" he roared, pulling it until the airman nearly choked. "Explain your bloody self!"

"I thought it wouldn't notice!" explained the poor wretch feebly, withering as the girls' flight watched his anguish and tried hard not to giggle – many of us failing miserably as we attempted to stare straight ahead.

The SWO paused and then, with a bellow that could have been heard as far away as the Big House, he blasted the three immortal words...

"My left testicle!"

Everybody shuddered and then, in case, we hadn't heard it the first time, he shouted it again.

"My left testicle! Open your coats, all of you. NOW!"

At least half a dozen had done the same thing and those airwomen who hadn't already succumbed to the giggles did so now.

Needless to say, the Guardroom did have a use that week and the hapless airmen could be seen reporting there at intervals throughout the day and doing extra fatigues for their pains.

The weather had turned really cold now and snow was thick on the ground. John and Paddy began decorating the office with various objects in their endeavours to bring a bit of Christmas spirit to us early. When they couldn't find any paper chains, then the covers of the cigarette coupons had to do, all strung together with paper clips.

The Officers in Command Accounts and even Groupy began surreptitiously bringing in the odd sprigs of holly and sticking them behind pictures in their individual offices.

There was never time to get bored. It was John that pushed me into participating in another festive event.

"I'm on the Entertainments Committee," he said one day when he was bringing round the coffee. "A few of the airmen and airwomen are getting together to give a party on St Nicholas's Day for the kiddies from the local orphanage. It's their Christmas."

"Of course I'll help if I can," I agreed, anticipating an afternoon's skive.

"Great! I'll ask Groupy if he will let you come down to the NAAFI to help decorate it. The children will be arriving at three o'clock."

That afternoon, a dozen or so of us transformed the NAAFI into 'fairyland'. It was rather strange to see one of the German airmen getting dressed up as St Nicholas whilst one of our own airmen became the traditional 'Black Peter', his trusty servant. I wondered what my granddad would think of that.

Our 'St Nicholas' was based at Rheindahlen with the German Air Force. He looked as though he had just stepped out of a war film – very fair hair and piercing blue eyes. His name was Freitamn, but we all called him Freddy. As with most of his countrymen we had met so far, his English was impeccable, but of course he would be using his own language for the part he would be playing with the children.

We were just putting the finishing touches to the tree when two coaches pulled up outside and dozens of youngsters either jumped or were helped out into the snow, accompanied by nuns wearing large white 'butterfly' headdresses.

The children's eyes popped open and they stared up the tree with their mouths agape. Freddy hastily dashed into another room so that they would not see him while they were having their tea. We served them with jelly and ice-cream and Christmas cake, and some, who were quite clearly of limited ability, had to be fed by the nuns. All were extremely well behaved and appreciated everything that was done for them.

After tea, Saint Nicholas and Black Peter appeared and handed out a present to each child. They seemed more interested in Freddy than the gifts, for their eyes lit up and they really believed that he had come to see them especially. I hadn't a clue what he was talking about, but that didn't matter. The children understood. They looked up at him in wonderment, at his long white beard and his Bishops cope and mitre. He was wearing a mask but I don't think any of them noticed that.

"*Bist du brav gewesen?*" asked Saint Nicholas to each child.

"*Ja ja,*" they replied, gazing at him in all seriousness. "*Ich bin gut.*"

"What did he ask them?" I whispered to John.

"I think he is asking them if they have all been good," he replied. Obviously, by the number of *ja, ja's* that Freddy received, they all firmly believed that they had been very good indeed! Afterwards there were carols, in German of course, and nothing I have ever heard before, or since, equalled the sound of those little children singing 'Silent Night' in their own language around the lighted Christmas tree, with such seriousness and total concentration.

St Nicholas and Black Peter giving out presents.

On the day after the Saint Nicholas party, Jan came to Germany. I had received a scribbled 'warning' from her, telling me that she was on her way, so I went on the RAF bus to the airport to meet her.

"I thought I would never get here," she grumbled, after she had changed her money at the cash desk, "but they decided to send me before Christmas after all. What's it like here?"

"There are plenty of men," I replied, knowing where Jan's priorities lay.

She was put into Block 3, with the shift workers, so it was inevitable that she would make a new circle of friends. Nevertheless, we spent a lot of time 'commuting' the few yards between the Blocks – after all, we had a lot of gossip to catch up on.

Then suddenly it was Christmas. The NAAFI and Mess started to prepare for those that must stay on camp for the festive period. Paper chains appeared in the most unlikely places and the trees outside the office blocks were suddenly ablaze with coloured lights. I could have gone on leave but I chose to stay behind, just that once. I knew about the traditional custom of the officers serving Christmas dinner, and I did not want to leave the WRAF at the end of my four years without having experienced this. The idea of some of the Flight Lieutenants dishing up my turkey, no matter how awful the cooks made it, was of enormous appeal to me!

Do you know what?" said Jan, as she sat on the edge of Rusty's bed, enjoying Mal's coffee, "we have to wear best blue for Christmas dinner. It's a bit off isn't it?"

"I don't know what I am going to wear *tonight*," I said, gazing into my cupboard, which was bulging with clothes, "never mind worry about Best Blue."

"Well, wear something reasonable," said Marilyn, because you will be allowed in the Men's' billet until one o'clock!"

The men in Germany were still in the old fashioned billets that we had been used to at Wilmslow, except that they did have central heating! They were not fortunate enough to be in blocks like us.

"I thought we were not allowed in the billets?" I exclaimed.

"We are on Christmas Day," said Mal, "and its Christmas Day at one minute past midnight tonight isn't it, so they are having a party."

"You crafty devil!" I laughed.

Rusty interrupted our conversation as she burst into the room and put a large parcel on my bed.

"You jammy bugger Ratty," she cried, "you have got a food parcel!"

"I have?" I yelled in surprise. "Oh my lovely Mum!" I tore at the packaging. "Oh look, she's sent a cake as well!

Our discussion about the forthcoming evening entertainment came to an end as we saw off the Christmas cake and an assortment of mince pies and sweets, and then, stomachs full, we lay on our beds, putting our part of the world to rights.

"I wonder what the Mess will cook up tomorrow," said Mal.

"You never know," I replied, "they might surpass themselves and give us something edible, seeing as the officers are there."

"I doubt it," said Rusty. "We'll probably just get the leavings."

The coloured lights in the trees around the office blocks twinkled brightly against the white canopy of snow as we trudged down to the NAAFI Beer Bar. The party was already in full swing with the jukebox churning out some Elvis Presley songs and the table creaking under the weight of the beer.

"Hi girls!" said Johnny, getting up unsteadily to greet us. "Happy Christmas!"

The Beer Bar was crowded and a haze of smoke enveloped the room, making it resemble a sleazy night club.

"You look as though you are having a happy Christmas already," said Marilyn, sitting down beside her boyfriend.

One of the others tottered off to get some beers in and we sat down with the rest of the crowd and were introduced to the people we did not already know. The only vacant chair for me was next to a tall, lean boy with black wavy hair, who was lounging back, his long legs stretched across the seat.

"Mind if I sit here?" I said.

He looked at me with a cheeky grin and casually removed his legs from across the chair. He looked a little older than the rest and it seemed almost an insult to call him a boy.

"Not at all," he drawled, peering at me with large green eyes that matched the sweater he was wearing. *'Now him, I could fancy!'* I thought.

Suddenly I felt like Shirley Jones when she first clapped eyes on Gordon Macrae in *Oklahoma!*

"Sit down for goodness sake," Marilyn's voice penetrated my dream, "you're making the place look untidy!"

Johnny began his introductions once more and, turning towards the 'green sweater' in the next seat he said, "this is Richie, he works with me."

"Hi!" he grinned, "Ah ye nae going hame for Christmas!"

"Oh no!" I sighed under my breath, *"not another flippin' Scotsman!"*

"Pardon?" he said.

"Sorry, I was thinking out loud," I replied. "Let's put some records on Pat, eh?"

The two of us wandered over to the jukebox and I selected 'Runaway' by Del Shannon.

"I wouldn't mind him for a Christmas present!" I whispered. "He is gorgeous."

"Sorry to disappoint," laughed Pat, "but he's married."

"Shit!" I exclaimed.

"Sorry mate," said Pat. "Lady wife is in the UK."

My evening had just been totally ruined. You would think that out of the thousands of blokes on this enormous camp I would be able to find *one* that I fancied that was also single. The occasional bloke that actually fancied me was either too young or too spotty. Older ones were either married or were after 'one thing' and when they realised that the 'one thing' was not going to happen they looked elsewhere – and not necessarily among other airwomen who were, in the main, still too afraid of getting pregnant to oblige. They had plenty of 'opportunities' in the local town, because, unlike us, the local girls were allowed out all night. It was maddening.

However, I still had the unusual occurrence of going into the Men's Billet to look forward to and Richie did put his arm in mine as we walked down the road at midnight, so it felt romantic, even if it wasn't going anywhere. Somewhere in the distance a clock struck midnight just as we were walking under the mistletoe that had been thoughtfully provided by one of the boys.

"It's Christmas day," said Richie, who was only partially drunk. There was a Christmas kiss, but that was as far as it went. I was not going to touch somebody else's property, no matter how tempting it was!

The billet had been decorated up and the beds put all around the side. Somebody had thoughtfully provided a crate of beer and sandwiches and there was a record player.

We airwomen only had an hour so we contented ourselves with a few dances and the novelty of being somewhere that we would not normally be permitted to go. One or two couples had the chance of some canoodling, but it was very public and all too soon the hour was up and we had to dash back or incur the wrath of a Duty Airwoman who had to stay up an extra hour for our benefit and wasn't too happy about it. Besides, we had a Christmas Dinner to look forward to.

Just for once the Mess did surpass themselves. We found that we did not have to go and get our dinner ourselves, as the tables were already set out, decorated with evergreens and with a bottle of wine and a packet of cigarettes for each person at the table. It seemed to be worth struggling into our Best Blue uniforms and white shirts after all.

The thing we really enjoyed more than anything though was to see the officers busy serving us 'lowly mortals' at our tables. Actually, they seemed to be enjoying themselves, but not as much as us! The sight of some of the Flight Lieutenants and Squadron Leaders I had worked for during the year dishing up the roast turkey and Christmas pudding was worth not going home for. After all, I had seen my Mum dishing it up for twenty years. This was another thing entirely.

I could not believe that the dinner had all been achieved by our usual Belgian cooks, but somehow they had managed it, and we wondered why the devil they could not do it for the rest of the year! It took us two hours to wade through it all and I am sure we came out of the Mess an inch fatter than when we went in. I put my spoon down after eating all I could of the Christmas Pudding and leaned back in my chair.

"Whew, I could not eat another thing!" I said, as a Squadron Leader whipped away my plate.

"I reckon they have brought in some RAF cooks to help them," said Trevor.

I would not have been surprised, because it was certainly not what we were used to.

"We'll all have to do the Nijmegen March in the summer to get all the weight off," said Chalky, as he stuffed his face with another mince pie.

That phrase 'The Nijmegen March' kept cropping up.

"Girls aren't allowed," answered Richie, "something about having to have a WRAF officer with them."

I wasn't in the least bit interested because there was no way that *I* was going to march one hundred miles, with or without a WRAF Officer, and that was that, although after what I had eaten, I had to agree with Chalky – we could have done with it.

The thick snows hung about through January and we all looked like yetis crossing the golf course in our duffle coats to work, but soon the winter weather started to lift. There was never time for boredom and there were the two cinemas to make up for the lack of television. It also didn't take long to get used to the size of the place or the unnatural amount of men in relation to women. But if we thought they would be queuing up for us, we were mistaken.

"It's always the way," said Jan one day, "the ones I fancy don't fancy me, and the ones I don't fancy *do* fancy me."

"What is more," said Pat, "even if you do find a bloke you fancy you still can't bring him anywhere near the WRAF Block."

It seemed as though 'the world and his wife' were hell bent on thwarting any attempts any of us might have at 'getting into dark corners' as my Dad would have put it. We, therefore, tended to spend most of our recreational time in a group rather than as couples, sometimes playing table-tennis or swimming in the outdoor pool at the YMCA, or even just quietly sitting in the WVS lounge reading the papers or playing records.

"Oh I am going to end up an old maid and die wondering!" I moaned to Jan one day when we were relaxing in the Weavers, along with about forty airmen.

"Well I am not going to let them put 'returned unopened' on *my* coffin," she laughed. "If I can't find myself a boyfriend out of *this* lot, I must be losing my touch."

Of course, there were a few girls, well known by the boys, who were not too particular, but the vast majority would not take chances. Besides, by the time you had run the gauntlet of the Snowdrops and their torches and the Duty Airwoman and her clock, not to mention Sergeant Payne if she happened to be around, you were past caring!

The boys, on the other hand, had much more freedom than us, so what *they* got up to after we had left them was another matter and we all thought it was extremely unfair.

"I see Phyllis has been shipped back to the UK at last," said Chalky.

It was pouring with rain and so a gang of us were sitting around in the Weavers one Sunday as usual, gossiping about each other and catching up on the newspapers – like old men and women 'putting the world to rights'.

"About time," said Johnny. "They have been trying to catch him for ages!"

I knew who 'Phyllis' was. His name was actually Philip, but everyone called him Phyllis – I thought out of fun, especially as he always took it in good part. He had black wavy hair and was rather good looking, but a lot older than the rest of us.

"Why? What's he done?" I asked innocently. There was much laughter all round, although some of the girls, like me, looked at Johnny blankly.

"He's a queer of course!" said Johnny. "But they had to catch him and prove it before they could kick him out!"

One or two of us still looked totally blank. Pat was with us and a couple of friends from her Block and Jan and Marilyn.

"Queer," said Johnny, "poofter, nine bob note…"

"It means he *goes* with other men!" said Mal patiently.

She whispered 'goes' under her breath.

"Oh, for goodness sake, I don't believe it!" I scoffed. I knew that you could get men who were 'girlie', and Philip was certainly that – I thought it was just an affectation – but to actually 'go' with other men! That I wasn't having. How?

"Dinna ask!" laughed Richie, who had just joined us at the table.

"Honestly!" laughed Johnny. "It will be in Station Routine Orders soon, you wait and see."

"Oh they can't put it in SROs," gasped Mal, "Don't be so silly."

"Yes they will!" said Richie. "He was a poofter, a shirt-lifter!"

"I still don't believe it," said Pat, as she took a slurp of her Coke. "There's no such thing."

"Oh yes there is," retorted Chalky. "You would be surprised. I bet Elvis is a poofter!"

He dodged out of the way as Pat went to throw the last few drops of her Coke all over him.

"Listen you," I said angrily. "I may have lived a sheltered life, but one thing I know for definite, for absolute bloody *definite* – is that Elvis is *not* a poofter!"

"What about Liberace then?" said Trevor. "Poofter – written all over him."

"Never!" I retorted. My Mother adored Liberace.

The conversation ended in roars of laughter as they each tried to outdo one another as to who they thought were poofters. I still wouldn't believe that you could get people of the same sex fancying each other, but my 'education' was, partially completed, at least, when the next lot of Station Routine Orders came out! It said that Philip and another chap had indeed been sent home and the word used to describe their misdemeanour was one that both I and my Mother used if we broke anything! Obviously, neither of us knew its true meaning! I did now and thus my education was further expanded – even further than my Mother's! We led a very sheltered life.

The weeks soon became months and I noticed that already the spring buds had disappeared and the trees across the golf course had put on their gowns of green and joined their neighbours, the fir trees, in making that particular part of the camp look like a country park.

I was playing table tennis with Mal at the YMCA when Richie came up the stairs, carrying a tray of steaming tea and some rolls. He placed them on the table and then looked at me with those twinkling eyes – the sod! He gave me a wry smile.

"I'm posted back to the UK," he said.

"Oh damn it!" I exclaimed.

"Next Wednesday to be precise!" he continued.

We had got rather attached to each other, even though there had been no 'hanky-panky' worth talking about and he had behaved like a gentleman.

"Flippin' heck, why are all the nicest ones married?" I said under my breath.

"Sorry hen!" he replied. "Never mind, Chalky fancies you."

"*I* don't fancy Chalky," I retorted, the conceit of the remark going right over my head.

"Have a cup of tea," said Mal. It was her answer to everything.

"But Wednesday is only five days away," I wailed.

"One lump or two," continued my friend.

"I've got to go on duty now," said Richie, as he finished his tea. "See you later."

I nodded dumbly as I kicked the table tennis ball that was lying, harming nobody, at my feet and watched him as he slowly walked back down the stairs and away to work on the other side of camp. It was all so infuriating.

During the spring, money had been spent on the NAAFI and we now had a huge Cocktail Lounge. A bit more palatable than the Beer Bar for airwomen who wished to behave like young ladies, we were told! So much so, that they even put the Beer Bar out of bounds to airwomen, which we all thought was a really male chauvinist thing to do.

The Cocktail Lounge, which had been re-christened 'The Queensway Club' also had a brand new dance floor and, just before Richie was due to depart, there was to be a jive and twist session with a band and a visit from a real disc jockey called Ian Fenner, who worked for the German branch of the BBC and introduced *Two Way Family Favourites* – a 'must' in any household on a Sunday in the UK if they had relations serving abroad in the armed forces. It was the launch of a new 'era' for our NAAFI.

Nobody was very impressed with the new arrangements though, but 'the powers that be' had thought that we had to be upgraded, so upgraded we were! The jukebox was relegated to the Beer Bar and our red Formica-topped tables were replaced with posh low coffee ones. However, the final straw came with the floor. It was so posh that we girls had to collect little plastic covers at the door to put on our stiletto heels to stop the new floor from being 'pinpricked' as we walked over it.

"Gee-zus Ker-riste, what a nightmare!" exclaimed Pat, as she wasted good dancing time by trying to push these things onto her shoes, while I handed mine over to the Duty Airman, who had the job of trying to fish around for the right size in a large box in front of him.

"Not my fault girls," he muttered, "you shouldn't have joined if you can't take a joke."

The heel covers were the worst invention ever and most of us spent time on our hands and knees retrieving them from under chairs where they had fallen off. True, our stilettos would have wrecked the new floor in a minute, but we had been perfectly happy with the old one. Besides, nine times out of ten we took our shoes off for jiving anyway. We really were an ungrateful lot.

The dancing was already in full swing when the object of my 'unrequited love' and Johnny and Chalky came into the Cocktail Lounge. Richie looked like something out of *Picturegoer* – in black trousers, a scarlet jumper and a yellow cravat that just showed over the neck of the jumper complementing his tanned skin – and he knew it. It was impossible to resist his charm and I was sure he was doing it on purpose.

The time flew by and even my displeasure at the plastic heel covers paled into insignificance at the idea that he would be going back to the UK tomorrow. There was a new record on the jukebox by Ella Fitzgerald called 'Every Time We Say Goodbye' and how appropriate it seemed to be.

"I keep saying it," he said lamely, as we got up for a dance. "I'm so sorry hen!"

"Oh it's OK," I smiled unconvincingly. "Plenty more fish in the sea – and stop calling me hen will you!"

The moment was ruined by one of the plastic covers coming of my heel and then we had to scrabble around looking for it. In the end we gave up and I danced in my stocking'd feet.

I handed the damn things in, or at least what was left of them, on the way out of the club and we walked back to the Block in the darkness, saying very little. Suddenly, he took his yellow cravat off, which he was never without when dressed in civvies, and put it round my neck and gave me a brotherly kiss and a big bear hug. I could see the silhouettes of other couples in the shadows saying their goodnights just a few yards out of range of the Duty Airwoman.

"To remind you of me," he smiled, and then, with a final wave, he walked out of my life forever. He disappeared round the corner out of sight and I was left staring at the empty space where he had been with the tears meeting under my chin and dripping onto the cravat, too young and unbelievably thick to even realise what a patronising gesture it had been!

8. *Be careful what you volunteer for!*

Life goes on, including mine. I still had a job of work to do at the Big House and so, the following morning, I strode purposefully across the golf course to work, trying not to feel too downhearted. The men outnumbered the women at about two hundred to one – I was doing something wrong somewhere in fancying what was out of bounds! John came into my office with a cup of tea and more sympathy.

"There you are," he said, "never let it be said that I don't do anything for you!"

I must have looked like a wet weekend.

He parked himself on the corner of my desk and rested his feet on the open drawer of the filing cabinet, casually pushing Groupy's correspondence to one side as he did so.

"Listen," he said. "I have an idea to make you forget all about that twit!"

I bristled at the idea of the lovely Richie being called a 'twit'.

"What is this brilliant brainwave of yours," I sighed. I could have done with getting on with my typing.

"Do the Nijmegen march next month," he giggled.

"Do the what?" I exclaimed. "You are not honestly suggesting that I should do that hundred mile route march thing that they are all going on about? Besides, airwomen are not allowed – remember?"

"Well maybe we can change their minds," said John. "I know two or three of the airwomen want to have a go. Maybe we can get up a team."

"Sod off John!" I laughed.

I had never done a day's sport in my life that I could avoid. Even at Wilmslow I had managed to keep it to a minimum. I was to sport what custard was to chips.

"Give it a go… you can practice first," he went on, totally ignoring my protests.

"Go away John. I've got work to do!"

"It will be a whole week in Holland!"

"I don't care if it is a whole week in Hong Kong High Street," I retorted. "Go away John!" But I was beginning to weaken. A whole week in Holland sounded good – and I had heard how lovely the Dutch were to the British.

"I *dare* you to do it!"

That was fatal. I should have remembered that the last time that I was dared to do something got me into the Air Force in the first place.

"But airwomen are not allowed," I repeated.

He jumped off my desk quickly as Groupy came in with some more typing for me to do.

"Haven't you got any work to do, young man?" smiled the Group Captain.

"I'm trying to get her to do the Nijmegen March Sir," he explained.

"Airwomen aren't allowed to Sir," I said patiently.

"Well maybe we can pull a few strings," said Groupy. "I think the objection is that you have to have a WRAF officer with you."

I didn't really *want* him to pull a few strings, but I did make a point of finding out all about it.

The March was something that had been going on in the town of Nijmegen in Holland since 1909 and probably before. It had originally been a sporting event for the Dutch but it had taken on a whole new meaning since the war and included Arnhem and Grave and other areas of significance, particularly to our parents' generation. It was a really mammoth event and thousands of servicemen, women and civilians took part in it, to try out their stamina and to have the honour of representing their country over a period of four days. Up to forty or more nations were involved in it, and it was growing year by year as the news about it travelled. It was, and would remain, the biggest march in the world.

In 1909 there had been just over three hundred taking part, but this figure, over decades, would increase to fifty thousand, at which time the Dutch would make that the limit.

It was always a source of amazement to us all that it did not eventually make it to British Television, even if only on the News. It was on *Pathé News* at the cinema though.

Throughout the year, minor one-day marches were held in the surrounding Dutch villages and towns, usually on a Saturday and nearly always consisting of 25 miles. The people that got the medals for these marches would build up a collection to wear when they went for the most important and coveted medal of all – the one with the orange and green Nijmegen ribbon. It was the 'cup final' of the summer's marching in the Netherlands.

The RAF had taken part before, but WRAF had never done so. There was always one objection or another.

John seemed to be fighting a losing battle, for despite his efforts he could only manage to find five airwomen to show any enthusiasm and there was certainly no encouragement from WRAF Admin. A 'team' had to consist of no less than twelve. Anything under that number and you had to march as an 'individual'. They were having enough of a job trying to get twelve *men* from Headquarters, never mind the same amount of women, although there were plenty of teams going from the Army and from the NATO forces at Rheindahlen and also from other RAF Stations in Germany. Just as it was with the Band at Medmenham – they wanted us to make up the numbers for a Headquarters team.

"Come on a mini-march," he said one day when he came into my office with some typing for me to do. "At least it will be a whole day in Holland and you can give it a try."

I finally agreed, if only to shut him up.

A whole day in Holland was tempting and so, much against my better judgement, I finally joined the other five girls and the boys at the crack of dawn to get the coach to a place I had never heard of called Bergen-op-Zoom.

Rheindahlen wasn't far from the border with Holland and these days there were no hold-ups at the crossing – just a bored look down the bus from the uniformed Dutch border guard and then we were there in the quaint little village, which was all dressed up in flags and flowers for the occasion, and with barrel organs and brass bands playing loudly as if to outsmart each other.

We dutifully marched behind the RAF team all through the countryside, knowing that we were only there to make up their numbers.

Where we 'belonged' – bringing up the rear!

We had to take big long strides to keep up with the boys and sometimes they forgot about us following along behind them and we almost had to run to avoid a gap forming between us and them. It was all worthwhile though, especially when, at the end of it all, we marched the last mile or so behind a rowdy, brassy Dutch band and there were people cheering us from all sides.

"I don't like this idea of us marching along at the back though," I moaned, as I took my beetle-crushers off and sat down on the pavement. "We used to march with the men when we were in the Signals Command Band."

The RAF Team Leader was a tall, lean officer called Flight Lieutenant Curry.

"We can try it out girls," he said, "but you will have to take longer steps and the men will have to take shorter ones."

There were cries of objection all round.

"Oh no Sir," said a ginger-haired boy called Bill. "We can't march with a load of women in with us – the other teams will think we are ponces. Can't they have their own team?"

"Don't be miserable, airman," snapped the Officer.

The arguments went on and I hardly noticed my feet swelling so that I could not put my beetle crushers on again. By the time the coach arrived back at camp, with some of the boys still arguing, I had no choice but to walk back to the block in my socks, carrying my shoes in my hand.

Pat Seymour was waiting for us.

"Jee-sus Ker-rist Ratty!" she exclaimed. "You are all bloody bonkers!"

I didn't care. There had been a real adrenalin rush at Bergen-op-Zoom and, although I still had to be persuaded to do the Nijmegen March if we were eventually allowed to, I had enjoyed the day and wouldn't mind doing it again. What I did *not* bargain for was coming face to face with Sergeant Payne at the door of the WRAF Block...

"Airwoman!" she yelled. "Where do you think you are, Margate Beach?"

"I have just been marching Sergeant," I muttered. The other girls, who had the sense to keep their shoes on, disappeared quickly into their respective Blocks.

"My feet are swollen," I went on.

"More fool you," she growled.

"I am going to do the Nijmegen March in July," I heard myself say.

A grin split her face from ear to ear and she penetrated me with her dark eyes. Then she dissolved into peels of sarcastic laughter before turning her back on me. It was the final push I needed. The next one-day march was at a place called 's-Hertogenbosh' and I had already mentally put my name down for it. I would show the cow!

There were many difficulties to be ironed out, not least the very idea that the RAF and WRAF would march as a mixed team. It was unheard of. Even the Central Band was separate.

There was the RAF Central Band and the WRAF Central Band and 'never the twain should meet' – yet anyway! We girls certainly could not enter a team on our own – there were not enough of us. In the meantime, in the background, Groupy and Flight Lieutenant Curry were pulling strings to see if we could go without a WRAF Officer.

With none of these things yet resolved we still went ahead and tried to design a suitable uniform for ourselves so that the six girls were in something cool and yet matched the boys.

"I would not have believed it would be so fraught with difficulty just to take a mixed team to Nijmegen," grumbled John one day when he came into my office. "Talk about bloody red tape – anyone would think we were arranging the Berlin Air Lift!"

However, after much argument and letters from the WRAF Officer giving permission, not to mention the blessing from the Ministry of Defence, it was decided that the boys would wear their best blue trousers with open-necked shirts, white webbing belt and best cap. The girls were to wear best skirts, pale blue blouses with the union jack sewn on the sleeves, best caps, beetle crusher shoes and white ankle socks.

Our belts were our special pride and joy, though. You could only buy them in the NAAFI but they had recently become an option as part of the summer uniform. They were air force blue canvas, about two inches wide and had a small zipped pocket in the side for our Identity Card and did up with a leather buckle in the front. There was just enough room to pin our mini-march medals all around so that they jangled from our waists.

Finally, the loose ends were tied up and we six girls did a mental 'V sign' to Sergeant Payne as the permission arrived for us to take part. There was still an ongoing argument about the girls marching at the back, but we were thankful for small mercies and kept quiet – for the time being anyway. Some of the boys did not want us at all, but had to accept that without us they could not go as a team and nobody wanted to go as individuals, so they kept quiet too.

We had our last briefing at the Education Centre before we left Germany for Holland and the town of Nijmegen. As I sat in the lecture room with my other team mates and listened to Flight Lieutenant Curry I couldn't help but smile at the way life turns out. Pat was right, I was stark raving bonkers!

I looked around. John from our office was there, along with the other lads that I knew by sight, plus a Sergeant who I did not know at all. The five other girls were Laney, a blonde girl from Block 2, Jean, a Scot, who was quite a bit older than the rest of us; sitting at a desk behind them were a very slim brown-haired girl called Val and little Cathy. The latter had dark auburn hair and was quite short, which meant that she had to take enormous strides to keep up. Last, but definitely not least, was Sandy – a gorgeous-looking girl with a figure I could have killed for – who worked in Stores. She had long, thick, black hair which she rolled up on top of her head when in uniform, but which was flowing loose down her back at the moment, as we were all in civvies. She also seemed to have friends in the tailoring department, because her uniform always seemed to be more tightly fitting where it mattered than anyone else's I knew! It looked as though it had been tailored especially to suit her curves. *My* uniform was tailored too – but there was tailoring and then there was 'Sandy's tailoring'!

I came back to life as Flight Lieutenant Curry began explaining the march to us.

"The March, as you all know, is a *march* and not a walk," he told us unnecessarily. "We march the whole way, just as you have been doing these past weeks at the smaller events. The route will take you 25 miles a day over a four-day period."

"Tell me something I don't know," Laney whispered.

"You march in a circle," he went on. "The first day starting to the North, the second the East, the third to the West – that's the worst day – and then on the fourth day we march to the South of Nijmegen. Each night we end up exactly where we started, thus forming a giant clover leaf."

"Bit of a pointless exercise," joked Mac.

"The starts are staggered," continued the officer, giving him a withering look, "each team gets a starting time which it must stick to – you will find that some teams start as early as 4.30am and yet there will still be teams marching off as late as 9.30am, so there is not a long gap, in Nijmegen itself, between the last to start and the first to finish."

He made the point that we would be representing not only RAF Germany but the whole of Great Britain and so we were to be on our very best behaviour. The boys would stay at the huge tented camp at Heumensoord, some way from the town, and the girls would be staying with women from other countries in one of the local schools, where the classrooms had been turned into dormitories for the duration of the March. The team would meet up together each morning at the square where the March started from.

Then he told us a bit about Operation Market Garden and how, although the March had been started many years before the war, it was of even more significance now, especially to the Allied Forces because of all the troops that were buried there in the War Graves.

I briefly recalled Sergeant Oliver at Hereford telling us about that and then put it to the back of my mind. There was a party in the NAAFI, or Queensway Club as it had to be called now, and most of us were only twenty or so. We had different priorities just then and we were anxious to get the meeting over and done with.

We left the Flight Lieutenant to go back to the Officers' Mess and went into the Club, carefully avoiding the highly polished dance floor and thus the need to put little plastic tips on the heels of our shoes.

"What do you think of my idea now?" said John, as he bought a tray of drinks to the table.

"I'll let you know when it's all over," I replied.

"You must be mad!" exclaimed Rusty. "I'm darned if I would do it!"

"All I hope is," said Jean, "that we have decent weather. I shall just die if it rains!"

"Oh, we should be lucky," said Mac. "After all, it *is* July."

I hoped that these were not 'famous last words'.

The following morning we were in an RAF bus, heading across the border and towards the town of Nijmegen. We occasionally found ourselves either in front of, or behind, other Air Force buses going in the same direction. We certainly were not the only team going from Germany, but we were the only 'mixed' team. There were plenty of all-male teams – from Geilenkirchen, Bruggen and Wildenrath – and also entries from the Army and NATO.

In fairness, the boys did their best to hide their embarrassment at having girls marching with them, but there were one or two that did not hide their feelings.

"People will think we are a load of fairies," grumbled Fred, a rather good-looking fair-haired boy from the Communications Centre.

"Listen airman!" said Flight Lieutenant Curry, getting quite cross. "The Israelis have put in a mixed team and I would suggest that you do *not* call *them* 'fairies'."

Fred shut up and settled down in his corner of the bus.

During our ride, we learnt more about what to expect. The accommodation would be very sparse, as the town was coping with thousands of marchers, not to mention all the people who were on a National Holiday for the event.

It took most of the day to get there, as there was plenty of traffic, but as we drew closer we saw the huge curve of the iron bridge in the distance, famous for the battles that were fought on and around it during the war.

There was an air of festivity everywhere, extra flags flew from the buildings and armchairs and tables had been brought out from private houses and placed along the side of the road without any fear of them being taken. Nearer to the centre of the town, large wooden stands had been erected and two huge bandstands occupied an area in the market square. In fact, it was just as our officer had described it. The coach pulled up outside a red brick school building.

"Right, all the airwomen out!" bawled the Flight Lieutenant. "You have two days for sightseeing and I shall let you know our starting time as soon as I know myself; I'll contact you tomorrow. Anyway, no doubt these fine honourable gentlemen (he pointed to the rest of the team in the back of the coach) will be calling at the school to escort you out."

"Oh well, we will *all* look forward to that!" laughed Sandy, as she jumped out of the coach and deliberately wiggled her bottom at the boys.

"I hope you will be still jumping and wiggling like that on Friday when the March is finished!" chuckled the officer, knowingly.

"I'll do my best," she giggled.

As the coach pulled away and left us, surrounded by our luggage at the entrance to the school, a Dutch Army captain came running down the steps towards us. She was very slim and smart in her grey uniform with gold epaulettes.

"Ah die Englander," she beamed. *"Velcolm, velcolm."*

She led us down a long corridor to a classroom, where bunk beds had been erected in place of the desks. The desks themselves were piled high in the school corridor. On the blackboard, written in large letters in English were the words 'Welcome to Nijmegen' and underneath 'tea can be obtained in the Hall whenever you require.'

"Jeez," grunted Laney, bouncing on the nearest bed, "these beds are hard!"

I heaved my kitbag up onto one of the top bunks and struggled to climb up with it.

"Guess we have to use the children's loos if we want to have a wash," said Sandy, as she picked up her towel and washbag. She was back in a short while.

"They are so small," she smiled. "Still, it's better than the men have got, I'll bet."

"Did you notice," said Jean, "they have got the weather forecast up on a board downstairs. It says it's going to be hot."

"That's all I need!" I replied, as I stretched out on the top bunk. "I'll just go red and stay red forever!"

"Better than raining," said Cathy, as I jumped down again.

We all trooped downstairs to the large school hall, where long trestle tables had been set end-to-end in rows. Already there were scores of girls in varying types and shades of uniform, talking in every nationality, bunched together in little knots around the room.

A young Dutch Sergeant came up to us and told us to help ourselves to whatever we wanted from the counter that had been set up at the end of the hall. The tables were piled with thick slices of bread and butter, and in cups at the side of these were chocolate hundreds and thousands, which we were supposed to spread on the bread.

It was Val who took the first sip of the drink provided – it was in a large urn and turned out to be a dark-looking mixture which we thought was flat coca-cola. Val took a tentative sip from her cup, only to suddenly lean forward and choke, making awful grimaces.

"Ugh, whatever is it?" she spluttered. "It's awful stuff!"

A Danish girl sitting at the next table to us started laughing and leaned over and spoke in perfect English.

"It's especially for the marchers," she said. "Lukewarm un-milked, salted tea."

"Oh no!" gasped Val. "They are trying to poison us as well!"

The girl giggled.

"They say it is going to be very hot and this is to make sure you get enough salt, for you lose a lot marching in warm weather. Have you done the march before?"

"No," said Sandy. "It's our first time."

"Well good luck!" was the reply.

I wasn't sure whether her words were meant to be genuine or sarcastic, but she had a kind smile on her face as she said them, so I gave her the benefit of the doubt.

We spent the following day, Monday, walking around Nijmegen and generally feeling like a million dollars. As far as we knew, we were the only British military girls taking part in the March, with the exception, I learned later, of a team of Policewomen. Therefore we turned out to be quite a novelty, both with our hosts and with the visiting teams. Everyone wore their uniforms and they were proud to do so, and often small children ran up to us, asking for our autographs. We sometimes found it would take fifteen minutes to walk as many yards because of the autograph hunters. The boys, out of devilment, put names like Elvis Presley or Marilyn Monroe down in the little autograph books held out by the kids – little knowing at the time that inside a month the second of these two celebrities would be dead. The children collected the names of marchers like other kids collected car numbers. It was all one big game.

All day the town was packed with people – and the cafés were doing a roaring trade in those who just wanted to sit under the open air umbrellas, have their beers and watch all the soldiers, sailors and airmen passing by in their droves and always in their uniforms, many adorned with medals already awarded from other marches. We saw crowds of men in smart green uniform, who were the Swiss. We also saw a small group in immaculate pale cream who were part of the very popular Israeli team, the only other mixed military team in the March.

There were Americans and Canadians, sprawled out under the canopies of the open air restaurants. There were groups of Dutch, Germans, Belgians, French, even Australians, and there were Danes, Norwegians and Italians, and, of course, among them all, our own British Army, Navy and Air Force, including the Scots Guards and Gordon Highlanders.

We almost got to a stage where we became worn out with the advances of the foreign soldiers, all of whom wanted to talk to us and buy us drinks, or to jive in the open air dance squares throughout the town. We could walk into a café or Dance Hall and find that we were, quite often, the only military women present and yet we were perfectly safe with the male members of our team never too far away as they looked on in amusement. Nothing that we had done before at the smaller marches could have prepared us for this.

The Dutch undoubtedly loved the British and every time a Band Leader saw our uniforms with the union jack on our sleeves he would immediately lead his musicians in a rendering of the National Anthem or Long Way to Tipperary. After all, the liberation from the Germans was still very fresh in the memories of anyone just a couple of years older than we were. It was all good fun and we loved every minute of it.

"My goodness," said Laney, "now I know how the Queen feels – won't it be *awful* if we don't complete the first day after all this?"

"These odds are definitely uneven," grinned Fred. "I would much prefer it if the situation were the other way round and we were the only men!"

"Trust you," giggled Sandy, "you are just jealous!"

"No wonder they didn't want us with them," said Val. "They didn't want us stealing their limelight."

"Oh, by the way", said John, "I nearly forgot, the bus will be calling for you at the school at 6.30 this evening to take you to the Tattoo."

"Oh thanks!" I cried. "*Now* you tell us! We'd better get back and get ready!"

The boys began to look for a taxi to take them back to their tented camp and left us to go back to the school to smarten up for the forthcoming event.

The old RAF bus arrived outside the school at exactly 6.30pm with the boys already stretched out inside with their feet up, trying hard not to crease their best uniforms.

"Our team has been chosen to represent the Air Force in the march around the Arena," said our Flight Lieutenant, proudly, as the coach pulled away and weaved in and out of the narrow streets on its way to the Stadium.

We were totally unprepared for that.

"Oh it's OK," laughed the officer. "When I give the word you just form up in threes down on the Arena and march around once and smile sweetly at all the people cheering you!"

I thought he was joking, but he wasn't.

The Stadium was a large sports arena, just like Wembley, and it didn't take me long to realise why we had started so early to cover such a short distance. It was like the approaches to Wembley on Cup Final day; cars and coaches were bumper-to-bumper all the way along the road and thousands of people were all rushing to the Stadium on foot in order to ensure they got inside and got a seat. Many more civilians, knowing that they would not stand a chance of getting inside, were content to crowd around the fields on the outskirts of the place in order to see the soldiers and the Bands forming up, and the coach-loads of personnel coming and going.

The seating arrangements inside were roughly split into four. The Royal Box side was occupied by Senior Officials, Officers from the participating countries and the local press and Dutch television cameras. All the teams taking part made large splashes of colour in the area opposite the Royal Box.

A huge square of green to my right told of the Swiss, whereas squares of brown, cream and fawn on my left were the various other armies, and everywhere there were people making up great patches of navy, air force blue, sky blue and white. The other two sections, at the 'goalpost ends' of the arena were occupied by thousands of civilians who had managed to get seats for the occasion and at this moment they were singing away lustily.

In the centre was a huge grass area, normally used for football and athletics, surrounded by the running track. In a long line, spaced evenly apart, in front of the Royal Box were a row of twenty or so white flagpoles and, standing to attention in front of each one, was a Dutch soldier. We all sat down in our places and waited for the proceedings to begin. I found myself sitting next to John. Already I was glad that he had convinced me to do this.

Suddenly I heard a band strike up, and from the huge opening underneath the Royal Box, there emerged the band of the Dutch Air Force, resplendent in bright blue jackets and equally bright trousers. They marched onto the arena and the singing of the crowd turned to cheers as they played the 'Vierdaags', the special march tune of the 'four days'. They counter-marched up and down and eventually came to a halt in front of the flagpoles. As they halted, hundreds of children ran out into the Stadium, some carrying bunches of flowers, others with the flags of the nations taking part. They skipped around to the tune of the Band, making patterns with the flags and flowers, finally finding their way to the edge of the arena where they spaced themselves all around the edge, waving their flags and flowers aloft.

More bands followed. First the German band marched on to subdued but polite cheers. After them, the American Army band, thrilling the audience with their unconventional jazzy marching. Then there was a Belgian band and then a Swiss one. There were soon a dozen or more bands massed on the grass area.

Then, quite suddenly, the music stopped, a small pause, and then, coming from the direction of the opening under the Royal Box we could hear another tune. We knew the tune before the band appeared. We could name that tune in one! It was the Royal Air Force March.

To us, at the start of the sixties, Holland might just as well have been China it felt so far away. It even felt like a long way from Germany, even though it was just over the border! On top of that, most of us had not been home for months, so the sound of an English band brought a lump to our throats immediately, but when the occasion was this one, and the band in question just happened to be the Central Band of the Royal Air Force that had played for most of our Passing Out Parades, the red blood in our veins turned to Air Force blue in an instant!

As they marched smartly into the stadium, their blue uniforms with the gold braid almost looking pinkish in the setting sun, the floodlights that had just come on reflected in their gleaming instruments. The large square of Air Force blue in the stands now erupted as the entire RAF contingent leapt to its feet. Airmen from all over Germany and the UK and also Air Training Corps, screamed together and waved frantically.

"It's ours! It's ours!" yelled Cathy. "Oh, aren't they lovely!"

Suddenly, all the British, the Army as well, were standing up and cheering fit to burst our lungs. I grabbed hold of Laney as water filled our eyes.

"Oh Laney!" I yelled, as we excitedly waved our hats in the air. "Aren't they smashing. Hooray, hooray!"

"And guess what?" whispered John. "They are here to play especially for us."

The massed bands of the different countries continued with their display, expertly counter-marching with each other and forming patterns across the grass and around the running track. Here I got my first glimpse of the enormous cry for peace in the world that the Nijmegen Marches had become. All these different nationalities that had been at each other's throats less than twenty years ago were joined together as one in the music of the massed bands, accompanied by the children with their flags and flowers of all nations and creeds.

Next there was the ceremony of the hoisting of the flags of every nation on the flagpoles along the side of the arena. This took an hour, for twenty-one nations were taking part this year. As each flag was hoisted, so the national anthem of that country was played, while we all stood to attention and the officers saluted. We heard the French and German National Anthems, the Star Spangled Banner, our own, and many others that we had never heard of.

In turn the flags were raised, the NATO flag, the Union Jack, the Belgian flag, the red flag with the white cross of the Swiss, the Star of David for the Israelis and the red, yellow and black German flag, the Canadian and others.

When the last flag was raised and the last national anthem played, the military in the audience began to move forward. Hundreds of soldiers leapt over the light barricade and took their places in threes around the running track. Flight Lieutenant Curry beckoned to us and we too ran down the steps and onto the track, where we formed up behind a team from the Dutch Air Force. Just for once, we girls spaced ourselves evenly among the boys.

"No arguments," barked our Officer. "We can't have the girls being left behind while you blokes forget they are there."

There were no arguments this time, not even from Bill.

The music started again and we began marching around the arena in our teams, a small gap left between each group. The front team almost met with the rear group, forming a huge circle around the running track.

We were not the only RAF team taking part in the march, but we were the only one down on that running track. The other RAF teams were in the stands, screaming and waving at us.

Then, all at once another sound was added to the one of the Massed Bands. To our complete and utter delight it was the RAF Laarbruch Pipe Band – they marched out of the entrance and joined the marchers at just the precise moment we passed and took their places in front of us. The other bands stopped and just the skirl of the pipes filled the night air.

We marched smartly, head and arms up to shoulder level.

"Oh, Sergeant Payne – weep a silent tear!" I thought.

Despite our efforts we couldn't help grinning broadly at each other as the pipes played and the Dutch crowd rose to their feet as we passed them.

Flags and handkerchiefs were waved at us and even the Senior RAF Officers on the saluting dais by the Royal Box were smiling broadly. The salute was taken by our own Air Vice Marshal, who had come to Nijmegen especially from Headquarters. All I needed just then was a Rolls Royce and I could have given him a queenly wave. Instead I settled for a smart 'eyes right' and they were eyes that were already welling up with tears.

This was the finale of the Tattoo and the marchers were the stars. In the end there were six bands all playing at once, but the roar of the crowd gave them plenty of competition. It was all for us. The comical part was that we hadn't even started the March yet.

Of course, in years to come, there would be occasions bigger and more elaborate, as communications and technology progressed, but to us then, on that particular day, in that year, this was just the 'bees knees' and unlike *anything* that any of us had ever seen before, nor dreamed we would ever see again.

The deafening cheers and the music roared on and on in my ears long after the Tattoo ended, but the first day of the March was in the morning…

9.   *The Nijmegen March: Days 1 and 2*

Tuesday 18th July 1962: I awoke to the sound of dozens of people outside our classroom running up and down the corridor in their efforts to get ready and I could hear a the sound of a band coming from the direction of the main square. I glanced with half-open eyes at Sandy, who had just come in from the washroom.

"Oh I'm not getting dressed yet," she said. "The toilets are jam packed with Danish girls, so I'll let them get on with it, they start before us."

I dragged myself out of bed and began to put some protective plaster on my heels, and the other girls followed suit.

"Well, at least we can get our feet done," said Val. "As long as I've got my feet done and my shoes and socks on, I don't care."

"You would look a picture striding around Nijmegen in your beetle crushers and jim-jams!" I laughed.

Eventually the Danish girls went on their way and we got washed and dressed and ran downstairs to our breakfast of cold tea and hundreds and thousands on bread, which by now we were getting used to, although sometimes there was cheese or ham to make a change.

As we breakfasted, dozens of girls were arriving for a snack, whilst others were leaving ahead of us. All were looking very smart in their various uniforms. As groups of them went out of the door we wished them good luck – in any language 'good luck' can be understood.

"We had better get going too," said Jean, being the oldest and naturally taking charge. She grimaced once again at the taste of the tea. "The lads are going to be at the start at 7.15, so hurry up."

We pinned the medals we had gained from the smaller marches around our money belts, carefully put our I.D. cards in the zip side of the belt and walked down the road towards the huge square, where there was a profusion of flags and bunting. As we walked down the steps of the school to the cries of good luck from the captain and her staff, the sound of the bands became more pronounced and we could hear the cheering of the crowds of people who had come out to watch.

The market square, a large penned-off area which was usually filled with people selling produce and cattle, had been cleared and instead was bustling with military personnel of many nations. Some teams had left long ago and still more were lining up in rows, three abreast, waiting to start. All the time the marchers were leaving and heading down the road towards Nijmegen Bridge and open country. The civilian marchers left from yet another starting point but would merge with us later along the route. It was all very orderly. Even the civvies had 'uniforms' of a sort, with each team wearing the same outfits and marching in step. Nobody 'walked'!

There was also a special section for the 'under sixteen-year-old' teams and, believe it or not, the 'over sixty-fives'. They actually did a total of seventy-five miles, or 30 km a day, doing mostly the same route as us, but taking a diversion to cut five miles off each day. There were teams from the Air Training Corps, St. John's Ambulance Cadets, and Scouts and Guides from the Netherlands and any other country who had applied to take part.

At the other end of the age range, there were teams of 'old soldiers' who knew these roads and country lanes well. Many of them, no doubt, had been involved, during the war, in the defence of that area and its aftermath, on both sides.

Then there were the totally daft teams, in our opinion anyway, who marched fifty kilometres a day! They followed the main route but branched off to do an extra bit each day, rejoining the main throng of marchers later. You had to have twelve in a 'team' with a leader. There were actually fourteen of us including our 'cycle orderly',

To one side of the square the buses and coaches that had brought the men down from the tented camp were lined up. We had no difficulty in spotting our own air force blue

Headquarters bus, with the roundel on the side, and the boys nonchalantly leaning against it waiting for us. We were still in the era when any person in the Armed Services could walk down any street in Britain, and in most parts of the world, proudly wearing their uniform. The very idea of covering it up or being afraid to wear it on public transport would have been treated as a joke!

The sections of people starting out on the March were split into various groups and each had their own track to start from, where a small hut was erected. We all lined up, behind the team from RAF Bruggen and in front of a German Army team in Track four. To the right of us, in Track five, the British Army teams were starting to line up and to the left there were scores of Swiss waiting to get on their way. The German Band (bless 'em) struck up the Air Force March the minute they saw that we were ready to move off!

"RAF Germany – by the left – quick march!" hollered Flight Lieutenant Curry.

An official wearing the bright orange and green armband that we were to become so familiar with in Holland, came out from his little hut, his home for the day, and punched our team card, rather like a bus conductor! Immediately we marched off to the sound of the band, with the boys, some of them reluctantly, accepting the girls in their midst and not tagging along behind. At intervals along the road and at each junction there was a large wooden board, with coloured wooden arrows pointing the way, so that we each followed our own route, and didn't end up on anybody else's. We had to follow the green arrow for the 40 kilometre a day military route. There was also a red arrow for 50km Military – but there was no danger of us following that one! There was a white arrow for the 40km civilian marchers and blue for the 30km civilian. These Marches had been going a long time and the organisers were experts. It went like clockwork.

We followed our green arrow, stepping out briskly and were soon overtaking RAF Bruggen.

"Slow down!" yelled our officer, who marched at the side of us. "It's a hundred miles you know, not a quick trot to the NAAFI and back!"

The band stayed with us all through the town and soon we were marching over the famous Nijmegen Bridge, with its huge arched steel structure that is so recognisable. All traffic over the bridge had been directed to a 'contra-flow' and would remain so until the day's marching had finished. Once over the other side of the river, we were into open country lanes, where, for the most part, traffic was forbidden.

Then we came to a right-hand fork, taking us towards the little village of Lent. Even at this early hour, people had come out of their cottages and were sitting on their kitchen chairs to watch us march past. Many were having their breakfast, but when they saw us they jumped up and waved enthusiastically.

I felt very proud to be British. We lived in a very happy time, with comparatively few worries and hang-ups and it was all down to the servicemen who had been here for such a different reason when I was a baby. I was even more determined that I would do this as a 'thank you' to them. Was I growing up?

For a few hundred yards the band continued to play but suddenly they stopped and peeled away to the left, leaving us to continue on our way without them while they marched back to the town centre, presumably to play for somebody else.

The flat Netherlands countryside stretched out ahead of us and the morning mist lifted to show us the long ribbon of people stretching out both in front of and behind us – far into the distance the ribbon stretched, far beyond the sight of human eye, the squares of colour mingling with each other in the distance and becoming clearer in the foreground. There was very little in the way of buildings to block the view. It looked like one long and colourful river, and there was the steady thump, thump, of marching feet and the occasional burst of singing and hand clapping to spur each other on and put a spring in our step.

For a while, all categories of marcher were together, but then the blue wooden arrow pointed to the left and, just like traffic leaving a motorway, so the 30-kilometre civilian marchers turned off and disappeared out of sight. Already the sun began to feel warm on our backs, but we were quite fresh and happy as we gently joked with our cycle orderly or made rude comments to the Bruggen team as we overtook them and they dropped behind us.

"Just 'cos you've got a secret weapon," they shouted wickedly.

They were referring to Sandy, who was marching in the middle at the front and wiggling her bottom as much as she could under the circumstances.

Now we were behind a team of American Army Medics, resplendent in a greyish uniform and wearing white helmets with red crosses on.

"I wonder if any of them knew Elvis Presley when he was in Germany doing his National Service?" said Val.

"Don't be daft," said Fred. "I shouldn't think so."

"Well, it was only two years ago," I said, leaping to her defence. "They might have done."

The conversation stopped as the Americans began to sing and soon we were joining in with them, to the latest Elvis number from his current film, G.I. Blues.

"D'ya ever get one of those days, boys,
D'ya ever get one of those days,
When nothing is right, from morning til' night,
D'ya ever get one of those days..."

We had great fun singing with them whilst we girls clapped our hands in time to the beat. The boys couldn't – they had rifles to hold, but the miles seemed to speed by and they were grudgingly realising that we were an asset to them rather than a liability.

We were still singing merrily as we marched along the top of a long dyke, and our cycle orderly decided to take a few photos of us. He rode on ahead so that he could be ready as we approached.

Poor Jamey was laden with haversacks containing first aid equipment, water bottles and also one or two Instamatic cameras, for we were not allowed to carry anything. At least the girls weren't. The boys, much to their annoyance, had to have packs on their backs as well as their rifles. He was so loaded down that when he went to get off his bike it overbalanced and the last we saw, as we marched past him, was Jamey, plus cycle, cameras and haversacks, all disappearing out of sight over the edge of the dyke! It was a jolly good job it was just grass and not a high one.

"Oh my camera!" screamed Laney, as she swung round and saw the flailing arms and legs of our cycle orderly rolling down into the ditch, much to the amusement of the teams in front and behind us. His language was international!

"We can't stop here", grinned our temporarily sadistic Flight Lieutenant, "your muscles are only just beginning to work properly – keep going – he'll catch us up."

"What if he doesn't?" shouted Mike.

"We'll wait for him at the first Rest Point," said the officer as he strode out. "Come on – he'll be all right. It's not a long drop."

"Charming!" cried Sandy.

We followed his orders and continued marching along behind the Americans, keeping in step whilst occasionally giggling at the recollection of our cycle orderly disappearing out of sight so suddenly.

We put still more miles behind us with no sign of him catching us up, when the American cycle orderly came racing towards us to say that the Rest Point was only one mile ahead. Sure enough, we looked up and in the distance we could see the large brown marquee with a red cross on it which was to become such a familiar sight to us all. Suddenly there was a new spring in the step of the American team as they entertained us with 'Deep in the Heart of Texas'.

We followed the human stream into a large open field where the marquees were situated and flung ourselves down on the grass, never minding that it was normally a cow field. Fortunately we escaped any accidents with cowpats! Within seconds, a nurse descended upon us and pushed mugs of salted tea into our hands, together with a hard-boiled egg each.

"Breakfast?" I asked.

"No, lunch," she giggled. It was still only 9.30am.

I never thought I would ever say it, but the tea tasted refreshing that morning and I ate the egg gratefully! The Dutch knew what they were doing.

The scene all around me looked like something from the film 'Dunkirk'. In fact, I could thoroughly recommend it to anybody making a war film as a possible saving in paying for 'extras' for the battle scenes! Thousands of soldiers and airmen of all nationalities were stretched out in this large field, their rifles thrown down anywhere on the grass, or neatly stacked together, butts downwards, to make little 'wigwams'. Dozens of nurses picked their way carefully between the inert bodies, armed with food and drink and first aid.

There were four massive tents with red crosses on, inside which were rows of camp beds, fortunately unused at this early stage. The toilets were simply holes in the ground with a tarpaulin sheet around them. People only used these if they were really desperate. It was preferable, where possible, to nip into a private house; the British, in particular, were always made welcome by the people sitting outside their homes and farms watching us go by. Occasionally we shared the loo with a couple of chickens or a goat, but we didn't care as long as we didn't have to use the ones at the Rest Points.

All the time the teams were entering the field on one side and leaving it for the second stage of the day's marching on the other side. We waited around and watched the Americans go on their way, but there was still no sign of Jamey.

"We will have to get moving in a minute," said our Flight Lieutenant, as he stood up and stretched his long legs. "We can't afford the time to wait around for him."

"I wonder where he could have got to?" said Laney. "I'm more worried about my camera."

"Well, there aren't any phones around here," Mac reminded us all.

"But what about poor Jamey?" replied Val, straightening her hat and tidying the wisps of hair sticking out underneath. Then, as if on cue, he arrived at the Rest Point, breathless and panting and a bit miffed at us for carrying on without him.

"Sorry," he gasped, as he put his bike down at the side of us, "that was a longer drop than it looked. I couldn't get out."

"Fine cycle orderly you are!" grunted our Flight Lieutenant impatiently.

Jamey looked really crestfallen but we found to our relief that all the cameras were none the worse for wear, or so we hoped. They were hard come by and very precious – seemingly more precious than Jamey at this moment in time. The only thing hurt was his pride.

"Bloomin' good when you have to rely on the Swiss to pull you out of the bloody dyke," mumbled Jamey. He really was not very happy with us at all and with good reason.

"Well come on everybody, on your feet!" shouted our leader. "We have not got all day, you know. There is a time limit of eleven hours!"

"We'll do it in half that," said Fred, with confidence, as he picked up his rifle.

"I hope so indeed! I certainly expect you to do it in six hours today ... and without rushing at it either," retorted the Flight Lieutenant sarcastically. "Now *will* you all get on your feet."

The boys knew how far they could push him and quickly stood up in their places, ready to march off. We waved goodbye to the friendly nurses and, to the echoes of the cheers of all the soldiers still resting, we joined up behind the other marchers leaving the Rest Point and continued on our way.

"Go on the British!" they shouted. "Go on the British!"

We now found ourselves marching behind a German team. There was no sign of any of the other RAF teams, but then they could be anywhere along the twenty-five-mile route.

The Germans, it has to be said, were not as cheery as the Americans, but they were polite enough. The people were polite to them too, but the measured clapping from onlookers as they passed turned, pointedly, into shouts and cheers as the British or Americans came into view behind them. In fact, there were many older Dutch who just stared fixedly ahead in silence and then nearly burst blood vessels when they caught sight of our RAF uniforms. It was sometimes quite embarrassing.

By now the sun was reaching its height and I could feel it burning onto my face and arms. I could feel my face getting redder and redder and my shirt began to feel damp. As we put the miles behind us, I began to long for a glass of water, but I knew we could not stop any more.

This was a time when Jamey began to earn his bike and make up for his earlier misfortune. Backwards and forwards he rode, collecting water from the kindly people standing outside their houses and passing it to us as we marched along. Sometimes he simply threw it at us and then ran back to return the cups and jugs to their owners.

Then the red and white arrows pointed in different directions – off to the right, taking the 50km military marchers and the 40km civilians even further north and through the outskirts of Arnhem, where they would pass the War Graves at Oosterbeek. We were relieved to find our route taking us to the left, as we had reached our farthest point away from Nijmegen and now were returning through the lanes, towards Elst and Valberg. We were doing well and we could see the teams stretching before us and behind us along the straight country road. I briefly wondered what it would look like from the air.

As we approached the junction at Elst, we rejoined the 'blue' route and soon, with the arrival of the others from our right, everyone was once again together going in the direction which would eventually take us along the dyke and into Nijmegen again. There were thousands of marchers, with hardly a gap between each team as one lot slotted in behind another, just like cars coming from a junction and joining motorway traffic. Suddenly though, John's voice broke into our singing.

"Laney, are you all right?" She was, unusually for her, in tears and quite clearly not all right. "Sir, sir, stop! There is something wrong with Laney."

"Halt!" yelled the Flight Lieutenant. We halted and moved to the side of the road to let the teams behind us get by. For a while we automatically marched up and down on the spot.

"What's the matter airwoman?" he said impatiently.

"My foot feels as though it is on fire Sir," swore Laney. "I think it is a blister. I can't believe it." She hopped on one foot." I have never had one before, and on the first day too!"

"Damn it!" said the Officer, never one to normally curse. "Sit down on the verge and let's have a look. The rest of you take advantage of this breather and lie down on the grass with your feet up against that fence over there."

We meekly followed his advice and I lay back and took the weight off my feet. I glanced across at where Laney was biting her lip as she tried to remove her shoe, showing that her heel was in a real mess. It was particularly annoying as the one thing that we did not want was for a girl to be the first to hold the team up.

"Well that's you out of the March," said Flight Lieutenant Curry.

"No!" cried Laney. "I'm not going to let the team down. We want the team medal."

"Never mind the team medal," said the officer, a little over anxious because he had been partly responsible for having the girls in his team in the first place, despite the lack of WRAF Officers (not that they would have made much difference).

"What's this Blondie?" drawled an American voice. "Trouble already!" It was the Cycle Orderly of another US team.

"I'm afraid she is finished," said our officer, looking at Laney's sore heel. It was an enormous blister that she had acquired. "She'll only hold the rest of the team up."

The rest of the American team halted at the side of the road and lay down on the grass verge.

"Gee whiz!" said the Cycle Orderly, fumbling in his satchel, "we can't have Blondie here dropping out, whatever next – my guys would be very upset!"

He produced a large hypodermic needle, whilst some of his compatriots joked with us and others took the time out to have a crafty cigarette and watch the other teams passing by, waving to everyone like long-lost friends.

"If you will permit me Sir," he said to our officer, "this is just a mild pain killer and should do the trick for Blondie until the end of the day's marching!"

"Oh marvellous!" he replied. "Thanks a lot – we haven't got anything like that in our equipment."

"Trust the Yanks to have everything," muttered Jamey under his breath.

Laney gritted her teeth while the American inserted the needle into a spot near the blister, leaving Flight Lieutenant Curry the job of putting a large dressing over it.

"There you are Blondie," said the Medic. "You'll be OK now. Just give it five minutes to take effect and then put your shoe back on."

Meanwhile a team of Cranwell cadets came by and jeered and shouted at us all sitting at the side of the road.

"We'll get you back," shouted Frank, "you wait and see!"

Laney struggled into her beetle-crusher.

"That was like magic!" She grimaced slightly as she put her foot on the ground. "It doesn't hurt anymore ... well, not much anyway!"

The Americans formed up in front of us and marched off, waving as they did so.

"Thanks a lot!" shouted Laney, as we all got to our feet with a very impatient officer hurrying us up. He was starting to get very anxious about these delays on just the first day. He took his place at the side of our team and we formed up in our threes again.

"RAF Germany – by the left – quick *march!*"

By now our limbs were quite stiff and it took some time to get ourselves moving comfortably. There was a Rest Point, but we decided that we didn't need it and carried on, this time through roads that twisted and turned through the countryside, the occasional cow on either side looking at the continuous stream of people in puzzlement.

Then the lanes began to give way to wider roads, and eventually villages, with bigger groups of people standing along the kerbside to watch the progress of the marchers. As the miles lessened, so the groups turned into crowds, until the road on either side was tightly packed with dense rows of onlookers, who cheered lustily as each team marched by. This put a new spirit into us and, despite the heat of the sun, we began to lift our heads up and sing loudly and even Laney had stopped limping and was striding out.

Suddenly we heard more singing behind us, in English! The song was "Maybe It's Because I'm a Londoner" in deep baritone voices. I turned round to see that the team from the Air Ministry in London had caught us up.

They were mostly older than us, being Senior NCOs, and they were looking red and hot but they were all singing merrily and swinging their arms to the beat of the song.

"Hello you lot!" said a Flight Sergeant. "Wait for us oldies!"

We cheered them as they fell into step behind us and we continued the last few miles together, another long stretch that took us almost back to Lent again. But Nijmegen Bridge was in the distance and we turned right to retrace our steps of the morning.

Once we were over the Bridge I knew then that we did not have far to go. Here, the various bands had been waiting to escort everyone home and they fell in at intervals between the marchers and played the rest of the way into the town. A Dutch Band dropped into a space about four teams ahead of us and soon we were marching briskly to the stirring music and the cheers of the people lining the route. Our first day of marching was over – our earlier troubles behind us now.

My legs felt like lead and my face was on fire, but all this was soon forgotten as I held my chin up and marched smartly behind the band, the traffic having been diverted away from the March route. We strode down the main street and in no time at all we were back in the market square where we had begun earlier that morning.

"RAF Germany – Halt!"

I fell against the railings that divided up the various starting sections and felt my legs immediately stiffen as Flight Lieutenant Curry had our 'checking in' card punched to say that we had completed the first day with our team intact. Laney pulled off her shoe and you could see the blood oozing through the plaster.

"This is stinging now," she cried. "I'm going to walk back without my shoe on and get it seen to before I do anything else."

"Ooh!" I grinned. "Good job old Payne isn't here, she would ask you if you were on your holidays at Margate."

"Stuff Payne!" said Laney as she clutched her shoe.

We stood for a while and cheered the other marchers as they came in behind us, and to our surprise these included the Israelis.

"Crikey!" I exclaimed. "I expected them to have been in long ago, they are behind us despite that stop we had!"

"Not really," said the officer patiently. "They started *after* you this morning."

"Oh!" I grunted, knocked down in flames. I watched them in admiration as they marched in. They were so smart in their cream uniforms and looked so proud of themselves.

They halted in front of us and waved politely and were immediately taken away in a bus. The girls were not in the school with us and the boys were not at the tented camp. Rumour had it that they were staying in a posh hotel with proper showers.

The Israelis.

The team from RAF Wildenrath arrived in and rushed up to us, patting us on the back and congratulated us for completing the first day of the March.

"Hang on," I laughed. "We have three more days to go yet!"

"I don't care," said a freckle-faced, ginger-haired boy, "we nearly died laughing back at camp when we found out that Headquarters team had girls in it – bloody poofters!"

He ducked the mock punch that came from Mac.

"I take it back, I take it back!" he laughed. "You did great – all of you!"

"Yah boo, so there!" chuckled Sandy. "We will show you!" She even managed to give them a sexy wiggle before hobbling off down the road, carrying her shoes.

"I think they are just bloody jealous," said Fred, as he watched Sandy disappear.

"Come on," said Laney, "let's catch her up. It's funny, but I just fancy one of those 'hundreds and thousands' sandwiches now."

We hobbled stiffly down the back roads to the school while the boys climbed aboard their bus to the tented camp. As we strolled along, crowds of people congratulated us and joked as they pointed to our feet and patted us on our backs. One or two held three fingers up on one hand and a thumb down on the other to indicate 'three days to go' – as if we needed telling!

We girls were the centre of attention. We tried to overlook the fact that the men did have packs on their backs and rifles to carry, but Cathy, particularly, was quite a little girl, and some of the men in the team were six feet tall. In order to keep in step the girls had to lengthen their stride quite considerably.

When we arrived at the school we found that the Captain had already arranged for a coach to take us to the showers at the nearby Army Barracks. With much difficulty I walked up the stairs to fetch my washing things and then back again to board the bus, while Laney stayed behind to get her blister fixed in one of the classrooms that had been set aside for the 'blister parade'.

The Army Camp was just on the outside of the town. Most of the soldiers were either in, or involved in, the organisation of the Marches and so the barracks were almost deserted when we arrived. We piled out of the coach and grinned inanely at a soldier who was 'guarding' the bathrooms. We had no idea what to expect and it was just as well. We were certainly not prepared for the sights that met our eyes. The Scandinavian girls were already in the showers and had absolutely no modesty at all!

We were very particular when we got undressed, and even in the WRAF Block we all took care to get undressed with a bit of decorum – at least turning our backs to anyone else in the room when taking our bras off, and taking our knickers down underneath our skirts! We must have been quite prudish really and the foreigners found us very quaint.

"My God!" I whispered, as a stark-naked girl walked past me, swinging a sponge bag.

"They don't care do they?" chuckled Sandy, who despite her perfect figure was swathed in a very large bath towel.

They made no attempt to put anything round themselves at all and there were all shapes, sizes and ages here, completely unabashed.

As Jean and I began to undress, pulling bras down sleeves, and knickers underneath skirts with extreme modesty, three Danish girls, as naked as nature intended, strolled up to us and, making no attempt to cover up, started to talk about the day's events. We didn't know where to look. We smiled politely and then I gathered the folds of my housecoat around me and ran for the showers, which at least were individual ones. I stripped off inside the little cubicle and slung my housecoat over the door, only succeeding in getting it soaking wet when I turned the shower on.

By the time we had been in Nijmegen another 24 hours we had got used to the uninhibited Scandinavians and were soon stripping off in the communal dressing room along with them. Perhaps not with *quite* such abandon as they did, but, nevertheless 'needs must when a shower awaits' and we did not have the luxury of a hotel like the Israelis.

"And so ends the first day!" said Val. We were sipping salted tea back in the school hall. "I bet we will not be this bright and breezy when it is all over though."

"I think it is all smashing!" I replied. "I'm glad I'm having a go."

"Well, let's make the most of it then," said Val. "I vote we go for a slap-up meal and have a good time just in case we are not in a fit state tomorrow."

"OK, but I am not wearing my beetle crushers," I replied. "I'm wearing my plimsolls."

"Me too," said Laney. "I don't think I will ever get a pair of beetle crushers on again. Gawd knows what I shall do in the morning."

"We'll think about that tomorrow."

"And the condemned man ate a hearty supper..." sighed Sandy, as she brushed her black hair and pinned it up under her WRAF hat. It seemed to defy the laws of gravity. She gave one of her wiggles and we followed her out of the door.

Within five minutes we were walking down the road, wearing a motley array of shoes with our uniforms and again receiving warm good wishes from everyone we met. The large open-air dance – or 'Blister Ball', as it was known – in the centre of the town near the Yellow Umbrellas, seemed wilder than ever, and despite our aching feet we were soon jiving and twisting in the main road in front of the Town Hall with its quaint red shutters.

There was every form of music imaginable. One minute it was a little local group playing what we called 'oomp-pa-pa' music, then it might be a couple of blokes from the Laarbruch Pipe Band with their bagpipes, or even a traditional Dutch organ. I swore I could jive to the alphabet if I had to and I set out to prove it.

However, we knew that we had an early start in the morning and so, following the instructions of our Flight Lieutenant, we left the Yellow Umbrellas and went for a good meal of mushroom omelette and chips in a little café nearby. The meal and the steaming black coffee that followed was like nectar from heaven – and we didn't even have to pay for it! One look at our uniforms and it was 'on the house', though we insisted on paying for our drinks. Whatever our forefathers did for this area, the residents were very grateful and showed it constantly.

We were in bed by 9pm and, although it was early, it didn't seem like it. Most people finished the day's marching by mid afternoon and went straight out around the town, so really 9pm was like midnight anywhere else. It certainly felt like midnight as I lay my head on my pillow.

"Everybody happy?" yelled Jean, as she turned the lights out.

"Yes we are!" we all answered back.

"How are the blisters Laney?" said Val.

"Beautiful!" answered Laney.

"I wonder," I yawned, as I snuggled down in my bed, "if it will be as hot tomorrow as it was today?

"Goodnight Jean!"

"Goodnight Ratty!"

"Night Cathy!"

"Go to sleep you lot!" yawned Sandy.

My last thought as I dropped off to sleep was the hope that I would not fall off that top bunk.

Wednesday, 5.30am. It was still quite dark when we walked down the road the following morning, but even in the early dawn the bands were playing and there were people out lining the streets.

"Nobody should be up at this time!" muttered Val. "It's not decent."

"The last time I was up at this time was in Recruit Training at Wilmslow!" I replied. I grimaced as I remembered Corporal Payne yelling, "Line up for breakfast – last one out of the billet is on a charge!" and us all falling over each other as we rushed so as not to be the last one. It seemed like a million years ago.

The boys were waiting for us in the usual place and soon we were on our way again, this time marching away from the river and towards the south. As we drew away from the still lighted streets we could only distinguish the team immediately in front of us, who were a NATO team that had travelled up from France. However, the familiar sound of 'Do You Ever Get One Of Those Days' meant that the Americans were somewhere up ahead and following behind us was one of the huge Swiss teams.

We continued marching along, singing our songs and clapping our hands, pushing more and more miles behind us as a pink and orange dawn started to light the way.

By the time we reached the first rest point it was daylight and I was glad to sit down on the grass with my feet propped up on one of the boys 'packs', which they were all equally glad to discard.

Even at this unearthly hour, the field was crowded with the Military and the nurses tripped in and out of the prostrate bodies with increased efficiency. The civilians in the march had their own rest points elsewhere, and we had yet to see them this morning.

"Ten minutes only!" cried Flight Lieutenant Curry.

It was barely enough time to catch our breath but it was silly to sit around for too long. We were forming a special relationship with our officer and we trusted him. Until now he had been 'the boss' and strictly adhered to the correctness of calling us all by our surnames or 'airwoman'. We, of course, automatically called him 'Sir' and always would do so, but gradually the gap between our worlds was narrowing and although he would always have our undying respect he quite often called us by our Christian names and became our friend. The boys, who shared the same accommodation with him at the tented camp, were like buddies, but not for one minute forgetting that he was our team leader and knowing that when we got back to camp we would have to go back to the old formalities and traditions.

"Well, come on you shower," he called, after our ten minutes was up, "let's get moving – shift yourselves!"

We wearily pulled ourselves to our feet and started off again down the road.

"Don't worry," he grinned, "there are another two Rest Points today, only eight miles to the next one."

A groan went up all around but we continued marching and singing at the tops of our voices. Many teams passed us and joked and patted us on the backs and many times we overtook these same teams further up the road, as they rested or had slackened their pace.

The sun grew hotter and hotter and it promised to be a real scorcher today. I was grateful that we had been able to start out early. We continued in our 40km circle in the direction of Wijchen, with the 50km marchers now branching off to do their larger circle, which would bring them back to us later in the day and further along the route. If we were bonkers then we thought they were even more bonkers!

On and on we plodded, heavier and heavier became my feet and redder and redder became my face. The road seemed never ending and, despite the cheers of onlookers, I felt that I would be spending the rest of my life on my feet.

As we walked along the top of the dyke, in the distance I could see the marchers out ahead and the horizon looked as though it was hundreds of miles away. I felt water splash against my face as Jamey unceasingly went back and forth with the bottles, but no sooner had my shirt been soaked than it dried out and then became damp with sweat.

Perhaps if I looked at the ground the miles would slip away quicker, but when I looked up the marchers far ahead on the horizon still appeared as though they were in the same place. However, gradually, oh so gradually, the clump of trees in the distance became nearer and finally, just beyond them, we could make out the familiar red crosses on the tents at the next Rest Point.

There was a huge cheer as we finally turned left and marched straight up to the tent where the tea urns were and flopped down on the grass. We drank the salted tea, but not as much as I would have liked because I was determined not to use those make-shift loos provided at the far end of the field.

There were film cameras here, from Pathe News, and I wondered if I might see myself one day at the cinema. There were also RAF photographers taking pictures for the Air Force News and for our local papers back home. But I did not get up and the photographers had to step over me to get the shots they wanted.

We didn't stay for long and were soon on our way again, accompanied by cheers from the inert bodies which came to life as we formed up in threes and marched off. We were fast becoming as well known and recognisable as the Israelis.

"Hooray, hooray! Keep going Headquarters!" they all yelled.

"Bloody old Headquarters poofters!" yelled somebody else, but only in fun.

We marched from the field and out onto the road again for the last lap of the second day, and once again all the Marchers were together, forming one continual river of colour and laughter and singing.

Surely the road must come to an end sometime, I thought, as the sun burned into my neck and the sweat ran down my shirt.

We came to an extra large crowd of onlookers and half a dozen young girls in Dutch National Costume ran into the road and sprayed us all with Eau de Cologne. This was wonderful and freshened us up no end, but it caused much laughter as the boys tried to duck from what they considered to be 'poofy stuff'. It was bad enough *marching* with girls but to have poofy perfume sprayed at them was the last straw. One or two of the Dutch girls even tried to steal a kiss from the Flight Lieutenant, much to his embarrassment and our amusement. He was marching at the side of us and very vulnerable to the attentions of the Cologne-squirting young ladies.

As the crowds increased, so the sides of the road became more and more festooned with popcorn stalls, ice-cream vans and programme sellers. Occasionally a van would weave precariously along the side of the road with a cameraman on the top, taking pictures. These and the official cars were the only vehicles allowed on the roads at this time and there were traffic detours everywhere.

"Oh, what wouldn't I give for an ice-cream!" sighed Val.

But we just had to look longingly while others enjoyed their ice cream cornets and plod on. The only thing we were allowed to touch were the paper cups of soup and Bovril that were thrust into our hands as we passed by, with someone further down the road holding out huge baskets for us to throw the empty cups into so that we did not have to break our march pace and to avoid any litter. They had thought of everything! That was one thing you did not see on these roads anywhere, despite the amount of people – litter! People did not drop rubbish at all and, despite the thousands of marchers and spectators, Nijmegen was as clean as a new pin.

Onwards and onwards we trudged, passing by the 'repair while you wait' shoe stalls and singing, always singing. We were told later that it was us girls that kept the boys going with our songs. When we ran out of popular songs we sang hymns. 'Onward Christian Soldiers' was one with a good marching beat and we sang that over and over again. 'We Plough the Fields and Scatter' was another, and on and on down this never-ending roads we slogged, changing the words to "We March the Roads and Chatter!"

Perhaps if I stared at the road and not ahead, the time would go quicker, but no such luck. I'd tried that before and it hadn't worked then – and it still didn't! We trudged on, ever onward. Oh, that I could sit down, just to sit down!

In front of us a huge Dutch Army team were singing loudly 'A Long Way to Tipperary' in their own language. We joined in with them in ours and on and on we trudged. Would this day never bloody end?

I looked at my watch, my new watch that only three weeks ago my Dad had bought me for my 21st birthday and I was so proud of. It was now thoroughly embedded in my wrist. It was twelve noon – was that all? I felt as though I had marched across Africa. *Just please let me sit down. All I want to do is to sit down.* Laney started clapping her hands above her head to get the blood circulating and ease the swelling. Soon the rest of the girls followed suit and we continued to march, looking as though we were doing 'morning exercises'.

Although there were no civilian cars about and no visible means of transport, there were still groups of people along the roadside. They must have walked from the villages to see the marching. You could tell when you were getting nearer to a town as the people became more numerous.

"Stop singing!" cried Jock. "Listen... I am sure I can hear a band!"

"He's hearing things now," whispered Mac, as he wiped the perspiration from his brow and put his rifle over his other arm for a change.

"Shut up and listen," said Sandy.

"It is, it *is* a band!" shouted Laney.

"It is, it *is!*" squealed Val.

Sure enough, in the distance, we could hear the faint strains of martial music and, as we marched on, the sound became louder and the crowds of people increased even more.

They were tickled pink at our new form of exercising to the beat of our songs. Soon we were to perfect it and it became almost compulsory as we marched through built up areas. We were becoming right show-offs as we spread out across the width of the street to make room for our outstretched arms. The crowd loved us and we loved them for spurring us on.

Then, as the road curved, we could see Nijmegen Bridge in the distance, and we fixed our eyes on it as our goal for the day.

"Not far now!" said Jock, stating the obvious.

My feet felt as though something had been dropped on them, but as the sound of the band became louder, so our steps quickened and it wasn't long before we were entering the town.

And there, waiting for us, in a side-street, obviously forewarned by Jamey that we were on our way, were the Royal Air Force Laarbruch Pipe Band! How we cheered when we saw them. We squealed at them and waved madly as the other band we had heard earlier marched on, gradually going out of earshot.

That glorious, wonderful RAF Laarbruch band. They were wearing their full ceremonial uniform with their special RAF tartan kilts and their Air Force blue fitted waistcoats and their specially-designed black forage caps with red ribbons down the back and the RAF badge on the side. They looked magnificent as they ran out from the side street and formed up in front of us.

There was a thump on the bass drum and a few sounds from the pipes and then they launched straight into 'Scotland the Brave'. We did not need to exercise our arms any more. Automatically they went up to shoulder height as we spread out right across the road again, a double arm width apart, and we gave it 'all the wellie' we could muster. My feet felt lighter and once again the aches and pains were forgotten as the adrenalin took over and shoulders went back, chins up and heads were held high.

Flight Lieutenant Curry took his official place at the front of us and proudly led his team back through the town at the end of the second day to the skirl of the pipes and the beat of the drum. We were marching as if we had just set out on a Queens Birthday Parade, or showing off to the public at the Royal Tournament.

It wouldn't have done for anyone to stand too near me though, because my shirt was steaming in the heat, but I didn't care, we were half way. We had marched fifty miles in step all the way with the boys. There was no turning back now. We would complete the hundred and get our medals, including the team one. The WRAFs would never, ever 'bring up the rear' again. They were part and parcel of the complete team.

I saw the familiar iron railings ahead. The official punched the team ticket, gave a quick count to make sure we were all present and correct and informed Flight Lieutenant Curry what time we had to be there in the morning.

Without even waiting for the command of 'halt' I leaned gratefully against the railings, not caring about the crowds all around me and the other teams finishing. All I wanted was water and a good pee without having to do it down a dug out hole, and not necessarily in that order!

"Six-thirty start tomorrow," said our Flight Lieutenant cheerfully.

There was a groan all round as he ushered the boys back to one of the fleet of coaches that were doing the round trip to Heumensoord and we began the short walk back to the school. I had taken my shoes off while he had been talking and quite happily went down the road in my ankle socks at the end of the second day.

"Well, well, well," beamed the Dutch Captain as we arrived at our lodgings and I sank down on the school steps leading up to the front door. "So die Englander haf completed de second day!" The expression on her face changed and she said kindly, "You must rest. It will be hard work tomorrow. The weather forecast is not good, I'm afraid."

"Charming," muttered Jean, as I stood up again and dragged myself into the school. "That's a good omen, I must say!"

"Everyone says the third day is the worst," I said, as I heaved myself up onto my bed. "We have to cross the 'Seven Sisters', which I believe are rather large hills."

"Oh no!" wailed Laney, checking her still very sore heel. "I don't want to know!"

I bathed my poor, aching feet and discovered that I had acquired a couple of small blisters also.

"Oh bugger!" I swore, "now I shall have to go on blister parade too."

I hobbled downstairs in my socks and joined the long queue of girls waiting to have their feet seen to. The queue stretched down the corridor and into a classroom, where two doctors and three nurses were working busily on the feet constantly put in front of them.

"*What a job!*" I thought.

I leaned wearily against the cool wall and began talking to a group of Danish Army girls who were in front of me.

"How did the English get on today then," said one of the girls as she gently removed her shoe and sock. "It was warm was it not?"

"It was warm all right," I agreed, "but we all got back in one piece. How did you get on?"

"Not too bad, but we have one girl out of the march and many men."

"Oh that's a shame!" I said, and then, just for something to say, "I wonder if it will hurt when they treat our blisters?"

She laughed wickedly, as if I had said something very silly, which of course I had!

"What do they do?" I asked in alarm.

"Well, they break open the blister and pour in iodine," said my sadistic Danish acquaintance.

"Good grief!" I cried. "I don't think I'll bother."

"You had better," she replied. "It is good – honestly."

The queue got smaller and I could hear yells coming from the small classroom and my hands trembled as I saw girls tearfully leaving the 'makeshift surgery' after the treatment. It sounded like a torture chamber and didn't look at all 'good' to me! Still, Laney had been alright in the end, so I had no choice.

"Oh it will be OK," said a Dutch girl just behind me. "Just hold onto the couch and it will be over in a minute."

I gritted my teeth and waited for my turn to come, but I didn't have to wait long. I entered the classroom to find that it had been supplied with five doctors' couches. Four of these were occupied with women having their feet seen to, all of them screwing their eyes up in pain. It was like a conveyer belt. I gingerly made my way to the fifth couch and lay face downwards on it with my bare feet dangling over the edge. My only consolation was that the bloke that was about to torture me was very good looking indeed.

"Don't worry," he said kindly, "you will finish the March."

If he had told me that Elvis was in the next room I would have believed him! I pressed the side of my face to the couch and held on tightly to the sides. I could feel the gentle hands of the doctor lifting my feet and 'closed my eyes and thought of England' in anticipation of the pain that was to come.

When it came it felt as though my feet had been sawn off. The pain seemed to run up my legs, along my back and into my brain, leaving me completely breathless. Did I scream? I don't know, but somebody took hold of my arm and gently pulled me off the couch. I looked down to see my heels completely encased in tape and the initial pain slowly ebbed away. That was it – done!

"Next please!" called the doctor.

"Bloody hell!" I gasped.

"Off you go," he smiled, ignoring my language.

I thanked him, though goodness knows what for, and dragged myself back up the stairs, using both hands on the banister rail. I felt as though I could not walk another yard, never mind another fifty miles.

"Bloody hell!" I exclaimed again, as I sank onto a bottom bunk.

"Works though, doesn't it!" laughed Laney.

"I dunno," I gasped. "I'll let you know when I come down from the ceiling."

"Well, we have only got another fifty miles to do," said Val.

The pillow I managed to throw at her just missed.

Actually, the treatment the doctor had given me was very effective, for within half an hour I could walk quite well, although I did not attempt to put my beetle crushers back on. Fired with a new enthusiasm, I dressed in a clean skirt and WRAF blouse and, together with Laney and Val, strolled down to the main part of the town. The place was crowded as usual and hundreds of marchers were lounging outside the cafés.

We found our boys, eventually, under the Yellow Umbrellas in the town square and they were already entering into the spirit of things, although on the instructions of our Flight Lieutenant, they were keeping the drink to an absolute minimum... or so they said!

Nearby, a large street organ was playing merrily. Adding to the general cacophony were some of the boys from the Pipe Band giving a tune on their bagpipes. Although it was still only early evening, the atmosphere was electric. I sat down beside Mac, Jock, Steve and John, gingerly holding onto my aching back as I did so.

"Hi girls," laughed Jock, who had now got over the embarrassment of having women in his team. "We know how you feel!"

"I bet you don't!" I grimaced, as I gently lowered myself into the chair.

"Come on," said John, "have a beer."

I truly could not have drunk a beer for a pension just then and so I ordered an orange juice from the waiter, who had been hovering close by. In no time at all he was back and put our drinks in front of us, refusing point blank to take any money.

"No, no," he smiled, "it's from over there." He nodded in the direction of one of the locals who had treated us and was grinning and pointing to our feet." The language of 'sore feet' was international. We took the offered drinks gratefully and shouted our thanks, much to the amusement of the boys.

"It's all right for you lot," said Mac. "At least you don't have to carry anything!"

"Tell you what," said Laney, with bravado. "I'll carry your rifle for you tomorrow!"

"Careful," I said. "Don't forget it's the third day tomorrow."

"I don't need reminding," she replied. "I just hope I'll make it!"

"You'll make it," said John, "or you'll get my rifle up your backside!"

We laughed and left the boys to their beer and strolled off back to the school for a good night's sleep. We slowly walked up the steps into the entrance of the school and peeped into the Head Teacher's office that the Captain and her staff were occupying.

"Come in, come in," she cried when she saw us. "We have just been watching you on television – look!"

The News was on showing various aspects of the day's marching. It seemed odd to see it on the television here in Holland and knowing that it would be impossible to see it in England.

"We just saw you at the Tattoo," whispered one of the nurses. "There you are again, see!"

Sure enough, there we were, in black and white, marching smartly behind the Laarbruch Pipe Band. We couldn't understand the commentary but it was enough just to see it.

"Oh don't we look funny!" laughed Val. "Oh look, there's you, and there's Mac, and there's Jock and Steve and Sandy, and oh – there's Jamey on his bike."

Soon the snippet of film was finished and we were watching the rest of the news, which included a story about the launch of 'Telstar' so that pictures could be beamed across the Atlantic. Just a few pictures beamed across the Channel would have done me!

"Good luck tomorrow," cried the Captain after us, as we left to go to our classroom.

"Thank you!" we called back, as we crept up the stairs like little old ladies.

"I don't want to be a pessimist," muttered Cathy, "but they have forecast rain for tomorrow."

"Oh shut up Cathy!" cried Jean. "It won't rain."

"Well it's written up on the blackboard downstairs," Cathy persisted.

This was true and it was with some trepidation that I climbed up onto the top bunk and snuggled down into the little hard bed that night. I wondered if I would sleep, but obviously I did, for the next thing I knew the bell was waking us up again...

10. *The Nijmegen March: Days 3 and 4*

Thursday 5.30am. I woke with a start to the sound of the school bell and realised as I lay in my bed that it really was the morning of the third day. I opened one eye and looked at my watch and I opened the other and caught sight of Laney, who was staring out of the window; she had already got her shoes and socks on, although she was still in her pyjamas.

"Morning Laney," I yawned.

Laney answered with three words that none of us really wanted to hear.

"Looks like rain," she said simply.

We all sat bolt upright in bed and looked at her in horror.

"Oh gawd!" I exclaimed.

"Sorry to break it to you," said Laney, "but at least it is not raining now – the sky is full of it though."

The hot sun was bad enough, but with the rain you get swollen feet, tight shoes, and sodden skirts flapping against bare legs, making them red raw. That was something the boys did not have to put up with, and we had no wet-weather gear as yet. It had been hard enough just to get the uniform organised and we certainly did not want to march in WRAF raincoats. We had already decided in advance that it was the lesser of two evils to simply get wet.

I climbed down from the bunk and straightened up but my back was so stiff I could barely bend down to put my shoes and socks on.

"My god, I feel about ninety!" I gasped.

"We must all be mad!" said Jean. "Completely crackers."

When we went down to breakfast we could tell from the gloomy faces of the other girls that Laney had been right. Rain had been forecast and everyone knew that this would be a day to remember.

The sky was grey and leaden as we hobbled down the road to the starting place and met the boys. The stands all around were already filled with people, all of them fully prepared with umbrellas and raincoats – but we couldn't carry such things with uniform. It wouldn't look right. It was probably just as well that we didn't have any wet weather gear, for it would only have been cumbersome.

Even as Flight Lieutenant Curry arrived and we formed up in our threes, the stiffness was still with me – I could barely move – but I could see that I was not alone.

The band was playing a slow march this morning and as we got the order to move off, everyone sang the same song in unison, language being no barrier, as they trudged along with their feet at the 'ten to three' position.

"Ooch-ouch, ooch-ouch," we all grunted. "Ah-oh, ah-oh, ah-oh..."

Gradually, oh so very gradually, the stiffness began to wear off and we were almost at proper marching pace again. We were off, towards the little village of Malden, with a very grey and watery dawn rising over the cornfields.

This time the route took us down the bank and along the towpath until we found ourselves being taken off into the open countryside again. We took up a steady pace behind a large Canadian Air Force team, many of them carrying their red and white flag with the red maple leaf upon it and other Canadians in camouflage, all with packs and rifles. The bands left us here and made their way back to town, while we went on our way and our singing had to take over, much to the amusement of our 'Commonwealth cousins.'

"Rain, rain, go away, come again another day," we chanted. The same chant over and over again to the beat of our feet. The Canadians must have thought we were totally barmy but they still joined in.

As the stiffness in our muscles began to wear away the sky got darker and the wind grew stronger. By now we were in flat, open countryside, going along the tops of dykes, with the canal on our right, and no shelter at all. The wind whipped our bare legs and tore through our skirts. How could it be like this in July?

Our fervent prayers were answered for a while, for we reached the first Rest Point and the rain was not forthcoming, although the sky was still very overcast. I felt a little more elated as the cheers from the soldiers already in the huge field greeted us and the Canadians went off to their own corner.

"Come on girls!" they yelled, forgetting the poor boys in the team, but by now they were used to it and in any case the main object of attention was Sandy. The rest of us were under no illusions. Even on this third day she somehow managed to look like she had just stepped off a catwalk. The news had travelled that Sandy was our secret weapon! That we put her out in front so that the rest of the team could watch her bottom wiggling to give them the incentive to go on. But it was all in good fun and she played up to it with enthusiasm.

I fell down on the floor just inside one of the marquees and left myself to the mercy of the nurses who hovered around. One laid a cup of cold tea at my elbow while another descended upon my legs and massaged them for all she was worth. However, we had hardly been there five minutes when our officer was hurrying us up.

"Come on!" he yelled. "You've rested long enough – let's get as far as we can before it rains."

"He's just a bloody sadist!" cried Frank, as he reluctantly pulled himself up.

"Oh good grief – what am I doing here?" I thought.

We struggled to our feet and very, very stiffly marched out of the Rest Point to still more cheers and good wishes from the soldiers and airmen. Our limbs had turned to concrete and so that other familiar tune had to start again.

"Ooch-ouch, ooch-ouch, ah-um, ah-um," we yelled until we began to loosen up yet again. The boys started their own version...

"Damn and blast, damn and blast."

A few of them would have used worse words, but they were aware of ladies and an officer present and most were polite in 1962.

"Look at those lucky buggers!" moaned Jock, as the 30km marchers started to peel away to the left. They had done their bit and now could take their 'short cut' to the village of Groesbeek. We had more to do yet...

The ribbon of marchers stretched out in front of us as we continued along the top of the dyke towards Plasmolen and then, quite suddenly, the heavens opened and the rain that had been threatening all morning, fell down. It fell in a sheet all around us and in seconds we were soaked to the skin.

"It's raining!" said John stupidly. I could have hit him!

"That," I replied cuttingly, "is the most unnecessary statement of the year!"

We could see the teams in front of us, all struggling against the strong wind and rain. Once, a first aid van passed by, all ready to pick people up who had fallen by the wayside, but on and on we plodded, our bodies bent almost double against the onslaught of the summer downpour, the boys holding their rifles and packs limply at their sides. Laney gallantly offered to carry a rifle for a while, but it wasn't long before she handed it back!

I found it difficult to keep upright against the terrific wind that roared across the dyke but there was no point in stopping, for there wasn't any shelter.

With our efforts against the elements we were too exhausted to talk or sing, so we plodded on, heads down, just following the feet of the person in front and grunting. Once we made a feeble effort to raise our spirits by linking arms and singing 'Well Didn't It Rain Noah?' followed by 'The Day The Rains Came Down' but neither were good marching tunes, so we left it and thought of something else with more beat.

Then the red arrow on the wooden board at the side of the road indicated that the Military 50km marchers had a bit further to go, a five-mile loop that would eventually bring them back to join us further down the road. They were welcome!

I learned later that many of the marchers doing the longer distance were actually foreign National Servicemen, using it as part of their training. I still thought they were daft though, even if they didn't have a lot of choice!

Onward, ever onward, we trudged. The weight of the wet hems in the girls' skirts acted like a whip against our legs and soon all of us had the backs of our legs lashed and bleeding.

The Israelis knew what they were doing, for their skirts were about three inches shorter than ours and it made such a difference to them.

It was Sandy who took the first initiative and rolled her skirt up around her waist so that it was about three inches above her knee and hid the folds of cloth round her waist with her belt. Well it would be Sandy, wouldn't it? She didn't know it, but she had just invented the 'mini skirt'. It certainly put a spring in the boys' steps as we all followed her lead and did the same, some of us achieving the desired effect better than others. Corporal Payne would have had a fit!

With new fervour we launched into our rendering of Johnny Ray's hit of a few years ago:

Just walking in the rain,
Getting soaking wet,
Torturing my heart
Just trying to forget...

My legs were going backwards and forwards automatically and I am sure that I was barely conscious of anything for most of the time. Surely this couldn't be me out there in the rain-lashed countryside of Holland? I must be mad.

"I'll ride on and see where the second rest point is," volunteered Jamey, bravely.

He battled to get on his bike and pushed off against the wind down the road ahead. I almost expected him to take-off like the wicked witch in *The Wizard of Oz*! He was away for ages, but when he finally returned it was to tell us that the rest point was still some way ahead and it was also getting very hilly. He rubbed his sore bum and decided to walk with us for a while.

Just the very idea that we were over half way was enough to make us stride out with renewed vigour. Soon the miles disappeared and our voices took on new volume when we saw the familiar marquees with their red crosses looming up out of the rain. We were always determined to go into the Rest Points with heads high and arms swinging, or doing our arm exercises. 'Showing-off' most people would call it!

"Royal Air Force Germany – Halt!"

I hobbled as far as the entrance to one of the tents and fell, exhausted, onto one of the scores of camp beds. My feet felt as though they were bursting through my shoes, the backs of my legs were all bloody where the hem of my wet skirt had been beating against them before we had hitched them up, and my hands were swollen. Flight Lieutenant Curry came and poked his head through the flap of the tent.

"Make the most of this Rest Point," he said. "We've got the seven hills ahead!"

"Oh hell!" grimaced Val, as she tried to wipe the blood away from the back of her legs. "I'd forgotten about that!"

A nurse crept up to the side of the camp bed that I had collapsed on and passed me a cup of the dreaded salted tea. My legs were killing me and I knew I had cramp. I felt as though hot irons were being drawn through me and I was grateful when another nurse started to massage my aching muscles again. I could not believe I was doing this. What had possessed me? Me! Who had avoided any sort of sport all my life. It seemed as though we had hardly arrived before it was time to leave again and Flight Lieutenant Curry was hobbling around the camp beds telling us to get on our feet. He wasn't exactly in first-class condition himself and neither was the sergeant who would have to take over from him if he fell out, though the likelihood of that happening was zero. With some difficulty we got into line and amid the cheers from all the other marchers we were ready to go again.

"By the left – quick march!" sang out the officer.

We fell in behind the Irish Guards and our spirits rose again as they laughed and joked with us. The rain had started to ease off and now the sun was beginning to dry our clothes.

Within a few minutes we came to a road junction and those doing the 30km, those under sixteen or over sixty-five, filtered in from our left. They turned left and joined the rest of us for the start of the seven hills.

We marked time ourselves to allow one or two of the teams to filter through in front of us and we knew that, behind us, other teams would do the same, until everyone was in procession together. They marched in threes, just the same as us, civilians as well as youth organisations and elderly 'old soldiers'. They didn't have to, but many preferred to. There were nurses, there were teams from various civilian organisations, the Scouts, Judo Clubs, St John's Ambulance, or just simply groups of people of twelve or more making up their own team, and everybody in step with those in the front. Individual marchers kept to one side to allow teams to pass them or occasionally a couple of marchers would overtake us, striding out but never running.

All the military personnel cheered and waved as we met up at the road junction and all the civilians waved back. Everyone was so friendly, even though most of us couldn't understand each other's language.

Perhaps it was at this moment that everything clicked into place for me about the Marches. I'd got plenty of aches and pains and blisters, but how privileged I was to be taking part in this annual event. I could understand why the Dutch were so particular about all the rules regarding the March and why it was so orderly. They didn't want it cheapened in any way by advertising or being used as a political platform. The March was much too dignified for that. There were thousands of foreigners here and every one of them was taking part in something that had started off as a sport for the Dutch but had quickly become an act of remembrance for some, especially today for the Canadians as they marched past their own War Graves just outside Groesbeek.

Here the singing stopped, as everyone, whatever nationality, reverently marched in silence until we were a respectable distance away. For five minutes or so only the thump, thump of marching feet could be heard.

I, momentarily at least, turned from teenager to adult as I told myself that I would be back to visit the British Graves at Oosterbeek one day. Then I was brought back to the present as Jamey came puffing up on his bike.

"Guess what?" he announced cheerily. "It's the Road of the Seven Hills just up there."

We all groaned together.

"Its all right for you!" wailed Jean. "You are riding a bike in comfort!"

"You're joking!" exclaimed Jamey. "I've got blisters on my arse the size of half crowns!"

All along the roadside we passed military and civilian people who had stopped for a short breather or who had dropped out. We saw the team from the Air Ministry sitting down at the side of the road while one of their number got his blisters treated.

"Yah boo!" yelled Paddy. "Come on you bloody old skivers, on your feet!"

"Skivers yourselves!" they laughed back. "We'll pass you further up the road, you'll see!"

Then the boys began another chant, especially for the Air Ministry NCOs, to the tune of 'Auld Lang Syne':

> *"Stand up yer bum!*
> *Stand up yer bum!*
> *Stand up yer bum or else!"*

Only at Nijmegen could they get away with such cheek!

We left the Air Ministry team amid laughter and cries of "oh my blinkin' blisters!", which they sang to the tune of the conga! We could still hear their voices in the distance when we saw the *Zevenheuvelenweg* (or Road of the Seven Hills) looming ahead.

This was a range of quite modest hills in the centre of the flat countryside but to me, on that third day of the March, they seemed no less than seven Mount Everests. When would this day ever finish?

"Right everybody, take short steps and lean forward," ordered our officer, whom we respected more and more with every minute.

We did as he bid and found that by using this method we could manage the hills and still keep in step as a team. I kept my head and eyes firmly fixed to the front as we chanted "oo-ow, oo-ow!" continuously.

"Take short steps!" shouted our officer, to the beat of our feet. "Take short steps."

"Oo-ow, oo-ow," we chanted.

When we reached the top of a hill, new muscles were put to work as we leaned back to come down the other side and the crowds of people on either side of the road egged us on by clapping and cheering. I remember somebody throwing some water over me. Just a couple of hours ago we had received more than enough water from the cloudburst that had drenched us but now I was grateful for the refreshing liquid running down my shirt. That hour was the longest hour of my life! I found myself thinking of the simple things in life – a comfortable chair to sit on, a cool bath, comfy slippers – oh yes, especially comfy slippers!

"Oo-ow, oo-ow," the incessant chant went on.

By the time we reached the top of the seventh hill, I felt all in, there was sweat in my eyes, my feet burned and the backs of my legs throbbed mercilessly.

"Listen," cried John, as we straightened up our bodies and started to take longer steps at the top of the last hill. "I can hear music."

"Balls!" panted Jock. "It's the trumpets of heaven you can hear – we are all dead!"

"No, honestly, listen!" he gasped. "I hear a band. I'm sure of it!"

I was quite convinced that Jock had been right and that it was heavenly music he was hearing and that Saint Peter would be waiting at the door, but I listened and sure enough, in the distance, I could hear the faint sound of band music. It was like a dose of medicine to us all.

We strode out, trying hard not to think of our stiff, aching bodies and as the music got louder so our steps became lighter. We were 'marching on feathers' as our hosts eloquently put it. Soon the crowds along the side of the road increased. Everyone was clamouring to see if their favourite team was complete after all the rain and the *Zevenheuvelenweg*.

"Bloody sadistic lot!" grinned John.

We could see them counting the people in our team and then a cheer went out as they realised that there were still the right amount! The cheers grew in volume and little children rushed out into the road and grabbed us by the hands and ran along with us until they had run so far away from their parents that they began to look alarmed, and with a cheery wave we pushed them off back to their mums and dads.

We automatically put ourselves into 'open order' so that a rank of three stretched the full width of the main road again, with Flight Lieutenant Curry marching down the centre white lines in the middle! There would be no traffic down this road today save for the marchers!

The end of the third day was near. I looked across at the rest of the team, who were all wearing cheesy grins, and laughed out loud. It was as if we had all been sprinkled with magic dust!

"We've made it again John," I laughed.

"We certainly have," he replied, as he picked up yet another child and marched along for some distance with the little girl in his arms, despite the fact that he was carrying a pack and rifle. Steve, next to him, did the same, and then they ran back, ignoring their aching legs, to deposit the children with their mothers. It was reminiscent of films I had seen of the liberation.

We marched down the main road with a German band falling in with our step and playing loudly in front of us. Possibly an odd sight to the older ones in the crowd, but nevertheless appreciated – they were a good band.

A cameraman was perched precariously on the balcony of a house, recording our passing for Dutch television, while some other bright spark lay in the road to film our feet! All the time the citizens cheered and waved and danced in the road. I turned my head to see what was going on behind me and saw that the team of Canadians had fallen into step with us, and behind them, I caught a glimpse of a civilian team of girls in pretty green summer skirts and white blouses. In front of the band was a German team and I guessed that further up the road there was the Army, for I could just glimpse the brown colour of their uniforms in between the grey of the Germans. The cheering rang in my ears and the pain in my feet was almost forgotten as I strode out with our goal, those railings at the finish, in sight.

The cheers grew even louder and police tried hard to keep the people back as we turned round a bend in the road and there was the Dutch official rushing out to count us and make sure our team was complete.

"RAF Germany – Halt!"

The cheering and clapping went on as more teams followed in behind us, but I just sat down, I sat down there and then on the stony ground with the people chattering and standing all around me and the sounds of the congratulations, music and cheers everywhere.

Laney and Cathy fell down exhausted beside me and then all three of us lay flat on our backs in the dirt in the middle of the Market Square, totally unable to move for the minute.

Two strong Dutch medics pulled me to my feet, probably saving me from being trampled on, as I came back to reality and opened my eyes again. The bus had been driven right up to the place where we had lain down, parting the crowd, who were still dancing and waving at the marchers, and it formed a wall for the Air Ministry team to lean on as they finished just behind us. The medics virtually lifted me onto it and pushed me into the nearest seat. I lowered myself down and leaned my sweating face against the cool window. Around me I could hear the sudden bursts of applause as each team rounded the corner.

The vehicle slowly moved through the throng of people and then onward, to take the boys back to the tented camp at Heumensoord before taking us to the school. This time we were not going to have to walk back, we had a lift, albeit the long way round via the boys lodgings!

This was the first I had seen of Heumensoord, and then it was only briefly through the windows, but it was enormous!

The brown tents that the boys were billeted in stretched, in long rows, as far as the eye could see. At the end of each row was a huge marquee with a red cross on its roof. To one side there were sections put aside for the toilets, which were dug out of the ground. We girls were infinitely better off in the school.

We must have looked a sorry sight as we arrived back at our lodgings, but then so did everyone else. Our clothes had been thoroughly washed and dried on our backs, we were bent double and could not straighten up after sitting on the bus for so long, and I could feel my feet bursting out of my shoes. All I wanted was a pee – and I wasn't the only one.

As we climbed slowly and painfully up the steps we looked at each other and erupted into hysterical and uncontrollable laughter.

"For God's sake, don't make me laugh or I'll do it in my drawers," I cried, as I crossed my legs and tried to make it to the toilet in time.

We were all in the same boat – none of us wanted to use the famous dug-out loos and it wasn't always possible to use a private house – not because we were not welcome but most of the time it just wasn't feasible. We finally made it without any 'accidents' as we all rushed to the school toilets together.

When I got back into the room I decided that I was not going to climb onto the top bunk. The desire for this novelty had gone. I lowered myself gingerly onto a spare bed and began the laborious task of pulling my shoes off. The treatment I had received at the blister parade had been successful, for I had not been troubled with those at all, but as I levered my feet out of my shoes the pain that covered my whole foot came out to reach me! I threw my 'beetle-crushers' into a corner and then sat on the bed and watched my feet swell! I could see them swelling up just as if someone was pumping air into them.

For a while we sat on the edge of our beds talking about anything but tomorrow, the last day of the March. None of us wanted to let the others know that we felt we could not march another step, never mind another twenty-five miles! We learned later that 152 people had dropped out on the third day. It was less than the 200 or so who had fallen by the wayside on the second day, so the rain had its uses after all. In fact, there was a rumour going round that two people had died on the second day in the heat. We found that very hard to believe but, in the fullness of time, we were to find out that it was true.

"I wonder what they are doing back at camp?" said Cathy.

"Jiving in the Naafi, I shouldn't wonder," I replied.

"I will never be able to jive again!" said Laney, looking ruefully at her swollen feet.

"What are you going to do when you get back to camp Ratty?" said Val.

"I am going to go to bed for a week," I grinned.

"Well…" said Jean, who was older and much more sensible, "I don't know about the rest of you, but even supposing it takes me an hour to get down those stairs, I'm going for a meal."

Exactly an hour later we had been to the showers and felt a bit better and then six 'elderly' airwomen were hobbling along the road in their socks to their favourite restaurant for their favourite Mushroom Omelette and Chips. It was a good job our lives were so active, despite my aversion to sport in all its forms, because, left to our own devices, we had chips with everything and the mushroom omelettes in Nijmegen were second to none.

As we groaned with each step we took, passers-by looked knowingly at our shoeless feet and our British uniforms and laughed. They were kind laughs though, and no language was needed. The meal did us good and, with some effort, we even made it to the Yellow Umbrellas and attempted to have a jive in our socks.

Some of the Bandsmen had brought their instruments to the square and played impromptu Rock and Roll tunes for us. We didn't care – we would have jived to the National Anthem if we could, blisters or no blisters.

We enjoyed ourselves, but we were quite glad to stroll back to the school and get ready for the morning. We were to have a 5.30 start, but all of us agreed that we would get up when we heard the early bell at 3.30am, for we were sure it would take us forever to get our shoes on!

I fell into a heavy sleep and dreamed of the Road of the Seven Hills.

Friday, 3.30am. At the sound of the first bell in the morning I opened my eyes and, after the initial surprise at finding myself still in one piece, struggled to get out of bed. My muscles had completely hardened now and I could barely lift my head from the pillow, never mind the rest of me. Only

Sandy, who, back at camp, was a very keen sportswoman, was able to get out of bed on her own, and then she assisted Laney.

The two of them endeavoured to pull the rest of us to our feet and, despite the aches and pains, it caused a great deal of laughter. We were glad we had decided to get up early.

We tried bending and touching our toes, only to find that we got stuck in that position and then had to pull ourselves back up with the help of a convenient door handle or bed post. Then we tried walking up and down the corridor outside where other girls, such as the Danish, were doing the same thing. It was a funny sight to see all them all, clad in a motley array of nightwear, creeping inch by inch up and down the corridor, many doubled over with laughter.

Then I had to try and get my shoes on.

"Ever tried to get size seven shoes onto size nine feet?" I said to Jean, as I pushed and shoved, with no success.

"Try this," she laughed, and produced a shoe-horn.

With the help of the shoe horn and a lot of struggling I managed to get my beetle crushers on, to find that I just could not walk at all.

"I would be better off without shoes!" I groaned. "At least I could get around all right then."

Sandy was in the same state as me, and the two of us hobbled painfully about the room, grimacing with each tortuous step. She could not even wiggle properly, and that, in itself, was a tragedy!

"And we still have to march another 25 miles," sighed Sandy.

"It's as much as I can do to walk to the loo!" I replied.

"Talking of which," interjected Val, "have you been to the loos at the Rest Points yet?"

"No fear!" I grinned. Most of the time we had managed to 'last out' but if push came to shove then we used one in a private house.

"I went yesterday, they are awful," she went on, "just holes in the ground, and everybody can see everybody else go!"

"That was why I was busting yesterday when we got back," I answered.

"Well I couldn't wait," said Val. "I had to go."

"Is there no privacy at all?" said Cathy.

"No," went on Val, "it's just a big box with four holes in so that four people can go at once over a pit in the ground."

"Ugh!" said Sandy, I'm glad I'm not 'on' at the moment."

I think we all said a fervent prayer to the same effect!

"Also," said Val, "the toilet paper is just like wallpaper."

Having exhausted the subject of the latrines at the Rest Points and thanking God that we were not 'on', we hobbled slowly down to breakfast.

"And the condemned man ate another hearty breakfast..." laughed Sandy, as she held a cup under the tap of the tea urn.

Girls were limping in and out of the hall all the time and those that had the bad luck to be out of the March completely still had their nightclothes on, while their feet were swathed in bandages.

Cathy ladled the usual hundreds and thousands onto her bread.

"Well," she said, "at least we are still all together."

"The Israelis haven't had anybody drop out yet either," said Laney. "They are terrific."

The Israelis were a law unto themselves though. They had brought their own medics and didn't mix with us, although they were always very friendly on the rare occasions that we saw them along the March. They were exceptionally smart in their expertly tailored uniforms and the girls in brown shiny leather boots, and all of them with smart black berets worn almost on the sides of their heads, which always seemed to be in place. They were a very 'handsome' team in every way.

We finished our breakfast and then hobbled down the steps of the school to the playground outside. Already we could hear the music and the cheering of the people, and we grunted and groaned in unison as we walked the hundred or so yards to the start.

Even more stands had been erected at the roadside, some of them being as much as twelve to fourteen tiers high. Tall scaffolding had been put up too and technicians were swarming all over it as they secured television cameras.

Flags and bunting hung everywhere and no less than four different bands, both civilian and military, were playing four different tunes in and around the start area. A general air of festivity abounded and, even at this early hour, the popcorn and newspaper vendors were doing a roaring trade.

We had put on fresh, clean uniforms for this last day and had on new white socks. Our shoes were starting to become museum pieces but nevertheless we had managed to shine them up with a bit of spit and polish. The Union Jacks sewn on our shirt sleeves seemed brighter this morning and all of us wore our medals from our previous marches pinned to the belts around out waists with pride.

Many of the teams had smartened up their uniforms and today the Irish Guards were taking a piper with them the whole way. Some of the Army teams who, until now, had marched in camouflage uniform were now in their full best uniform.

The Israelis were forming up in threes in front of us. They had changed into brightly coloured National Dress, and to crown it all were actually doing National dancing while they waited for the order to start! This, of course, pleased the crowd no end and the cheers and clapping rang out even more. We applauded and cheered with them, but it was all too much for John.

"Right," he laughed, "that does it! Let's give them some good old British National Dancing." He grabbed my arm and proceeded to jive to the band. Then, to the complete amazement of everyone, including myself, we jived as if on a dance floor, and soon the rest of the team followed. My limbs throbbed, but by the time the order came to get us into line, much of the stiffness had left me.

"RAF Germany, by the left quick *march!*"

We stopped our jiving and, to the sound of applause from those people round about, we hastily found our places in line and stepped out, best foot forward.

We got into step behind the Israelis and, to the tune of the Bands, we marched through the town, towards, but not quite going to, Heumensoord, where the men had just travelled from. Then we crossed the main St Annastraat, the wide street that we would be marching down in a few hours time on completion of the 1962 Nijmegen March. Already people were taking their places along the roadside, although it would be a while yet before the first of the Marchers would appear.

The July sun rose in the heavens and as the band peeled away and waved us goodbye, we strode on, singing loudly. By now we had almost exhausted all the songs any of us knew and were practically down to reciting the alphabet as we marched. We had to sing to keep the step and keep up some motivation.

The sound of 'Do Ya Ever Get One Of Those Days' told us that our friends, the Americans were not far behind us.

You're at a drive-in moo-ovie,
And with a cute brunette,
You're counting all the ki-isses
You figure your gonna get,
Closer, closer, and then she hollers 'no'!
D'ya ever get one of those dames
Who just wants to watch the show!

This gave us even more encouragement for it is very hard not to march with a spring in your step to that song. The Israelis lengthened their stride and we were beginning to lose ground. They had become almost our rivals, but joining in with the Americans' song increased our stride as well!

"Come on," said Paddy, "let's catch them up. Don't let them get away!"

"It's *not* a race!" yelled Flight Lieutenant Curry.

Nevertheless, after a while we did make some ground by taking longer strides and caught up with them again. Then, to our surprise and delight, they stopped at the side of the road and clapped and cheered as we and the Americans passed them. They were lovely but I felt myself flagging.

"Keep going old girl," whispered John. "You'll make it – 'cos if you don't I will prod you with my bayonet!"

I looked at the rifle over his shoulder with the bayonet clipped to the side of it and promptly straightened my back.

We reached the first Rest Point to more cheers and shouts.

"It's Headquarters team – hooray, hooray – well done girls!" everyone shouted. We felt like film stars. The boys were happy to take a back seat and actually stood to one side, leaving the girls on their own for a minute as we marched into the special area designated for us. Instead of being embarrassed, they were now proud to have us with them. I could see hundreds of men throwing their caps in the air and dozens of them rushed up and hugged us.

I wove my way through the mêlée, flung myself down to the ground and was thankful for the nurses who ran up and started pummelling away at my back and the tops of my legs. Laney shoved a cup of salted tea in my hand.

"We've done 85 miles," she said.

"My back tells me that," I replied, "and God's knows what I am going to do about my feet, for they are going to burst out of these shoes in a minute."

"Sandy's are too," said Laney. "You might have to cut them."

"What!" I gasped. "Cut my beetle crushers!"

The whole idea was sacrilegious! I'd become attached to them over the years, I had been issued with them in 1959! They would be museum pieces in the future, in a glass case!

The nurse finished thumping my back and I gently eased myself up and finished my tea. It was a mistake because *now* I was going to be forced to use those damn latrines.

"I've got to go!" I wailed. "Anybody else coming?"

Laney decided that she had better take her courage in both hands, so together we walked across to the tarpaulin latrines at the other side of the field. I picked my way gingerly across the grass, carrying one shoe in my hand.

They lived up to everything we had been told, but by this time I just couldn't care less about sitting down bottom-to-bottom on a four-seater loo. At least it was only a wee I wanted and the holes were deep! I did what I had to do and got out as fast as I possibly could, without looking to left or right, and not for the first time I was glad I wasn't 'on'.

We picked our way among the hundreds of inert bodies to where the rest of the team were lining up and I bent to try and put my shoe on. I managed, with a great deal of difficulty, but when I tried to form up I found that it was impossible to move my right foot.

I hung on to Bill, who was the nearest person to me, while Sandy struggled with her shoes.

"Oh no, what on earth are we to do?" I grimaced.

"Cut it!" said John "here give it to me!"

"My beetle crushers!" I cried. It was like seeing an operation performed on a pet cat as he cut a large piece out of the toe of my right shoe. Sergeant Payne would have had a stroke! Nevertheless John's Swiss Army knife did the trick and then, with a satisfied grin, he handed them back to me.

"After all my polishing and cleaning," I moaned, as I struggled to put them back on.

"What are you moaning about now woman?" exclaimed John. "You're alright. I bet there are not many in the Air Force who have open-toed beetle crushers!"

His handiwork had eased the pressure and I found I could walk OK again, so he did the same to Sandy's.

We waved a cheery goodbye to all the soldiers and airmen still coming into the Rest Point and started on our way again, passing a team of London Policemen, complete with their traditional tall helmets on their heads – certainly an incongruous sight in Holland.

Then it was the parting of the ways, as the green arrow indicated that we had to go off to the right, while those on the 50km route went to the left. There was certainly no chance of us following *them*.

On we slogged, helping each other along, the girls sometimes carrying the boys' rifles and the boys sometimes giving us a helping arm. How I wanted to sit down, just to sit down. I was ready to sit down there and then in the middle of the road and let everyone march over me. Just the simple act of sitting down became my only ambition in life. Even Sandy's wiggle was in danger of disappearing altogether.

We resorted to singing some of our old Wilmslow songs:

"They say that in the Air Force the pay is mighty fine,
They give you thirty shillings and take back twenty nine!
Oh, I don't want no more of Air Force life…"

All the way along the side of the road people were egging us on. Many had baths of water outside their homes and would either run out to us carrying paper cups or they would spray us with their garden hoses. We accepted all gratefully.

As soon as anyone spotted the Union Jacks on our arms, the cries got louder.

"Die Englander! Die Englander!"

The road seemed never ending and my body was snapping in two, but all along the route the citizens of Nijmegen and the surrounding villages egged us on.

"I can't go on," I wailed. "I can't go on – just let me sit down."

"Come on," encouraged Jock. "It's all in the mind."

"It's not!" I answered. "It's all in my bloody feet!"

The Gordon Highlanders, who were marching along behind us, laughed at our 'double act'!

"Keep going," giggled Frank. "Hey, did you hear the one about the Englishman, the Scotsman and the Irishman?"

"Oh don't," I cried. "It hurts my feet to laugh!"

"Hear that?" laughed Frank, turning round to the Scottish team. "It hurts her feet to laugh!"

There was more laughter from the Gordon Highlanders and for a few more miles we had smiles on our faces. We changed hats with them for a while, the Scotsmen marching along wearing ours while we sported their black and red forage caps.

We came to a road junction and were joined, once again, by all the civilian marchers as we entered the pretty little town of Cuijk. Here our spirits were lifted as the local 'oom-pa-pa' band spurred us on our way and all the people in the town square cheered and waved.

Then we had to cross a wooden pontoon bridge to take us to the other side of the river, a sharp left turn and we were striding along the towpath towards, we hoped, the final leg of the March. After all, we had done nearly ninety miles, marching all the time.

But soon the route took us away from the river, the trees disappeared and, as I looked ahead at what lay before us, my heart missed a beat. It was a long, white road, completely and utterly straight and flat, in marked contrast to the Seven Hills of yesterday. It stretched as far as the eye could see, without a break, and no trees or buildings for shade.

"Good God, we've marched to the M1!" exclaimed Mike.

We gave the Gordon Highlanders their hats back and fell in behind the long straight queue of teams. Onward we marched, and every time I glanced back I could see this straight road stretching out behind me and yet it also stretched out in front with no sign of an end. What a boring road this was! It just seemed to go on and on.

"*Keep Right On To The End Of The Road*" we sang, with parched lips. But where was the end?

Jamey came up to us on his bike, carrying full water bottles – he was our saviour.

"I know it seems impossible to believe this," he said, "but there *is* an end."

I looked up and the white road suddenly disappeared into some trees and we started to see houses again, yet although we were marching briskly they just seemed to be a mirage in the middle distance, never getting any nearer.

"*I'm going to die on this road,*" I thought. "*I must be flippin' mad to have let them con me into this. I am just going to peg out on this road!*"

Slowly, the trees seemed to get nearer. I could hardly see where I was going for the sweat dripping down and mingling with my watering eyes. Now my blisters were stinging and all I wanted to do was just sit down.

Once we reached the shade of the trees, we all but fell down and gratefully drank the water that Jamey had bought, together with a salt tablet to put back some of what we had lost.

He was full of himself. He had cycled to the last rest point of the March and now he was dying to tell us all about it, but nobody would give him a chance.

"It's all right for you Jamey," I cried. "You haven't got our feet!"

"You haven't got my bum," he retorted.

"I'd like to see a Dutch doctor get to work on your backside with his iodine," said Cathy unkindly.

Jamey squirted her with water and begged us all to keep quiet while he told his story.

"Listen!" he shouted.

"Come on everybody!" interrupted Flight Lieutenant Curry, who was as weary as the rest of us, and also had blisters.

"Get into line and he can tell us while we march."

"The last rest point is not far away," cried Jamey, as we started off again. "Then it will be only *five* miles after that. You should see it there, it is fantastic. I could hardly get my bike through," he went on excitedly, "there are thousands and thousands of people, and all the service and civilian people marching through – and all the bands."

He stopped for breath and walked along at the side of me, pushing his bike. "I'm not kidding though," he went on with renewed vigour, "it's bloody amazing! Honestly, there are just so many people, all waving and clapping and throwing flowers."

I marched on in a daze. Sometimes we overtook teams and sometimes teams overtook us. The Dutch love their marches and some really take them to the extreme. At one stage we passed two young girls dragging along a third girl between them. Her feet that were encased in bandages were hardly touching the ground.

"Crumbs," said Mac, "she's keen!"

"There is something even keener over there," said Flight lieutenant Curry. "Look at that."

And there, marching along, on his own, was an old man who was well over seventy. He had a long white beard and was wearing green corduroy trousers tucked into his sock – his *one* sock because the other leg was a wooden peg leg! I could not believe my eyes and the sight of him seemed to make all our efforts pale into insignificance! He looked like Long John Silver. He even had a crutch like Long John Silver but that was the only support he had. No-one was helping him and he was marching along slowly but with his head high and his shoulders back. His skin under his white vest was bronzed in the sun. The vest was virtually covered in medals, as was the green beret on his head. All that was missing was the parrot!

He waved to us and smiled when he saw our shattered expressions. I learned later that he had done every march since they had started in 1909, but that now he did the seventy-five mile route.

"Well," said Mac, "I think at his age and with one leg we'll *let* him do seventy-five."

"At least he has only got one foot to get blisters on," whispered Cathy.

We gained a new lease of life and resorted back to our Wilmslow song:

"They say that in the Air Force, the food is mighty fine,
Some cheese fell off the table and started marking time.
Oh, I don't want no more of ..."

On we went, and gradually the countryside became more built-up and the crowds of people began to increase. Music from the Bands became louder and began to take over from our singing, and we could see Nijmegen Bridge in the distance. Suddenly a policeman rushed up to us and guided us off the main road and onto a field at the left-hand side.

I glanced down the long road that was the last five miles before disappearing into the Rest Point and all I could see were people, millions of cheering people. We had marched ninety-five miles and the Rest Point was, in fact, only yards away from the crossroads that we had marched across that morning.

There was a marvellous feeling of comradeship as we strode into the field. Hats were thrown in the air and with one accord everyone leapt to their feet as we arrived. The field was situated at the back of the huge stands of people waiting for us to march through. It was roped off into huge squares, one for all of the RAF teams, one for all of the Army teams, another for the German Army, German Air Force, Danes, Swiss, Norwegians, Dutch, and so on.

There was a square for each of the nations taking part in the military section of the march.

Already waiting, in each particular squared-off area, were the Bands of each Country or Service taking part. In our own roped off area, the RAF Germany Band were waiting for us, the Central Band having now gone home to take part in the Royal Tournament. Also, there was the RAF Laarbruch Pipe Band. RAF Wildenrath and the Air Ministry Team had already arrived, as had Bruggen and Gutersloh.

Whilst this was going on, the civilians were sorting themselves out at their own rest areas, and others were simply marching through without stopping.

I sat down and watched as all the Swiss formed up behind their Band, together with a Standard Bearer holding aloft the red flag with the white cross at the head of the long contingent of about two hundred. They moved off, with the cheers of everybody around them, and as soon as they had gone the board where they had been was changed to indicate that another nation should line up there. It was run like clockwork.

Jamey informed us that the marchers had been coming through all day and that there were many more to come. We were the first women to arrive in. The Israeli team were back but then they had started out before us this morning so that didn't count. Not that it was a race, I kept reminding myself!

The Army started to form up behind their band. Some of the Army teams had made arrangements for their best red jackets to be brought to this Rest Point so that they could march through in their full ceremonial uniform. Other teams were tidying themselves up as best as they could for the final five miles.

We were no exception. Tired though we were, we hobbled to the first aid tent and brushed our hair and put on a bit of lipstick. We had managed to get a few important items like that into the purses of the belts we wore round our waists! I looked down at my open toed beetle crushers and decided that there was not much I could do about them.

The WRAF was in the process of changing its best hat from the 'coal scuttle' as we lovingly called it, to a forage cap similar to that worn by air hostesses. Not everyone had been issued with it yet but, just for Nijmegen, we had ours ahead of time, and we had worn it throughout the March – well most of the time anyway. Now all we had to do was to make sure it was on properly and that we were as tidy as we could be under the circumstances. Soon we were ready but there were still a few more RAF teams to wait for if we were to all march in together.

The Army teams were apparently ready to move off, and the cheers from the crowds increased as they formed up and began to move out of the field and onto the big wide street that led straight into Nijmegen town. They were a lovely sight in their best uniform behind the Guards Band. There were hundreds of them with buttons and badges gleaming in the sunlight.

As I stood there watching, still more teams came into the field and had moved to their allotted areas where they were to get ready. We cheered as they arrived irrespective of nationality. There were no winners or losers – just those that had completed the March, hopefully with a team intact, so that they could get the Queen Juliana Team Medal.

Some more Israelis came by, as immaculate as ever, and banging their tambourines. There were Norwegians, more Army, more Swiss and Danes. Then the German teams marched through, to the sound of polite applause.

"I wish the rest of the RAF would hurry up," said Jean, rubbing her legs.

I did too, so that we could get on our way. I paced up and down and every step was torture but I didn't dare sit down because I knew it would be worse for me when I did get up onto my feet again.

The Irish Guards arrived and then the London Bobbies, who got a special cheer from us, and then – thank God – the rest of the RAF teams, including the team from Geilenkirchen and from Wildenrath, and the team of Cranwell cadets.

"About bloody time!" said John.

"Hooray, hooray!" we all shouted. "Come on you bloody skivers!"

I don't think the Cranwell cadets took too kindly to being called 'bloody skivers'. After all, they were our future officers! Nevertheless, they were all grinning from ear to ear with the pleasure of having got to the last lap of the March. At last we could all line up behind the Massed Bands of the Royal Air Force.

We took our positions for the last time in threes, leaving a twenty pace gap between each RAF team. Each leader marched in front of his team, carrying the Royal Air Force ensign. We were afforded the honour of being the first team behind the Band and Flight Lieutenant Curry stood a few paces in front of us, holding the ensign aloft proudly.

"Royal Air Force – by the left – quick march!"

The magic of the Royal Air Force March! As if somebody had waved a wand, the pain and stiffness in my legs and back vanished, my blisters were better and I felt like a million dollars. We were 'marching on feathers' again.

A team of Danish Army, who were just arriving, marked time to allow us to move out into the wide main road to the deafening cheers of the people of Nijmegen. Suddenly I had Air Force blue blood again. As we automatically got into open order across the width of the road behind the light blue flag with its RAF Roundel in the corner, I stole a look at our team.

Heads were high, arms were swinging at shoulder level in a way that any drill instructor would have been proud of. But above all, everyone had a grin on their faces which stretched from ear to ear, and all had a damp look about their eyes – even the boys.

On either side of the road Dutch people were banked up on tiers that reached as high as the rooftops. People were hanging from lamp-posts and leaning from the windows of tall buildings. We passed a Monastery and all the Monks were at the windows, waving and cheering. Children dodged the policemen and ran into the road to grab our hands, only to be hauled back quickly and people were dancing to the music.

All along the route were the deafening cheers, almost drowning the band and sounding like a huge rolling sea against the rocks. The thrill of marching behind any Royal Air Force Band never diminished. Just at that moment it felt as though every minute of the last three years in the Air Force had been meant to culminate in this. I felt as though I would willingly scrub floors every day rather than have missed it, and Sergeant Payne could shout at me as much as she liked!

There were so many RAF, that way back behind us, the Laarbruch Pipe Band were also playing their hearts out for the Air Training Corps cadets and for Wildrenrath and Bruggen. We couldn't hear them because we were so immediately behind our own bands, but we knew they were there just the same.

People ran out and pressed bunches of flowers into our arms and young girls ran up and stole kisses from the boys. Now I realised why it was called the Via Gladiola! There were flowers everywhere, which were mostly gladioli.

We marched for over an hour, but it didn't seem like that, and the nearer we got to the end, so the louder the cheers grew and the tiers that the people were standing on got even bigger! Then, almost before we knew it, there was a sharp bend in the road and there, on our right hand side was the saluting dais. The stand where it was situated was something like fifteen rows high and there were scores of senior officers sitting there, looking magnificent with all the gold braid and medals.

As we got closer, so a tall and very smart figure uncurled himself from his chair and stood to attention, the golden oak leaves on his cap glinting in the sun. It was the Air Officer Commanding RAF Germany, Air Vice-Marshal Gordon Jones.

"Royal Air Force – eyes right!"

We smartly turned our heads and eyes to the right in unison and the officer saluted back, grinning broadly as he did so.

Then he caught sight of the Headquarters team immediately behind the Band and even he pushed etiquette to one side and his salute turned into a hearty wave.

I glanced across at Laney. Tears were coursing down her cheeks, tears that looked odd with the broad grin she was wearing. I thought I would burst with pride. All the Military on the stand were waving to us.

As the road curved still further, with my head and eyes to the right I could see the long column of RAF behind us, the Cranwell cadets with the white bands around their peaked caps, the Air Ministry, Bruggen and many more. One long contingent of Air Force blue, interspersed every so often by a Royal Air Force ensign, and even further back still, the Laarbruch Pipe Band.

"The Final Day"

I was just twenty-one years old and I reckoned I felt as the Queen must have felt when she drove down the Mall on Coronation Day. Although I bet she never had feet like mine!

By now, everything was beginning to catch up with me, and I felt mentally and physically exhausted. Nothing now could stop the tears that were flowing unchecked down my cheeks, as still more people piled flowers onto me and the Band played the Dambusters March.

Cut me and I swear the blood would have been Air Force blue! The tears flowed even more as I wished so much that my parents could see me. But they would have to wait for my letter, and what a letter *that* would be!

The salute had been taken and the March was nearly over. We rounded the familiar corner towards the finishing place. The Israelis stopped at the side of the road and stood among the crowds to cheer and clap us – we felt very proud at this because they could just as easily have gone off back to the comfort of their hotel. Instead they had waited and were standing there clapping us. Even the boys were choked up and more than one had a very wet face.

"We've made it, we've made it!" cried Cathy, who could contain herself no longer.

"Royal Air Force – Halt!"

The hundreds of Royal Air Force personnel obeyed their team leaders to a man and there was an enormous 'thump' as everyone halted at the same time.

The band moved to one side and continued playing, until we were caught up by the Pipes and Drums, and then they took over to play for everyone who was still marching in. I felt someone press a medal into my hand – I never knew who it was – and then I lay down on the ground, clutching it, my flowers strewn across my chest and I cried and cried.

All the pent up emotion of the last four days and the magic of that last five miles, was too much for me. I just lay there and cried into the dust and stones, while the cheering and the excitement went on all around.

I was lifted bodily from the ground and opened my eyes to find myself staring into the face of an enormous Dutch Police Officer who was just in the process of saving me and Laney from being trampled on. He stood us on our feet and once more we were in among the crowd of marchers, each of us congratulating the others. All around us were the Air Force teams all laughing and crying at the same time.

Flight Lieutenant Curry appeared out of the crowd and proudly showed me the team medal, a large golden coin with the head of Queen Juliana on it. What a lot of blisters *that* represented.

I could see amid the throng of people, Cathy being carried by two medics and, just visible through a huge armful of flowers, was Sandy, with tears streaming down her face. All the time the water would not stop pouring from my eyes.

Laney stared at me with a stupid look on her face.

"We have marched one hundred bloody miles!" she gasped. "Just think, one *hundred* bloody miles!"

Again there were more hugs and more bunches of flowers were pushed into our arms.

Before I could say any more I was being man-handled by the Dutch policeman, towards the Hospital tent at the side of the square and then suddenly I was away from the heat of the sun and in the shade. I could see that the other girls had been brought in, despite their protestations.

Actually, there wasn't much wrong with us, but we were grateful for the attention. Then, as the adrenalin rush started to subside, so I began to realise just how much my feet and legs ached. I didn't care though, for in my hand I still held my Nijmegen Medal, although I hadn't even looked at it yet. I opened my fist for the first time and looked at it as if it was some delicate butterfly that I did not want to escape.

There it was – proof, the green and gold ribbon with the bronze Nijmegen medal attached to it. A little object turned out in its thousands for the Marches, but as precious as a diamond to anyone privileged enough to take part in the event. The medal awarded by Queen Juliana herself.

The good-looking policeman loomed up and, despite my efforts to put him off, he lifted me up into his arms. I was sure that the effort would give him a hernia, but he managed it as if I was half my actual weight. It boosted my confidence for the next twelve months!

I was still holding the armful of flowers. I turned to the nurses as he begun to carry me through the door. I felt such a twerp!

"Here," I said, "you have the flowers, I think you are smashing!"

They shook their heads and tried to push them back, but I insisted. In the end they took them and the policeman carried me to a waiting car. Laney was pushed in beside me and in a daze we sat there as it slowly wove in and out of the throngs of people.

Even as we drove along the back roads to the school, more teams were finishing, accompanied by even more bands.

All we could hear was military music, cheering and clapping. The car pulled up outside the school and willing hands helped us to hobble across the courtyard to the steps, where the Captain was waiting for us.

"Congratulations English girls," she beamed.

Laney, Jean and I sat down on the steps at the end of my first Nijmegen March.

Throughout the school corridors there were great tin baths full of flowers and girls with blistered feet and aching legs were dancing around, waving their medals.

As we made our way up the steps and to our room, the Danish crowded around and hugged us and then some Swiss girls bobbed their heads from behind their door. Eventually we managed to get to our dormitory and what flowers that were left we put in buckets of water.

I lay on the nearest bed and stared at the ceiling and let my limbs change to cement. I lay there, already composing my letter home to tell my Mum and Dad all about it. Gradually, the girls dozed off, but I was awake, still clutching my medal.

It must have been nearly an hour later when there was a gentle tap on the door and there, resplendent in his smart uniform, was none other than the Air Commodore from RAF Germany, who had accompanied the Air Vice Marshal to the marches. I could not believe that somebody so exalted should be there, in our sleeping quarters, and us in all our glory, half undressed and probably stinking.

"It's alright airwoman," he whispered, as I struggled to try and get to my feet and straighten my uniform, "don't get up."

I was dumbfounded.

"I just came to tell you that we are very proud of you," he grinned, "and if there is anything you need you are just to say the word – is there anything?"

"No Sir!" I whispered, still dumbfounded.

"Well don't forget," he twinkled, "if you want anything, just ask."

He crept back to the door, like a naughty child.

"I'll leave you in peace now," he said, and gently touched his cap as he closed the door.

"Who was that?" whispered Jean, who had hidden under the covers.

"The Air Commodore, I think," I answered. "It was all so quick!"

As more girls returned from the marching, so the noise throughout the school increased. One by one our team 'came to', quite mortified at the idea that the Air Commodore had caught them unawares, even though we all agreed that it was jolly decent of him to go to the trouble. It occurred to me that they might not have any trouble in getting a team for Nijmegen together *next* year, not that I would be around for it. The four years that I had signed on for would be up by then.

We all had a good wash, for we needed it. We couldn't be bothered with the showers any more, or the sight of the Scandinavian girls running around stark naked. Then, still wearing our marching uniforms with our medals pinned to our blouses, we walked in our plimsolls or sandals to the nearest restaurant.

We had imagined that we would have a quiet meal away from the centre of the main activity, but we had imagined wrongly! The restaurant was packed with marchers and soon people of all nationalities were talking to us, some in perfect English and others with English spattered with sign language, but nobody was complaining, for I certainly could not speak their language.

"Well, this is the life," said Val. "Who's coming back next year then?"

"I'll be demobbed by then," I replied, mournfully. It was a sobering thought.

That night, the town of Nijmegen celebrated. Irrespective of blisters and swollen and aching legs, the thousands of marchers celebrated at a giant "Blister Ball" held throughout the town. Hardly anyone wore uniform shoes and there was a band or a barrel organ at every street corner. All evening the military bands that had played throughout the March entertained us in the streets. The beer flowed and the locals gave the marchers a night they would never forget.

We managed to get some seats under the Yellow Umbrellas. Eventually the boys from our team arrived. They knew where we would be.

"Well," said Mike, "back to camp tomorrow!"

"Oh shut up you old misery!" said Laney. "I want to stay here!"

"Frankly," I said, totally honestly "I shall be glad to get back into my own little bed in the WRAF Block and sleep."

"Groupy's going to be pleased next week," said John, "with two of us creeping around like pensioners. He is going to have to ring for us an hour before he wants us!"

I felt as though I had been away for months.

Around us the bands played and beer appeared in front of us from nowhere. Boys from the RAF Laarbruch Pipe Band arrived and gave us impromptu tunes on the bagpipes. The Americans came by and laughed and joked for a while. The Danish boys appeared and tried to chat up Sandy, though they spoke little English. Dozens of other nationalities, all too numerous to mention, passed by the yellow umbrellas that evening. The whole town was at the 'Blister Ball' and the language of 'ooch-ouch' was universal!

We dragged ourselves back to the school late that night. Even so, the streets were still as crowded as a Saturday afternoon in London at Sales Time. We were in time to find the Dutch Army Captain and her staff sitting in the office of the School, reading the papers and looking a bit solemn. Then we learned that the rumours about the two people that had died on the second day were true.

"They were very stupid," she said, as she pointed to the picture in the paper. "I expect they drank too much beer when it was too hot."

She leaned over and chatted to one of the nurses in Dutch and they both nodded together. One of the victims was Swiss and the other an Army cadet.

"There is always somebody silly," she went on, when she saw our shocked expressions. The other nurse sitting with her also spoke to the Captain and she translated.

"She thinks they had too much beer and not enough salt." They all nodded in agreement.

We were a little subdued when we took off our marching uniforms for the last time and climbed wearily into our hard little beds in the classroom, but I was asleep as soon as my head touched the pillow.

I awoke in the morning to find that I just could not move. We all had a hilarious time trying to pull each other out of bed again, all the time with Sandy extolling the virtues of regular sport.

It was all right for these sporty ones. Since Wilmslow I had studiously avoided any form of unnecessary activity, apart from jiving, of course. It hadn't always been possible but I had done quite a good job of it until now!

Soon though, we managed to get motivated and it wasn't too long before we had collected our belongings together and were ready to go back to Germany. The only two deviations away from the correct WRAF uniform were the Nijmegen Medals worn proudly on our jackets and the fact that we were all wearing white socks and no shoes.

All along the corridors the girls from other nations were busy getting ready for their journeys back to their respective countries and every few minutes a head would pop round the door to say goodbye to us. We'd never see them again and we'd known them for less than a week, but we all felt like long lost friends parting. All that remained now was to bid a fond farewell to our host, the Captain and her staff. We all hugged her and gratefully accepted their helping hands onto the RAF bus. The boys were already on board and we waved frantically out of the window at the Captain and the girls still left around the entrance to the school.

Our driver took us through the now deserted streets of Nijmegen past the empty stands, past the coloured flags and bunting, on past the Sports Arena where we had seen the Tattoo, and then on, past Nijmegen Bridge and onto the road that would lead us back to Germany and the WRAF Block. There was no chance of going to Arnhem to see the War Graves. That was on the agenda for another time. Anyone stopping the coach and looking into it at the border would have seen, at a glance, where we had come from though, for they would have seen a coach-load of RAF personnel stretched out horizontally along the seats of the bus, most of them asleep. All of us were too tired to talk, but anyone wishing to take a blood sample from these inert bodies would have found that the colour was, most definitely, Air Force blue!

The real significance of the area that we had marched over was lost on most of us, but not for long. We had been unable to visit the War Graves at the time of the March, after all, nobody wanted thousands of 'beetle-crushers' all over the place. Instead each team had respectfully marched by in silence. However, some of us did go back to Oosterbeek, near Arnhem, as we had promised ourselves.

As we looked at the giant white cross which guarded the rows and rows of white headstones it was hard not to be emotionally affected and tears filled my eyes. The names meant nothing to me, but the ages on each stone spoke volumes – most were younger than those of us in the Headquarters team. They were just young lads that had fought tooth and nail to defend that area from the Germans. All *we* had done was *march* over it. I could hear the birds singing in the nearby trees and I could smell the scent from the pink roses planted lovingly about the place. It was an awesome sight and, once again, I felt very proud that I had been part of the Nijmegen March.

Nijmegen Bridge.

11. ...ad Astra

When I arrived back at camp it was to find Rusty in the throes of packing and moving into a single room. I looked at her empty bed with all the blankets pulled off and lying crumpled on the floor.

"I can't turn my back for a minute can I?" I grumbled, "Where are you off to madam?"

"Corporal to *you* airwoman," she chuckled. "I'm off to a single room."

"Yeah, it's a good job you are back missus," said Mal. "I thought I was going to be left here all alone."

The fact was that Rusty had indeed got her Corporal's tapes through. It wasn't that surprising really – I was qualified as well but she had been in longer than me *and* had picked the right number when we had to toss up for our jobs when we had first arrived at the Big House. She had ended up working for an Air Commodore – it did make a difference! The down side was that she would have to move out.

"Anyway, just look at her with her medal up," said Mal, looking at my best blue jacket as I sat down stiffly on my bed. "Come on, come on, tell it all to Auntie Mal."

We were soon joined by Pat, who had seen the bus arrive at the WRAF Block to drop the marchers off.

"I still think you are bloody bonkers," she said, "absolutely bloody bonkers."

"So do I," added Mal, as she picked up my 'open toed beetle crushers' gingerly as if they were about to bite her.

"Wait till old Payne sees those," giggled Pat.

There wasn't much peace for me to catch up on my beauty sleep. First one and then another had to come in and find out how we got on and then somebody came in with an envelope that had just come down from the Photographic Section. The camp photographer had taken pictures of our triumphant march through the town and these had been quickly developed and sent to the WRAF Block. I gazed at my copy. It showed the smart marchers armed with piles of flowers and crowds of people waving at them. We certainly did not look as though we had marched one hundred miles in that picture. Only the pained expressions on some of the faces gave the game away.

Mal had reverently placed my beetle crushers on my locker in a place of honour.

"I think I should put those in a glass case Ratty!" she said, catching sight of my gaze, "as a memento of your efforts!"

"They're a memento alright," I grinned. "It's a good job I don't have to put those out for a kit inspection any more."

"Oh those days are over now, I think," mused Mal, "now that we can wear court shoes I don't think we'll see many more days of bulling beetle crushers – except for parades, that is."

"And Nijmegen," I added.

"And Nijmegen," she laughed.

A few days later there was a letter from home, enclosing a cutting from the local paper with the sensationalised headlines, 'Local girl takes part in March on which two die.' The rest of the story was mainly about the event and there was a picture that made me look a lot smarter than I had felt when it had been taken at the Rest Point.

"Silly buggers!" said John, when I went to work and showed him the cutting. "Beer, heat and long-distance marching do not mix."

"Now I realise why we had all that salted tea," I replied, "and" I said as an afterthought, "thank goodness for our cycle orderly – I never could have done it without him."

We both agreed that Jamey had been the star of our team.

None of us was very pleased at what they had been doing to our NAAFI throughout the summer. Not only were we having difficulty in calling it the Queensway Club, despite the large neon sign they had put outside, but, in our opinion it had lost its 'charm'!

We happened to like the lino floor and the wooden tables with the red Formica tops. We liked the counter where we could get hot cheese pasties and frothy coffee. Most of all, we happened to like going in the Beer Bar, which was now, much to our disgust, out of bounds to airwomen! If that wasn't enough, to add insult to injury, the corporals lost their club and, instead, became part of the Junior Ranks Club. The days of having their own little bolt-hole had gone and they were as annoyed to lose their segregated status as we were to have them in our domain all the time. However, the powers-that-be thought they knew what was good for us and that was that. It was all in the cause of bringing us up to date.

We were an ungrateful lot because it must have cost thousands, especially the floor. We wondered how long it would take for the 'powers-that-be' to get the message that the little plastic heel covers did not work. Still, they tried.

I couldn't help feeling that they could have saved the tax payer a lot of money if they had just left our airmen's NAAFI as it was and the Corporals' Club as that was. Anyway, it didn't bother me too much at the moment – I couldn't get my winkle pickers on anyway and nobody minded plimsolls on the fancy floor.

We were quite the celebrities of the moment as gradually the team appeared in the Queensway Club, sporting their medals and telling their stories. We had only been away a week but it felt more like a month, especially now Rusty was a corporal.

"Typical," she said, as we sat in the restaurant, drinking Coke, "just when I get my tapes they do away with the blinkin' Corporals Club!"

"Never mind," I replied sarcastically. "You would have been lonely in there and we *do* have a lovely shiny dance floor!"

John hadn't been far out when he forecast that Groupy would have to ring for us half an hour before he wanted us. Both he and I were like little old people with rheumatism, but at least he had his shoes on. I was still 'excused boots'! I once met him walking, so slowly, down the corridor, carrying a tray of coffee, whilst I was hobbling towards Groupy's office in my plimsolls, as usual. We just burst out laughing at each other and the coffee went everywhere.

"Do your feet still hurt when you laugh," he giggled.

"No," I laughed, "but my blinkin' back does!"

Gradually everything settled down and the effects of the March began to wear off as we got back into our routine. There was only the memory remaining and that very special medal with the green and gold ribbon – and a pair of very dodgy 'beetle-crushers'.

Rusty's bed did not stay empty for long. Within a week we were joined by Kay, a slim, auburn-haired dental nurse who was to work in Station Sick Quarters. The fourth bed in the room had been empty ever since I had moved in but not for much longer. I recognised Liz the minute she struggled in carrying her kitbag and suitcase.

"Oh my gawd!" I sighed, "It is old 'no-tact Liz'.

"Ratty!" she squealed, as she dropped down on the spare bed.

"That's a fine door stop you have got there," she grinned, pointing to the sanitary towel.

"It works," I replied, as I gave her a hug.

"Have you seen any mauve socks dangling past your window lately?" I asked.

"No," she giggled. "The girls that moved into your room at Medmenham were not as adventurous as you lot." She winked at me knowingly.

"I promise you," I laughed, "that bloke was too drunk to do anything but drink the water out of the goldfish bowl."

"Oh yeah, and that's your story." She began to unpack and make her bed space her own.

"It is, and I am sticking to it," I replied.

It didn't take long for the girls to settle in and as the months drifted by towards the winter some of us suddenly started to realise the passage of time. We were determined to make the most of our situation before we went back to the UK again and there were many debates about whether we should or should not sign on. It was the start of the sixties and were we missing it all – or would we miss what we had here? There were still restrictions regarding what time we had to be in the Block, even though most of us were now over 21. The men, on the other hand, could stay out as long as they liked, which we continued to think was singularly unfair.

"Mind you," I said to Mal one day when we were discussing the subject, "if I was at home, my Dad would expect me to be in by ten, never mind twelve."

"Too true," said Mal, "and I bet you wouldn't nip out of your bedroom window either."

I laughed. That was indeed true. Apart from breaking my neck, there wouldn't be anywhere to nip to in the quiet little suburb where my parents lived. Trying to outsmart the Duty Airwoman was one thing – outsmarting my Dad was quite another, even if I wanted to – which I didn't.

In fact, nipping out of the window had lost some of its charm – even here. As at Medmenham, it *was* possible to go out through the washing room window and disappear among the trees out of sight of any lurking 'Snowdrop' or Redcap. We couldn't get far though, not without a car, and very few airmen, and no airwomen, possessed such luxury. The nearest German hostelry open after the NAAFI had shut was Antiks Bar in the little shopping centre on the far side of the camp and it was a long walk. We had to run the gauntlet of too many people who were trying to 'protect' us to make it really worthwhile. It was better for the girls in Block Three, who were shift workers – it was much harder for WRAF Admin to keep track of them.

Jan was well able to climb through the washing room window at the back of her Block and then scurry away through the woods in the darkness to meet up with the boys and have an extra hour or two with them. There was one occasion, though, when it lost its attraction, even for her and it was a good job that Kay happened to be Duty Airwoman.

"All present and correct," Kay counted as she popped her head round the door at midnight and ticked us off in the book. "By the way, just to let you know, Jan is nowhere to be seen."

"Oh don't tell me she has gone out *before* bed check," I yawned, "she takes some chances!"

"It's after midnight now," said Kay. "I'll have to mark her as absent."

Usually the Duty NCO came round at midnight to check that the Duty WRAF was doing her job properly. We just had to hope that on this occasion she would be delayed, otherwise Kay would be in trouble as well. There was a whole host of people whose sole task was to keep us from any mischief and look after our welfare – and they took it very seriously.

"I'll go and check Block Two and pretend I got delayed somewhere, but if she is not back by the time I have finished I shall *have* to mark her absent – I'll have no choice."

Kay disappeared and Mal and I kept watch from our back window to see if we could detect any signs of anyone lurking in the woods. Not that we could see much, as a cloud covered moon tried to shine through the trees. Suddenly, I caught sight of some figures approaching the back of Jan's block and then heard whispering as the boys tried to hoist her up through the window. They were clearly all drunk.

"Come on quick, jump," hissed one of the figures, pushing her from behind.

"Oh gawd," said Mal, "somebody's coming. Look, there's a torch over there."

The boys clearly saw the flashing of the torch too and gave Jan an almighty push and she promptly fell straight into the open washing machine! The clattering and the swearing that followed was enough to wake the dead and we could hear her from our vantage point at the window.

"Bloody Snowdrops!" cried one of the boys, as they ran off into the darkness.

"Ouch – bloody hell!" yelled Jan. "Who the hell left this bloody thing here?"

It was a very large machine with the type of lid that came off completely, but worse, much worse, it had a churning mechanism, like a pole, coming up from the middle. The result was very painful as well as very noisy. However, her room was just across the corridor from the washroom and so she was able to hobble inside undetected, but very sore indeed!

The following morning she realised how lucky she had been. Kay, as Duty Airwoman, had turned a blind eye, the boys were able to outwit the Snowdrop and, more to the point, the Duty NCO was late visiting the WRAF Blocks. It was a combination of lots of good luck.

She was badly bruised but was not going to suffer the indignity of reporting sick. She came into our room the following evening, still feeling battered.

"I bet that's done your virginity in, Jan," I smiled.

"Huh," she grunted, "I didn't plan to lose it like *that* though."

Afterwards, we did slow things down a bit – we felt that we had made our point. However, we did think it was very unfair that the boys could choose what time their parties finished and we could not and that they had the Beer Bar, so we felt we were owed the occasional foray into places out of bounds to us after we should have been tucked up in bed.

And so the weeks went by – happy weeks – weeks of carefree parties in the Queensway Club and dances and late nights in the little bars in the surrounding villages when we could get away with it. Sergeant Payne never did find out, or if she did she never let on. In the main she left us alone, probably because she was too busy out gallivanting herself.

Sometimes we would go to a little place just on the outskirts of the camp where a pub sold a drink which we called 'rainbow juice'. It was made up of different coloured liquors all resting one on top of the other to form stripes. I am quite sure it had a proper name, but it was always 'rainbow juice' to us. We spent many a happy hour in this place and it became the favourite haunt on pay day, when we would have half chickens and chips and eat until we could have popped. It made up for the crap they fed us in the Mess.

The fuss over us doing the Nijmegen March was not entirely over. Our team was summoned to pose on the very grand steps of the Big House to have our photo taken for the *Air Force News*. We all felt very proud and I suddenly found myself wishing I could do it all again.

We six girls had paved the way for others though. Never again would there be any scraping around to get a complete WRAF team and never again would it be impossible to get a WRAF Officer to go with them. Once the news spread as to what the marches were all about and what a great time we'd had, there would be plenty of people willing to give it a try and be proud to do so.

I sat on the RAF bus coming back from Dusseldorf Airport after being at home for Christmas and watched the scenery while half listening to the sound of chattering from new people posted in and from families coming back after the festive season. I'd had one Christmas Dinner being served by the officers last year and that was enough. This time I chose to have it served up by my Mum. It did, though, emphasise the fact that next time I would be home permanently, and it gave me a lot to think about as I gazed out of the window.

The change in my brothers had brought home to me the passage of time. Michael was a teenager now and Richard, who had been seven when I joined up, was already eleven and going to secondary school. Should I or shouldn't I sign on? The decision I would make this year would affect my life forever.

There had been a drizzle of snow at home but here it was thick and I wondered for a while if the bus would get through, but there were no worries. Suddenly I saw the big white sign at the side of the road which was now so familiar to me. It bore the legend *Headquarters Northern Army Group*, and then underneath, *Second Allied Tactical Air Force, British Army of the Rhine, Royal Air Force Germany (2nd Tactical Air Force)*. It *was* a very big camp but I was becoming very attached to it.

Mal had already arrived back from leave when I got in and, as usual, she was brewing up. There was a new clean sanitary towel around the door handles to stop it from banging.

"Well, this is the last time we shall be coming back," she said unnecessarily. "The next time we leave here it will be for good."

"State the obvious, why don't you!" I replied grumpily.

"I think I shall miss it," she said.

"Everything is changing though Mal," I had to remind her. "I am coming to the conclusion that time does not stand still for anyone." Now it was me stating the obvious.

Pat Seymour came bouncing into the room. She reminded me a bit of Tigger in Winnie-the-Pooh. She never altered.

"Jeezus Ker-iste!" she blasphemed, as usual. "Did you see the new fashions at home this time?" She walked across to where my fluffy petticoat was lying on my bed, its yards of stiff netting taking up most of the area, and pushed it to one side.

"This is out of date now," she laughed, as she sat down.

She was right, of course. It had been more than six months since my last lot of leave, just before Nijmegen. With no television to speak of and little interest in newspapers and magazines, we were very cloistered in Germany and it was only a trip home on leave that brought us all up to date. The lovely petticoats and wide skirts and plastic belts had given way to the 'sack dress'. I was horrified.

"Well, at least it is easy to make," said Mal, "it's only a length of material with a hole cut in for the head and arms to go through."

It wasn't a lot different from our sacks that we had worn for the Tramps Ball at Medmenham. We probably had invented the 'sack dress' without realising it back in 1960, in the same way as Sandy had 'invented' the mini before it's time on the Nijmegen March.

I looked at my petticoat lying on the bed, harming nobody, apart from the space it was taking up. It was a 'symphony' in puce, turquoise and blue net and worn underneath a 'circular' cotton skirt it was, in my opinion, the 'bees-knees'. It *was* going to have to go, though. I manhandled it back into the cupboard and made a mental note that I would have to have a word with Jan. She had bought an identical one at the same time as me and it represented the end of the fifties. It would have to have a 'decent burial'.

"Sad isn't it," I mused.

"Nah, we have to move with the times." Pat jumped up from my bed. "What do you think of those Beatles then?"

"Not a lot," I replied, "though to be fair, I didn't hear much of them. When they came on television my Dad turned it off and forgave Cliff Richard and Tommy Steele."

Mal and Pat both laughed.

"Oh, the Beatles will never replace Elvis," said Mal, "but I do like them."

"I agree, nothing could replace Elvis singing 'Love me Tender'," I answered. "Or is it that we are just getting old." I took Pat's arm. "Let's go and see who's in the NAAFI." I turned to where Mal was busy taking her rollers out and combing her fair hair. "Are you coming Mal?"

"It's the Queensway Club," she corrected me. "We *have* to call it the Queensway Club or The Junior Ranks Club."

We put on our heavy white duffle coats over the top of our civvies and braved the elements.

We found some of the RAF boys and one or two of the German Air Force lads in the Cocktail Lounge, giggling over something they had seen in the paper.

"Here you are girls, look at this," grinned Chalky. "Seems they have put the pill on the market now. You will have to get some and then we can have our wicked way with you!"

"That's old news," I retorted. "It has been out for nearly a year, but if you think any of us would walk into Sick Quarters and *ask* for it you can dream on."

"Nice try mate," chortled Brian, who had just sat down with us.

It was the subject of conversation quite often in the Block and sometimes controversial, but we all agreed that none of us would ever go and ask for it – not unless we had a ring on our finger.

"It says here that it will be freely available for all women and then we can have free love," joked Chalky. "Go on – how about it? It's what it says here."

"Not a chance," said Pat. "I could never ask for it unless I was married … or at least engaged."

"Nor me," said Mal. "Sick Quarters would think I was a tart."

"Sorry chaps," I smiled. "If you want your wicked way with us you will have to marry us."

"That's blackmail," replied Fred with a wink.

"Oh well," said Frank, "we can always go down the Reeperbahn and find a real tart."

We were quite sure they did anyway, and the conversation, as always, ended in laughter as the boys stalked off to the Beer Bar. It was though another indication of how times had changed in four short years.

There was thick snow on the ground and it was hard to tell one nationality from another as everyone had their duffle coats covering their uniforms when we went back to work after the holiday. We tramped backwards and forwards across the golf course to the Big House, making well-trodden pathways in the snow. There was a bus provided but invariably we walked and threw snowballs at each other, arriving at work breathless and invigorated for the day.

The Big House really was an awesome sight and, although we were very small cogs in the scheme of things, it would be difficult not to feel proud to work in such a place. Of course it wasn't the sharp end. There were plenty of people who had been on operational stations to remind us of that! – Chalky for one.

"Oh, you have to be at the sharp end to know what the Air Force is all about," he would say. "Now, when *I* was at Waddington..." His sentence was usually cut short by somebody throwing a beer mat at him.

We weren't at the sharp end and we were not at war as our forefathers had been, but we still felt special, and whether I was sitting in Groupy's office and taking down his letters in shorthand or typing sheets of accounts, it was all part of the greater scheme of things and you couldn't help feeling like part of a huge family.

The roads out of the camp were so icy that no one wanted to bother with the night-life in the town and so more dances were held on camp. Jive sessions, old time, fancy dress, nothing was forgotten. I threw myself into these activities with a vengeance, determined to make the most of my last few months.

At one of the dances that took place nearer to Easter, Jan and I decided to finally part with our precious frothy petticoats. They represented our teens, and we loved them, but it had to be done – the fashions had moved on. We turned them upside down and adapted them, with ribbons and pins, into the frothiest and most outrageous of Easter Bonnets and walked into the Cocktail Lounge wearing them – to the great amusement of everyone there.

When the dance finished they finally found their way to the dustbin and it was the end of an era.

As the days ticked by we tried to make the most of our last few months. We would start the evening in the Queensway Club, which I still insisted on calling the NAAFI, then go on to the Cinema, usually to see Elvis, then on to Antiks in the German Shopping Centre if we were lucky enough to skip out of the window. None of us were very rich but the drink was cheap, for the service people anyway, and we all had cigarette coupons for even cheaper fags if needed – it didn't occur to anybody that they might be bad for us. And if we ran out of money it didn't matter – we made do and shared – just as we did at Medmenham.

Kay, working in Sick Quarters, opened up a whole new world for us too, as through her we got to know a new circle of friends among the Medics and Ambulance Drivers.

Time flew by, as time always does when you are not sure whether you want it to or not, and I took to buying souvenirs at the little German Shopping Centre that was on the other side of the camp, and which I had, until now, hardly ever visited. I was behaving more and more like a tourist nearing the end of a holiday.

Our shopping excursions further away from camp usually consisted of a bus organised by the WVS to Roermond, which was just over the border in Holland, or to the market town of Venlo, where we could get the latest fashions quite cheaply from C&A's. Jan and I even managed a trip to Cologne on the train, which was an adventure in itself, when left to our own devices.

Reality finally caught up with us once and for all when Mal's date for going came through. I knew that I had exactly two weeks after her. It didn't seem possible.

"Ah well," she sighed. "I s'pose I'd better get me gear packed…"

"At least your number is dry now," said Liz from the corner, where she was lying on her bed, reading *Air Force News*.

"I suppose it is!" replied Mal a little wistfully.

She hooked her washing bag over her arm and walked out into the corridor, singing,

"Falling in love again,
Never wanted to.
What am I to do?
I can't help it!"

in the style of Marlene Dietrich in 'The Blue Angel', oblivious to the strange looks from a couple of new arrivals who were just coming up the stairs after the inevitable meeting with WRAF Admin and our dear Sergeant Payne.

But as Marilyn's posting date approached she became more and more down-hearted and the kettle in the corner worked overtime.

"I don't want to go!" she said. "I'm going to miss everything so much!"

"Sign on then," I replied.

"I would if I thought I could stay here," she replied, "but I might get somewhere horrible like Wilmslow."

"Heaven forbid!" I grimaced. "I think if I got Wilmslow I would shoot myself."

"There won't be any Wilmslow much longer," laughed Liz, "the death-watch beetle have let go and they are they pulling it down. Don't you lot *ever* read the Air Force News?"

"Since when, Nellie know-all?" I retorted.

"Recruit Training is moving to a new place called Spitalgate," said Liz, patiently, "and they are doing away with the billets, everyone will be in blocks like this!"

"Ooh!" cried Kay, Mal and I in unison.

"Fancy them having blocks!" I exclaimed, ignoring Liz's patronising look. "Gosh, I bet they won't know they are born, they'll be having a room each next!"

"I know," said Liz, "joined up before our time didn't we?"

"I don't know," mumbled Marilyn. "I don't think we did. I think it's a shame if they really are closing it down, despite how we moaned about the place, the WRAF is losing its individuality."

"Well you are a fine one," retorted Liz, "you don't want to get posted there and yet you don't want to see it closed down – you don't make sense – what *do* you want, the place preserved as a museum?"

"Probably," answered Mal, wistfully.

We sat and wrote on pieces of paper the 'pros and cons' of signing on, but still ended up none the wiser, and the days drifted by relentlessly.

On Mal's last night in the Block it was my turn to make the black coffee. She all but fell through the door after saying goodbye to her boyfriend. She looked like a panda with mascara smudged all over her cheeks where she had been crying and she was very drunk.

"Oh I don't want to go!" she wailed. "He'll find himself a new girlfriend as soon as I'm gone, you wait and see."

"Come on," I sympathised, "get this down you. We'll keep in touch."

"Oh you'll forget me when I'm gone too," she cried, feeling very sorry for herself. "Out of sight, out of mind."

"Oh shut up the lot of you!" moaned Liz. "You'll have me at it in a minute."

Kay came into the room and found all three of us in tears. That was more than anybody could stand and so she decided to join in rather than try and beat us. We were, therefore, a sorry lot when the Duty WRAF came round on bed check.

"For God's sake, what's up with you lot?" she asked.

"I don't want to go home," cried Mal.

"And we don't want her to go home," I added.

She raised her eyebrows to the heavens and closed the door on us. She was new, she didn't understand. She hadn't got her number dry yet.

The following day there was another empty bed space, this time in the far left hand corner of the room and the kettle lay unused on Mal's locker. The sanitary towel on the door handle remained as a memento. Within days of leaving us, we received a letter from her.

"You'll never guess what," she wrote. "Bloody Sergeant tore up my 'twelve-fifty' at Innsworth, bloomin' sacrilege it was!"

"Oh, and she only just got her number dry!" laughed Kay.

Of course, our precious Identity Cards had to be destroyed. After all, they didn't want anybody else using them and pretending they were us, but I could understand the finality of it. They went everywhere with us, even round the Nijmegen March.

As Mal left, so June arrived in Germany and for a short while at least, three of the 'J's were together again. Not that we saw much of her as she and her corporal were in married quarters in the local town. By now they had a little baby girl and she was occupied with being a mum.

"Well, at least she found herself a bloke, even if it *is* him," said Jan one day, after she had paid a visit to see our friend. "She has done better than either of us – we haven't found anybody to write home about at all."

This was true. How anybody could be on this huge camp where there were so many men and still come away without one beggared belief. We both looked in the mirror together.

"We are not that bloody ugly are we?" I said.

"Nah," replied Jan, "too bloody fussy – that's us."

"Oh it's just as well," I went on, "I do think those that have tied themselves down have missed such a lot."

"I think you are right," she agreed. "Still, it would have been nice to have had the choice!"

"Never mind," piped up Kay. "You may find someone at your demob party Ratty."

"Bit late then," I retorted, "when I am off home on the following day."

Naturally enough, my demob was an excuse for a party, and the Sick Quarters crowd were very adept at putting on parties! How the time had flown. Four years had seemed like an eternity when I had joined on 4th July 1959. Yet it had whizzed by – a blip in the scheme of things. Kay and Liz still had a year to do and Jan had six months.

The event was due to take place on the evening before my departure in the Green Room. We were allowed to use this room so that we did not spoil their lovely new 'Junior Ranks

Club'. Now that the NAAFI had gone 'posh' they were particular about having boozy parties in the holy portals of the Cocktail Lounge, and as girls were not allowed in the Beer Bar we had to seek an alternative. It served them right!

Despite my miserable frame of mind it didn't take long for things to get underway. Everyone was there except for Jan, who had gone on leave and just could not get a flight to be back in time. She was due to return the following day, just as I was leaving. She was furious but there was nothing she could do about it.

Of course, Pat was demobbed too. We had joined up together and we would be leaving together. Even John from my Section turned up during the evening with his girlfriend.

"Do your feet still hurt you when you laugh?" he grinned. It was a perpetual joke with him.

"Oh John," I wailed, "I don't want to go!" Another couple of months and it would be time for Nijmegen again. The alcohol was beginning to have its effect on me.

"They will have an all girls team this year," he said, rubbing salt into the wound. "No more trying to keep up with the boys."

"Cheeky bugger!" I laughed. "More like *you* keeping up with the girls."

He laughed and filled my glass from the bottle he was holding.

"You'll be back!" said John. "I bet you come back!"

"No chance!" I grinned through my tears. "I'm not going through all this again. Once I'm out, I'm out and that is – *it!*"

"You'll be back!" he repeated. "Come on now – you have *got* to get the crown to your medal!"

The 'crown' was a further addition to the original Nijmegen medal to show you had done it twice. After that, you got a number to go on the ribbon and then, depending on how many marches you had done, you could progress to the silver and then the gold medal.

"I don't think so," I repeated, a little unconvincingly. "I'll manage without the crown."

"You'll be back," he repeated. "If not next year, then one day you will."

"No I won't," I replied.

He laughed and put his arm around his girlfriend and they wandered off together, just as two of the medics from Sick Quarters appeared in the doorway of the Green Room, wearing white waiter's jackets and carrying huge trays of champagne for everyone to toast me with. They had thought of everything.

By the end of the evening both Pat and I were quite the worse for wear but there were many willing helpers to get me along the road to the Block. I looked around for her but she seemed to have disappeared in the general direction of her own accommodation. We had an extension of an extra hour but even if I had been in any state to climb out of the window I had no intention of doing so. I did have a plane to catch in the morning.

The night air hit me as we crossed the main road. I looked across at the Queensway Club with its neon sign outside and further down the road I could just make out the sign of the Astra Cinema where, not long ago, I had seen Elvis Presley in 'Blue Hawaii'.

The experience was still fresh in my mind and I burst into a chorus of 'Can't Help Falling in Love'. Kay and Liz joined in as we crossed the road together with Chalky, Trevor, George and even Mal's boyfriend, Johnny, who still hadn't quite got used to not seeing her around. All of us were singing and the sound must have been awful. There was no sign of Pat anywhere.

"Miserable bugger," I thought, "she might have waited for me."

We saw a couple of Snowdrops walking in our direction and quietened it down a bit.

"Shh!" hissed Trevor, "they'll put us all on jankers!"

As it happened, they just laughed and let us go on our way but, true to form, Sergeant Payne was waiting for us, diligently doing her job as Senior NCO in charge of us wayward airwomen.

"What's this?" she snarled, looking at the spectacle of me being hauled bodily into the Block.

"It's all right Sarge," said Chalky, in his drunken stupor, "she's just upset at leaving!"

"It's a good job she *is* leaving," she replied. "I am not having any drunken airwomen in *my* Block!" She said it as though she had personally designed and built it.

Even in my inebriated state I managed to give her a withering look and I thought for a minute she was going to put me on a charge. She didn't, and marched off in the direction of the Senior NCO's quarters, probably glad to be rid of me and not willing to risk delaying my departure still further by having me 'up in front of the beak'!

The boys gave her the V sign behind her back as Liz and Kay grabbed my arm.

"Do you know," I slurred, "she was almost the first bloody NCO I met when I arrived at Wilmslow and she is the last bloody NCO I meet on my last bloody day!"

They dumped me at the door of the Block and the three of us climbed unsteadily up the stairs to our room. Kay put the kettle on and we were just about to enjoy our coffee when there was a tap on the door and Pat bounced in, carrying some interesting smelling packages under her arm.

"Thought I'd forgotten you didn't you?" she grinned. "Here you are – catch!"

All the time I had been cursing her for not waiting for me she had been busy. She had got a bike and gone down to the German shopping centre and had come back with half chicken and chips. How she managed it without falling off was a mystery to all of us because she was really quite drunk.

"Honestly," she slurred, "I was wobbling all over the place but I kept on the cycle track with the lights off and nobody saw me – at least I don't think so."

I almost forgot how miserable I should be as I sat up in bed eating, what was, by now, a nearly cold supper which I would not have touched if I had been sober.

"How did you get in?" said Liz.

"Took the bike round the back and chatted up the Duty Airwoman silly!" replied Pat.

"What a silly question," giggled Kay.

One thing was certain, my parents were reasonably tolerant, but there was no way that either of them would entertain the idea of me sitting up in bed and eating half chicken and chips out of a newspaper when I got home. They would be horrified. It suddenly felt like the last supper and it really was a miracle that Pat had managed not to get caught. People were definitely turning a 'blind eye' tonight.

We had drunk too much and had eaten too much and we totally forgot that Pat still had to get back to her own Block. The Duty Airwoman had taken enough risks – we couldn't ask her to take any more and all the Blocks had been locked up by now. There was nothing for it but to creep downstairs and push her through the laundry room window.

"Shh, don't wake anybody!" I giggled, as she landed on the ground at the back of our Block.

Kay and I leaned out of our window and watched her as she crept along to her own accommodation and scrambled in through the laundry room window, which she had had the forethought to leave on the latch before cycling off for the food. She had also made sure that there was no washing machine in the way.

"Night Pat!" I whispered into the darkness.

"Night all!" she hissed back. "See you in the morning, booted and spurred."

We had an afternoon flight so I went to 'clear' from the Section. I wished the word 'clear' would apply to my aching head! I felt so sad when I went round to everyone – Groupy, the Squadron Leaders, Mac and John and all the Corporals and Frau Braum. I did not like saying goodbye at all.

Groupy stood at his door and waved as I walked down the corridor and everyone else followed his example. As I turned the corner to walk down the maze of corridors to get out of the Big House I looked back to see every door of Command Accounts open and people waving at me. I handed in my pass at the door and tears pricked my eyes again as I walked out of the gates and across the Golf Course. The two Group Captains I had worked for would be a hard act for any civilian boss to follow.

For a long time I stood there, on the highest part of the green, just looking back at the building behind me. I wanted to form a complete picture in my mind that I would never forget, so that in years to come I could call upon it. I stared for quite five minutes at the enormous Big House with its rows of flags outside and the long iron railings. I made a mental picture of the Post Office next door to the building, and the trees bordering the married quarters over to my right.

I looked at the Camp Theatre and the Army NAAFI that hadn't gone 'posh' yet. Then, as I continued my walk I looked at the Sports Grounds and the Swimming Pool, the Cinemas, The Malcolm Club and the Junior Ranks Club. I was determined not to forget. I wanted to have a photograph in my mind for ever. After all, maybe one day some bright spark in the Government would decide to pull it all down – you never know. They seemed to be gradually doing so everywhere else!

I walked back past the Mess, which was still 'keeping the draught off the parade ground' and caught sight of Pat coming from the other direction. She too was clearing from the camp and saying her goodbyes. The bus was already waiting for us when we met up and turned the corner towards the WRAF Blocks.

"Jeezus Ker-riste, look at the time!" she exclaimed, and ran towards her Block. "Just going to get my luggage – see you in a minute."

There was just time to fly upstairs and, with the help of anybody who happened to be about, struggle down with my luggage and pile it into the boot. Sergeant Payne was looking out of the window as we climbed aboard and she gave us a wave. We waved back – she wasn't all that bad really, or was it that we had just got used to her?

It didn't seem like five minutes before we arrived at Dusseldorf airport and we stood with the families and watched our baggage being carted away to be loaded onto the aircraft. We waited in the departure lounge for our flight to be called and, just as I was thinking how sorry I was to have missed Jan, I saw her through the glass partition that divided the 'departures' from the 'arrivals'. We shouted and screamed at each other, but we were being pushed our separate ways, so we waved and moved on. Kay, who had come to see us off, walked with us to the entrance and looked at our glum faces.

"Oh come on you silly old devils!" she said, "its not all bad. Just think, I am on Duty WRAF tomorrow – you two aren't."

I didn't know whether to wish I was on Duty or to be looking forward to going back home and starting a new chapter in my life. My encounter with Bill Haley on Waterloo Station felt as though it had been on another planet.

There was, however, no time for further thought as the air hostess pushed us on board the Viscount and we both shouted our goodbyes. I took my place and looked through the window. Jan had somehow found her way round to the railings where Kay and one or two others were standing and they were all waving energetically.

"Bye!" we shouted, even though they couldn't hear us.

It was a good job that the rest of the passengers were mostly families or people going on leave, otherwise they would have thought we were crackers, waving madly with the tears rolling down our faces unchecked.

Suddenly the engines took on a different note and we were moving across the runway. The girls became tiny dots, still waving, and I wondered if I would ever see them again. The great machine lurched forward and soared off into the sky and soon we were way above the clouds. I leaned back against my seat, in floods of tears, and marvelled, yet again, at how fast the time had gone since we had signed on.

It's easy just to think of all the good things and forget the nasty bits – and there were experiences that I *would* rather forget – I'd done my fair share of cleaning the loos, washing down the passages and scrubbing tables, but even those chores had been accompanied by laughter. But just now it was the good things I thought of as the aeroplane sped us towards home.

I was having very selective memories on the day I left Germany for the last time and already that statement about your last station always being 'the best' was proving to be true – yet again. Pat settled down in her seat next to me, lost in her own thoughts for a while.

As for me, I remembered Wilmslow and the square bashing and our field day, the laughs we had and the NAAFI with the jukebox that always played 'Lipstick on your Collar'.

Then Hereford with, among others, Tommy, Pat and Wendy, and the jukebox that always played 'Why Am I So Starry Eyed' and 'Travellin' Light'.

Then there was the laughter at the New Year's Eve Ball and poor Tommy getting posted to Cranwell, of all places. I could see his face now with the look of total disgust! I didn't even have to wonder where *he* was now – I knew – with his National Service over he was playing bass in a very famous jazz band indeed. He had been right about that, at least.

The picture in my mind switched to Medmenham – God's Little Acre – the four J's and ghost hunting and canoeing on the river and my efforts at being the next Eddie Calvert.

Then there was Germany, with The Big House, my first introduction to The Nijmegen March and the delightful Dutch people. As for the jukebox at Rheindahlen? Why, anything by Elvis Presley of course!

"Will you all fasten your safety belts please!"

"Oh lord, we're here!" exclaimed Pat, as the aeroplane started to drop out of the sky. "That went quick." Pat's voice cut Elvis from my mind and brought me back to the present with a jolt.

The aeroplane descended below the clouds and we sped along the runway. There was only one more 'lap' to go – to report to RAF Innsworth to be officially demobbed. This was where we would have to hand in our uniforms and our precious 'twelve fifties'. I never wanted to see the gates of an RAF Station less.

I tried to tell myself that the WRAF was changing and it would never be the same the older I got. It was a weak argument, but my thoughts kept me occupied and Pat and I sat in silence and continued on our journey. We were really a contrary lot – the more the 'powers-that-be' tried to, in their eyes, improve our lives, the more we wanted the opposite.

When we were given the posh new Queensway Club, we longed for the old NAAFI, with the cheese pasties and the Beer Bar. Moreover, when Rusty became a corporal and got her own room as a result, she was never in it, much preferring to be with the 'gang', and I was willing to bet that if we were allowed to stay out all night we would not take up the offer. After all, it would take all the fun out of jumping out of the window! There was no pleasing some people.

It was early evening by the time we arrived at Innsworth and showed our passes at the Guardroom. I suddenly found myself thinking of that first day, four years ago, when we had all hovered like frightened rabbits, as the Snowdrop welcomed 'the lambs to the slaughter!'

I thought of the rest of our flight and smiled inwardly as I thought of Haggis and her 'research' into who amongst us were still virgins. Well, at least, I thought I had smiled inwardly, but obviously I hadn't!

"Well *I* don't think it's any bloody thing to smile about!" said Pat, as we struggled once more with our kitbags and suitcases. Then I laughed out loud.

"Do you know, that's the very first thing you said to me when we arrived at Wilmslow!"

"No!" she exclaimed "Was it really?"

With that, we both collapsed into helpless fits of the giggles as we walked towards Stores and the General Office. Passing airmen looked at us as though we were mad.

"I was actually thinking about Haggis and her billet check for virgins," I whispered.

"Well, to be honest," said Pat, "I don't think things have changed that much – blokes are all talk. How about you Ratty?" she went on, "did you survive intactica?"

"Yeah!" I replied.

"Really?" she cried in mock horror, "how *did* you manage that?"

"With a great deal of difficulty," I laughed. "What about you?"

"Not even on the washing machine!" she giggled.

"How dreadful!" I joked as we walked down towards the Stores.

"Give me time!" said Pat, "I've got a few years before I have 'returned unopened' on me."

"Well, we can get The Pill now," I reminded her. "Free love and all that."

We fell into further uncontrollable mirth, although we automatically began to simmer down when we saw the big burly corporal who was waiting for us in Stores. It was a reflex action.

"Come on you two!" he grunted, "It's nearly my teatime! Go into those cubicles and put on your civilian clothes and then hand all your uniform to me except your WRAF handbag and your passion killers."

"Oh Corporal," exclaimed Pat, "Why don't you want our lovely passion killers?"

"Not service issue any more," was the gruff reply. He quite clearly had little sense of humour.

We meekly did as he told us, wiping the tears of laughter from our eyes at the same time. Without knowing it, we had turned from teenagers to young women and had learned that you don't necessarily have to lose your virginity to do so.

I dressed in my straight, shapeless, sack dress that finished just above the knees and a short jacket. I still didn't think it was as nice as my 'fifties frills' but it was cool and supposedly the height of fashion. I was quite pleased about being able to keep my WRAF handbag though, as I had grown quite attached to it. I shoved the passion killers inside it and put it in my suitcase.

"Well ladies," he then said, kindly. "Now, you only have to collect your pay and hand in your 'twelve fifties' and you will be civilians."

"Gee thanks!" I replied, and our moods changed rapidly as we both dejectedly made our way to Pay Accounts, where we were given our last lot of wages.

"Right lassie," said the Pay Accounts Sergeant to me, while Pat was signing for hers, "Your 'twelve fifty' please!"

I looked at him square in the eye and held on tight to my Identity Card. He was tall and dark and looked too young to be a sergeant. How dare he take my 'twelve fifty'. It was like an umbilical cord holding me to the RAF, which I now felt was part of me, and I could understand how Mal had felt. My hand became hot and sweaty as I wrestled with my innermost thoughts. I could refuse to let him have it, as even now it wasn't too late to change my mind. I moved from one foot to the other still looking him straight in the eye, wanting to ask that I be allowed to stay, but the words just would not come.

"Your 'twelve fifty' please airwoman!" he repeated.

I handed over the card, telling myself not to be so daft.

"Thank you Miss," he said, and then promptly cut the card in half.

"Bloody vandal!" whispered Pat.

He looked at the notes on his desk.

"You can hand in yours in the morning, Seymour," he said to Pat. "Says here that you are staying overnight."

I suddenly felt quite jealous that she was still officially an airwoman a day longer than me, but she would never get a train to get to her home that same night. I could.

We said our goodbyes on the steps of the Block as *Top of the Pops* echoed through one of the windows and that group called The Beatles were singing 'From Me to You'.

"You will write, won't you," I said.

"Of course I will," she retorted.

I gave her a final hug and she disappeared into the WRAF Block and I was left alone to get the train to London. I had very little left belonging to the Air Force, except my memories.

It began to drizzle with rain as I walked past the men's accommodation, where it looked like some new recruits were getting a ticking-off from a sergeant. They looked so young and sorry for themselves.

The weather echoed my spirits as I turned and watched the lads go on their way, looking a bit sheepish – goodness knows what they had done to upset the sergeant. I happily would have swapped with them because *I* knew something that they didn't – your last station is always your best.

Suddenly, the Duty NCO marched out and began to lower the Ensign and I automatically stood to attention along with the recruits as it was hauled down. Then I felt quite silly when I realised that I was wearing civvies and had an umbrella in my hand.

Once the flag was lowered the airmen went on their way and I quickened my pace, waving to the Station Policeman in the Guardroom as I reached the gate. I turned back and had a last look at the sight of an RAF Station settling down for the evening before I crossed into the civilian world.

The dark grey clouds were trying in vain to hide the faint orange and gold of the sunset, making the rain-washed parade ground sparkle in the evening light. The lights along the road and in the surrounding buildings went on, and also those in the WRAF Block. Even now, it still wasn't too late to change my mind ... but no, I had to move on with my life. I had one step to take that would take me into another world. And it really *was* 'another world'. Four years ago, Marilyn Monroe had still been alive, as had Buddy Holly and the Big Bopper. If anyone had told me that within a year President Kennedy would be dead and that Elvis would not last beyond the next decade, I would have thought they had gone totally and completely stark raving bonkers!

I saw the bus in the distance and struggled to the bus stop, giving a last look behind me at the Camp gates. The conductor, I am sure, was quite used to seeing tear-stained 'new' civilians at *this* stop.

"Going home?" he said kindly.

"Yes, for good this time!" I replied.

Well, at least there would be no more goodbyes. If there was anything I hated more about the Air Force than scrubbing corridors at Wilmslow it was the 'goodbyes', especially at this time of the evening. I wasn't sure which was worse, saying goodbye to your friends when they move on, or saying goodbye to your parents on some cold and draughty station and then travelling back to camp down dark lonely roads when everyone else is snuggled up watching television.

I fumbled around in my purse for my fare and my coins chinked against my Nijmegen Medal with its green and orange ribbon.

"What's that?" said the Conductor, "the George Cross?"

"I don't think so!" I laughed. "The Blister Cross, more likely!"

By the time I had finished telling him what it was we had arrived at the station and I struggled with my suitcase.

"Why did you join up in the first place?" the friendly chap said, as he rang the bell for the driver to start off again.

"My Dad bet me ten bob!" I answered, seriously. The bus started to move away.

"Was it worth it?" he called.

"Oh yes!" I shouted back with feeling, "every single bloody penny!"

The vehicle moved out of sight and I struggled onto the platform, along with some people who were clearly still in the RAF and some civilians. The umbrella was a nuisance along with my case and handbag so I decided to put it away and delved into my jacket pocket for my plastic rain hood instead. I felt something silky which had not been there before we went to Stores. I pulled it out to find it was a tatty pair of grey passion killers. There were roars of laughter from those nearest to me. Pat must have put them in my pocket when I was handing my kit in.

"The sod!" I said out loud.

I was spared any further merriment from the people on the platform by the arrival of my train. I shoved them back into my pocket, vowing that one day I would get my revenge on that reprobate, but just for now I had a journey to make – home to the family I loved.

My parents would be waiting up for me and, with a bit of luck, it would be roast lamb with mint sauce for Sunday Dinner at the weekend, which was a bit of an improvement on cold chicken and chips in the WRAF Block.

But still I thought, *"I do have the crown to get for my Nijmegen Medal."* I wrestled with my thoughts as the train sped through the dark countryside nearer and nearer towards home. *"On the other hand, there is always next year – or the year after – isn't there?"*

~ END ~